MODERN HUMANITIES RESEARC
NEW TRANSLATIC
VOLUME 14

In Defence of Women

To Mamie

with best wishes,

Joanna

MODERN HUMANITIES RESEARCH ASSOCIATION
NEW TRANSLATIONS

The guiding principle of this series is to publish new translations into English of important works that have been hitherto imperfectly translated or that are entirely untranslated. The work to be translated or re-translated should be aesthetically or intellectually important. The proposal should cover such issues as copyright and, where relevant, an account of the faults of the previous translation/s; it should be accompanied by independent statements from two experts in the field attesting to the significance of the original work (in cases where this is not obvious) and to the desirability of a new or renewed translation.

Translations should be accompanied by a fairly substantial introduction and other, briefer, apparatus: a note on the translation; a select bibliography; a chronology of the author's life and works; and notes to the text.

Titles will be selected by members of the Editorial Board and edited by leading academics.

www.translations.mhra.org.uk

In Defence of Women

Translated by Joanna M. Barker

Modern Humanities Research Association
New Translations 14
2018

Published by

The Modern Humanities Research Association
Salisbury House
Station Road
Cambridge CB1 2LA
United Kingdom

Copy-Editor: Simon Davies

First published 2018

ISBN 978-1-78188-774-5

CONTENTS

INTRODUCTION

Throughout the seventeenth century, Spain was a closed society, standing aloof from cultural developments taking place elsewhere in Europe, and wrapped in memories of its glorious past. But the beginning of the following century brought a new king, a new dynasty and a new age. The influx of people, books and ideas from beyond its borders gave Spain its own, all too brief, age of Enlightenment.

At this time of momentous change, the three authors represented in this volume — one male and two female — made their own contribution to the Europe-wide debate over the nature of women and their position in society. The first of these was Benito Jerónimo Feijoo, a Benedictine monk who was an admired scholar and a prolific author. Over the course of nearly thirty years, Feijoo published a series of essays and letters on an enormous range of subjects, in an attempt to shock his nation out of ways of thinking he regarded as ignorant, archaic and dangerous. Among the most controversial was his argument, stated in his *Defence of Women* (1726), that women were intellectually equal to men, and that the entrenched opposition to this view was the result of unjustified prejudice.[1] This essay sparked a pamphlet war that continued for twenty-five years.

Feijoo showed an enormous breadth of knowledge of other writings on the subject of women, drawn not only from classical authors but also from English and French philosophers of his own time and the previous century. He illustrated the error of the conventional deprecation of female abilities with a list of women who displayed courage, discretion and the ability to govern, and others who were known for their intellectual or artistic skills. What was unusual was that he drew these women from his own country's history and from contemporary Europe, showing that such women were not merely legends from a dim and distant past.

Feijoo was not afraid to oppose even Aristotle, whose authority was still unquestioned among Spanish scholars and theologians, countering his pronouncements on women's inferiority with logic, reason and example. His

---

[1] Benito Jerónimo de Feijoo, 'Defensa de las mugeres', in *Theatro Critico universal, o Discursos varios en todo género de materias, para desengaño de errores comunes* (Madrid: Viuda de Francisco del Hierro, 1726–1740), I (1731), ch. 16, pp. 331–400. Modern edition by Victoria Sau, *Defensa de la mujer: Discurso XVI del Teatro crítico* (Barcelona: ICARIA, 1997).

open-minded approach, combined with his vast reading and fascination with new ideas, appears remarkable coming from a man who spent most of his life as a cloistered monk; and the fury with which male contemporaries attacked his argument demonstrated that they were fearful of his influence.

Sixty years after Feijoo's *Defence of Women*, Josefa Amar y Borbón submitted a paper to the Madrid Economic Society of Friends of the Nation, in which she demanded that women should be admitted as members and allowed to participate fully in the Society's activities: her *Discourse in Defence of the Talents of Women, and their Aptitude for Government and Other Positions in which Men are Employed* (1786).[2] Amar came from a family of physicians at the court in Madrid, and benefited from an education that was unusually broad for a woman of her time, which enabled her to win a reputation as a translator of works from other European languages. She nevertheless displayed unusual self-confidence in publicly entering a debate with some of the most influential men in the country, countering their views with succinct asperity.

The importance of education to Amar was reflected in her major original work, the *Discourse on the Physical and Moral Education of Women* (1790).[3] This book advocated a broader education of women and defended their value to society as wives, mothers and teachers of their children. It demonstrated her grasp of all the major written contributions to the subject from antiquity to her own day, and added a particularly female voice drawn from her own experience. Amar also gave a lead to other women by becoming an active citizen in her home town of Zaragoza.

At the end of the century, Inés Joyes y Blake added her voice to the debate. She was a descendant of Irish immigrants, and lived in and around the port of Malaga. She lived for many years as a widow, and we have no evidence that she ever wrote for publication until, late in life, she decided to translate from English a work hitherto unknown in Spain: Samuel Johnson's *History of Rasselas, Prince of Abissinia*. To this she attached, in the form of a letter to her daughters, an outspoken attack on the vacuous nature of contemporary women's lives and the pernicious effects of the sexual double standard.[4]

---

[2]   Josefa Amar y Borbón, 'Discurso en defensa del talento de las mujeres, y de su aptitud para el gobierno, y otros cargos en que se emplean los hombres', in *Memorial literario*, Madrid, 8, 32 (1786), 399–430. Modern editions by Olegario Negrín Fajardo, in *Ilustración y educación: La sociedad económica matritense* (Madrid: Editora Nacional, 1984), pp. 162–76; and by Maria Victoria López-Cordón Cortezo, in *Condición femenina y razón ilustrada: Josefa Amar y Borbón* (Zaragoza: Prensas Universitarias de Zaragoza, 2005), pp. 265–96.
[3]   Josefa Amar y Borbón, *Discurso sobre la educación física y moral de las mugeres* (Madrid: Benito Cano, 1790). Modern edition by María Victoria López-Cordón Cortezo (Madrid: Ediciones Cátedra, Universitat de València, Instituto de la Mujer, 1994).
[4]   Inés Joyes y Blake, *Apología de las mujeres*, epilogue to *El príncipe de Abisinia: Novela*, translation by Joyes of Samuel Johnson's *Rasselas* (Madrid: Sancha, 1798), pp. 177–204. Modern editions by Mónica Bolufer Peruga, in *La vida y la escritura en el siglo XVIII: Inés*

Joyes was critical of men's behaviour, but she also challenged women to recognise that youth and beauty were ephemeral, and to develop a form of self-respect that was not based only on the flattering attentions of men. She encouraged women to support each other through firm friendships, and not to fall into the trap of becoming competitors for male approval.

As the century progressed, these three authors brought a new perspective to the Spanish cultural world, demanding that women should be granted a place in the public arena, and that their voice should be heard.

Women in Spanish Culture and Society

Spain had not stood aside from the long-running debate over the nature of women and their position in society. During the sixteenth century two Spaniards, Luis de León and Juan Luis Vives, had published lengthy works on the subject that found a receptive market both within Spain and elsewhere in Europe. The main theme of their works was to exhort women to be chaste, submissive to their husbands and devoted to their domestic duties, and they were still regarded as authoritative two hundred years later.

Luis de León (1527–1591) was an erudite Augustinian friar whose scholarly and religious career was repeatedly interrupted by the attentions of the Inquisition. His first and most serious transgression, which led to over four years of imprisonment, was to translate the biblical *Song of Songs* from Latin into Spanish and present the manuscript to his cousin, Isabel Osorio, who was a nun in Salamanca. Translation of the scriptures into the vernacular was forbidden by the church, and putting them into the hands of women had been particularly condemned by the Council of Trent.

León's most popular work was composed for his newly-married niece, and was entitled *The Perfect Wife*. This first appeared in 1583 and went through six editions in the following fifty years. It had a second lease of life in the late eighteenth century, with three more editions between 1773 and 1799. Josefa Amar quoted from it approvingly, if selectively, in her 1790 *Discourse on the Physical and Moral Education of Women*.

León's book praised marriage as an honourable estate ordained by God, and explained that God's most important requirement was that human beings carry out the obligations of the state in life for which He had designed them. Women are ordained to be wives and mothers, and should strive to achieve the perfection of the model wife described in Proverbs 31. 10–31. The perfect wife should study how to free her husband from care, and be hardworking, in particular spinning and weaving to provide the clothes required by her

---

Joyes: *Apología de las mujeres* (València: Universitat de València, 2008), pp. 275–98; and by Helena Establier Pérez, as epilogue to *Historia de Rasselas, príncipe de Abisinia* (Salamanca: Ediciones Universidad de Salamanca, 2009).

household. She must stay at home, not visiting other people's houses and not allowing other people into her own house, for fear they should introduce new ideas and customs that might upset the domestic equilibrium. Women must particularly protect their daughters from contact with strangers, for once they are tempted by desire, their natural female weakness and lack of self-control will lead them straight to corruption.

León was aware that he had a difficult task to persuade the 'delicate ladies' of his time to engage in the manual work of spinning and weaving, since they believed that while this might suit the wife of a labourer, it was not relevant to them. He was particularly incensed by upper-class women who lay in bed till noon and then took three hours painting their faces, and then went out visiting and participating in mixed company. He exhorted women to be silent, mild and discreet: they are not made for study or learning, nor for anything difficult or complex; their sole duty is domestic, and this should be the limit of their understanding.

The popularity of *The Perfect Wife*, which became a regular gift for brides, was rivalled by that of *The Education of a Christian Woman* by Juan Luis Vives, published sixty years earlier.[5] Vives (c. 1492–1540) was, like León, from a family of *conversos*, or converted Jews, who were regarded with suspicion by the Inquisition: as a child he had seen his aunt and cousin burned at the stake on the charge of operating a clandestine synagogue. His father was also executed in 1524, and though his mother had died in 1508, her remains were exhumed and ritually burned twenty years later. Vives left Spain shortly after his mother's death, and unsurprisingly declined to return to the country for the rest of his life. He studied in Paris and spent much of his life in Bruges, with frequent visits to England, where he became friendly with Erasmus and Thomas More, and was appointed a lecturer in Cardinal Wolsey's new college in Oxford (now Corpus Christi).

In 1523 Queen Catherine of Aragon, the daughter of Queen Isabella of Castile, engaged her countryman to provide a programme of studies for her daughter, Mary Tudor, specifically tailored to the requirements of a princess.[6] In the same year, Vives published a book that tackled the broader question of how women should be educated. The *Education of a Christian Woman* was written in Latin, a language few women were taught, and appears to have been addressed to their male guardians. It proved even more popular than *The Perfect Wife*, with eight more editions over the following sixty years, as well as translations into French, German, English, Italian and Dutch. It was translated into Spanish by Juan

---

[5] Juan Luis Vives, *De institutione feminae Christianae* (1523), bilingual edition by Charles Fantazzi and Constant Matheeusen, 2 vols (Leiden: Brill, 1996–1998); English translation by Fantazzi, *The Education of a Christian Woman: A Sixteenth-Century Manual* (Chicago: University of Chicago Press, 2000).

[6] *De ratione studii puerilis* (A Study Plan for Children, 1523).

Justiniano and published in seven editions from 1528 to 1584.[7] Josefa Amar also quoted from this text in her *Discourse on the Education of Women*, but observed that it was difficult to find, and recommended the book be republished.[8] Her suggestion was taken up by her own publisher, Benito Cano, who brought out a new edition in 1793.

Like León, Vives condemned jewellery, cosmetics, banquets and dancing. Young girls should dress plainly, eat simple food and be beaten regularly: 'indulgence corrupts boys, but it is the utter ruin of girls'.[9] He disliked coloured clothes on the grounds that God did not create scarlet sheep, and instructed that dolls should be taken away from girls since they might teach them the desire for ornaments and finery. Girls should not be permitted to 'be infected with a proclivity to talkativeness'.[10]

Again like León, Vives insists that women learn how to work with wool and flax. In fact, spinning was something of an obsession for him: a woman should never be seen without her basket of wool. This was related to the common male fear of female idleness, for once a woman has finished her household tasks, her thoughts are dangerously undisciplined.

Where Vives diverged from León was in his advice that girls should be taught to read: their reading matter should, however, be limited to the scriptures, the Church Fathers, moralising classical authors and Christian poets. He was conscious that he was pushing against the tide of current social attitudes: for example, he insisted that feast-days and banquets, where men and women mix together socially, were worse than pagan customs, but was aware that they had become so firmly established that there were few who, like him, stood against the popular frenzy. He raged against the immorality of love poetry, yet admitted that by his day no one expressed even slight displeasure at such writings.[11]

It seems that Vives, an earnest scholar of thirty-two, was driven to distraction by chattering, giggling girls, wasting their time reading romances and discussing the latest fashions. How he wished they would shut up; laughter, he thunders, is the sign of a frivolous mind: 'let her take care that she does not laugh too freely'. He was bewildered by other men who praised women for their witty conversation; in his opinion, this 'is something that is welcomed and respected by the ordinances of hell'.[12]

---

[7]   *Libro llamado Instruccion de la muger christiana*, trans. by Juan Justiniano (Zaragoza: Bartholome de Nagera, 1555); reprinted with introduction and annotations by Elizabeth Teresa Howe (Madrid: Fundación Universitaria Española, 1995).
[8]   Amar, *Educación*, p. 175.
[9]   Vives, *Education of a Christian Woman*, p. 278.
[10] Vives, *Education of a Christian Woman*, p. 56.
[11] Vives, *Education of a Christian Woman*, pp. 136, 77.
[12] Vives, *Education of a Christian Woman*, pp. 129, 130.

At the time Benito Feijoo, Josefa Amar and Inés Joyes wrote their defences of women, these works by León and Vives were still the key prescriptive texts on the subject written by Spaniards. Their ideas had contributed to increased social restriction during the seventeenth century, when it was observed that Spanish women were kept in strict seclusion, imprisoned behind iron grilles by jealous husbands, forbidden to leave the house and constantly under the watchful eye of a *dueña*. Spanish literature and theatre of the Golden Age reinforced this view. The great dramatist Félix Lope de Vega (1562–1635) penned a number of tragedies now known as 'honour plays', in which adulterous wives were put to death, together with their lovers, by avenging husbands. Their constant theme was the stain caused by female sexual transgression to a man's honour, which could be restored only by bloody revenge. The most violent example is *The Commanders of Cordoba* (*Los comendadores de Córdoba*), where the husband in his murderous rage kills not only his wife and her lover, but every living being in the house, including the monkey and the parrot. He then goes to the king to confess his actions, and is rewarded with a new wife.

A woman's view was given by María Zayas y Sotomayor (1590–1661?) in her twenty novellas, published in 1637 and 1647 as *Exemplary Tales of Love* and *The Disillusions of Love*.[13] These tales are told by a group of noblemen and women gathered in a private home. In the preface to the volume, Zayas made an impassioned defence of women's equality and a plea for improved female education. She observed that the reason women were not as learned as men was not lack of ability but lack of practice, the result of being locked up, denied teachers and given nothing to occupy their time but needlework.

Zayas's tales became increasingly bleak, with the later ones containing high levels of violence against women: five of the seven wives in the stories die, and two others barely survive cruel punishment. Yet despite her desire to illustrate the harsh and unjust treatment of women, she did not suggest they might benefit from rising up against masculine authority, for the rules of society were too firmly set against them. Love and happiness were indeed illusions. Zayas's novellas remained immensely popular long after her death, with over twenty editions published in Spain between 1637 and 1814.

Outsiders' Views of Spain

For nearly three hundred years, from 1494 to 1763, Spain was at war with the other countries of Europe. Shifting alliances might change the identity of the enemy, but it was difficult for the citizens of other countries to travel to Spain, unless they were protected by diplomatic immunity. Foreigners therefore relied

---

[13] *Novelas amorosas y ejemplares* and *Desengaños amorosas*. See María de Zayas y Sotomayor, *Exemplary Tales of Love and Tales of Disillusion*, ed. and trans. by Margaret R. Greer and Elizabeth Rhodes (Chicago: University of Chicago Press, 2009).

on literature for their view of Spanish society, and Lope de Vega's revenge tragedies and María de Zayas's novellas helped to maintain the impression that Spanish women were strictly and violently oppressed.

Eyewitness accounts tended to confirm the view of the extreme restrictions placed around Spanish women. Madame de Villars, the wife of the French ambassador to Madrid from 1679 to 1681, had come from a Parisian society dominated by the salons, where women dictated the rules in matters of taste and behaviour. She found life at the court of Carlos II utterly stultifying, and wrote to her friend Madame de Coulanges that the young French queen was not permitted to ride, had to be in bed by eight o'clock, and if she left the palace, travelled in a carriage with the windows blacked out. It was only when her lady-in-waiting was changed that she was even allowed to look out of the window at the garden.[14]

A turning point was marked at the very beginning of the eighteenth century.[15] The year 1700 saw the death of King Carlos II, last of the line of Habsburg kings who had ruled the country for nearly two hundred years. Carlos, who was known to be physically and mentally feeble, left a will that granted his throne to Philippe de Bourbon, grandson of Louis XIV of France. The other great powers of Europe, Great Britain and Austria, were horrified by this union, which would give France control of the Spanish empire in South America, and jointly invaded the country in support of an alternative candidate, eventually unsuccessfully. This so-called War of the Spanish Succession lasted thirteen years; Spain's cities were besieged and its countryside ravaged by rival forces. Madrid itself was briefly occupied on two occasions, and the royal family forced to flee. It was not until 1714 that the new king, now styled Felipe V, was able to take full control of his realm.

With him came an opening of Spain to the rest of Europe, and an introduction of French fashions, ideas and lifestyles. Ladies adopted Paris fashions, to the distress not only of moralists but also of economists, who believed that the importing of French silks, lace and other luxuries was ruining local industry. Following the French example, society figures set up salons, or *tertulias*, where men and women mixed on terms of familiarity. In 1759, Carlos III came to the throne, having spent nearly twenty-five years as king of Naples and Sicily. His court introduced Italian influences, which included a further relaxation of relations between men and women.

However, the image persisted of Spain as a place where women were kept in oriental seclusion and men exacted bloody revenge, and it was something of

---

[14] Marie Gigault de Bellefonds, Marquise de Villars, *Lettres de Mmes de Villars, de La Fayette, et de Tencin*, ed. by Louis-Simon Auger (Paris: Chaumerot Jeune, 1823).
[15] For a discussion of the change in Spanish social practices regarding women between the seventeenth and eighteenth centuries, see Paloma Fernández-Quintanilla, *La mujer ilustrada en la España del siglo XVIII* (Madrid: Ministerio de Cultura, 1981), pp. 17–28.

a surprise to travellers who came to Spain in the latter half of the eighteenth
century to discover women mixing with men on easy terms. The German
traveller Christian August Fischer was struck by what he found:

> It is true that in Spain women were formerly in a state of the most abject
> slavery, insomuch that since the general civilisation of Europe Spanish
> jealousy has become proverbial; but in progress of time the manners of
> Spain, running from one extreme to the other, are almost become more
> free than in any other country. Women pay and receive visits, form their
> tertullas [sic] at will, go to public fêtes without consulting their husbands,
> spend the income of their dowries as they please, and demand besides a
> certain proportion of pin-money, which is stipulated in their marriage
> articles. In a word they not only know how to assert their rights, but enforce
> their pretensions with the utmost rigour.[16]

An English provincial clergyman, clearly unfamiliar with the concept of the
salon, was even more surprised:

> Whilst I continued at Aviles, I discovered, for the first time, that the visit
> is always to the lady; that the master of the family is perfectly at liberty
> to come or go; that there is no necessity to take notice of him; and that,
> if the daughter is handsomer than her mother, she may without offence
> occupy the whole attention. This idea I found afterwards confirmed in
> the great metropolis, by seeing gentlemen introduced to ladies of the first
> fashion, and visiting them on the most familiar footing, without the least
> acquaintance, or even personal knowledge, of their husbands.[17]

Alexander Jardine, a military man, was charmed by the company of the women
of Cadiz, describing them as 'perhaps the gayest, the most lively and agreeable
women in Europe'.[18]

However, others noted that women's charm was unlikely to be supported by
learning or other accomplishments. Henry Swinburne commented scathingly
that, 'for want of the polish and succours of education, their wit remains
obscured by the rudest ignorance and the most ridiculous prejudices'.[19]

One thing commented on with a mixture of curiosity and disapproval by all
travellers in eighteenth-century Spain was the custom, introduced from Italy,
for married women to have a *cortejo*.[20] This man would act as her constant

---

[16] Christian August Fischer [pseud. Frederick Augustus Fischer], *Travels in Spain in 1797 and 1798* (London: A. Strahan for T. N. Longman and O. Rees, 1802), pp. 174–75.
[17] Joseph Townsend, *A Journey through Spain in the Years 1786 and 1787*, 2nd edn (London: for C. Dilly, 1792), II, p. 37.
[18] Alexander Jardine, *Letters from Barbary, France, Spain, Portugal, Etc., by an English Officer* (Dublin: for Messrs. H. Chamberlaine, P. Byrne, J. Moore, and Grueber and McAllister, 1789), pp. 89–90.
[19] Henry Swinburne, *Travels through Spain in the Years 1775 and 1776*, 2nd edn (London: P. Elmsley, 1787), II, p. 218.
[20] For a discussion of the social institution of the *cortejo*, see Carmen Martín Gaite's *Usos*

companion, escorting her in public and acting as her devoted servant. As early as 1718, the Abbé Vayrac remarked that men were treating women as veritable idols and bowing to their every whim.[21] Whether the *cortejo* was a lover in every sense of the term was left deliberately ambiguous, but foreigners assumed the worst; to Swinburne it indicated at least 'the appearance of indelicate debauchery',[22] to Jardine it was an 'illicit love connection'[23] and the poet Robert Southey was disappointed that 'jealousy has been replaced by depravity'.[24]

Far from being forced into seclusion, women seemed to treat their husbands with an indifference bordering on contempt. Townsend noted that it was easy for a woman to hide a lover, since 'every part of the house is so accessible by day, and the husband is so completely nobody at home, so seldom visible, or, if visible, so perfectly a stranger to all who visit in his family, that the lover may easily escape unnoticed'.[25] The *cortejo* was expected to subject himself to his mistress's whims and demands: Fischer explained that a woman would reject a man's advances with disdain, for 'they must not be chosen, 'tis they must choose. 'Tis they that take upon themselves the part of the man, to whom they only leave the duty of complying with their wishes, and giving himself up entirely to their will'.[26] In fact, the role of *cortejo* appeared unattractively burdensome:

> To him a wish however slightly expressed, a caprice the most undecided, is a command, while the most inviolable respect for her whims and fancies, the most undisturbed submission of temper are sacred duties; in a word he must in all things be the passive agent of a woman whose ardent imagination often commands what is impossible with the most impatient egotism.[27]

We can see that this relationship is the mirror image of that described by León and Vives in their conduct manuals. Had Spain somehow become a society where women were dominant and men submissive? The truth was, of course, more complex. The numerous pamphlets that appeared in response to Feijoo's *Defence of Women* strongly rejected the possibility that women might be equal to men in intellect, let alone in any other way. Women were still married off to much older husbands chosen for them by their families, and the practice of the *cortejo* applied to only a limited section of society. Amar and Joyes were

---

amorosos del dieciocho en España (Madrid: Siglo Veintiuno de España Editores, 1972).
[21] Martín Gaite, *Usos amorosos del dieciocho en España*, pp. 2–3, citing Vayrac's *État présent de l'Espagne* (Amsterdam, 1718), I, p. 56.
[22] Swinburne, *Travels through Spain*, II, p. 218.
[23] Jardine, *Letters from Barbary*, p. 107.
[24] Robert Southey, *Letters Written During a Short Residence in Spain and Portugal*, 2nd edn (Bristol: Biggs and Cottle for T.N. Longman and O. Reeves, 1799), p. 54.
[25] Townsend, *A Journey through Spain*, II, p. 143.
[26] Fischer, *Travels in Spain*, p. 170.
[27] Fischer, *Travels in Spain*, pp. 171–72.

anxious to warn their contemporaries that the attentions paid to them by men would disappear once they were no longer young and pretty, and if they did not find something fulfilling to do, they were destined to a lonely old age. Joyes was particularly cynical about male flattery, seeing it purely as a seduction technique; the sexual double standard meant that only women would suffer if they succumbed to such a ruse.

Feijoo and Amar engaged closely with written sources in trying to convince their readers of women's talents. Joyes was less self-consciously intellectual, but was clearly an acute — and concerned — observer of contemporary social behaviour. They were writing in a century when new ideas were sweeping through Europe, and all three felt compelled to add their voices to the debate.

Spain in an Age of Reform

Upon the death in 1700 of the last Habsburg ruler of Spain, the first of the new Bourbon line, King Felipe V, found a country that had suffered a century of stagnation and was regarded as the backwater of Europe. The glories of the sixteenth century, when Spain had been the dominant military power in Europe and founded colonies in Florida, Cuba and south-east Asia, as well as Mexico and most of the mainland of South America, were long gone. The import of gold and silver bullion, far from enriching the country, had led to rampant inflation: Madame de Villars had complained in 1680 that her husband's allowance as French ambassador was reducing so rapidly in value that they were unable to make ends meet.[28] Spanish agriculture, industry and trade had fallen far behind France and Britain, and it was foreign merchants who benefited from the trade between Spain and its colonies, whilst the gold brought by the fleet in its annual voyage was hardly enough to pay the debts the crown had incurred for its increasingly unsuccessful wars.

In fact, the country once feared by the whole of Europe had become the butt of its neighbours' contempt. Spaniards were mocked as lazy, ignorant and superstitious. The *Short Account of the Destruction of the Indies* (*Brevísima relación de la destrucción de las Indias*, 1552) of Bartolomé de las Casas, widely translated into other languages, had made public some of the atrocities inflicted by the conquistadors during their subjugation of South America, and led to a belief that the Spanish character was uniquely cruel and vindictive. It was assumed that the Inquisition was all-powerful throughout the country and had stamped out all freedom of thought, leaving Spaniards in woeful ignorance of the changes going on in the world around them. The population was falling and large areas of the country lay uncultivated, a condition attributed to a propensity for idleness in the Spanish character. The deluded Don Quixote,

---

[28] Villars, *Lettres*, p. 52.

eponymous hero of Cervantes' famous novel, seemed to stand for all that was wrong with the country: a man who believed himself to be noble and heroic, but was in truth a forlorn and pathetic creature.

Once the War of the Spanish Succession came to an end in 1715, Felipe and his French advisers were able to turn their attention to reforming the Spanish administration and replenishing the depleted treasury. Unlike the centralised French state, Spain was a loose collection of provinces that jealously guarded their privileges, the most important being their exemption from the obligation to pay taxes to Madrid. Large tracts of land were owned by the church and by absentee landlords, and agriculture was neglected, so the country often had difficulty in feeding its population. Trade and industry were under-developed, since Spain had depended on importing resources from its South American colonies.

The Inquisition was still influential in Spain, though it was not as dominant as it had been in the past. It organised an auto-de-fé to welcome Felipe V to his new realm, but the king declined with distaste the pleasure of watching heretics burn. Moreover, in 1714 Felipe dismissed the Inquisitor General from his post and commissioned a report which concluded that the Inquisition should be restricted to a spiritual role. One significant result of this was that the power to prohibit and censor books was transferred from the church to the crown.

Although Felipe V intended to rule as absolute monarch, like his grandfather in France, he also wished to encourage the cultural development of his new realm. The intellectual elite of Madrid were able to discuss in their *tertulias* the new ideas circulating in the rest of Europe. In 1714 the king approved the setting up of the Royal Academy of Language, designed on the model of the Académie Française, which, like its counterpart, set out to produce an official Spanish dictionary. A number of regional academies, both literary and scientific, were established.

Felipe's successor, Fernando VI, continued the attempt to modernise the state by stimulating commerce, and established a Royal Academy of Fine Arts. But it was under the next ruler, Carlos III, that Spain made the greatest efforts to join the mainstream of Enlightenment Europe. By contrast with his two predecessors, Carlos was a hard-headed man who already had twenty-five years' experience of rule over the Kingdom of Naples. The grandees of Spain, the old nobility who had been accustomed to being the royal advisers, were sidelined in favour of new men from the lower orders who were determined to reform and modernise their country. José Moñino, later to be made Count of Floridablanca, oversaw the expulsion of the Jesuits from Spain and the imposition of royal control over the Inquisition. François de Cabarrús, a French financier, founded the first Spanish central bank, as a means of bringing the state's finances under control. Pedro Rodríguez, a lawyer of obscure origin, became Count of Campomanes, and wrote influential texts on political economy, promoting methods to revive industry and the arts. Another lawyer, Gaspar de Jovellanos, turned his attention to agriculture and published a lengthy report on the state of farming throughout Spain, with detailed recommendations for land reform.

All of these eminent figures found themselves, perhaps to their own surprise, caught up in the debate about the role of women in society. The challenge to contemporary assumptions initiated by Benito Feijoo in 1726 continued to influence both men and women in Spain until the century was over.

Reconsidering the Spanish Enlightenment

It has long been a widely-received opinion that Spain did not have an Enlightenment. The country was known for its many internal customs barriers, and Voltaire sneered that there was one at the gates of Madrid especially designed to prevent the entry of new ideas.[29] As has already been discussed, Spain was something of a closed book to foreigners during the eighteenth century, and it is still often assumed that the country continued to slumber under the weight of monarchical absolutism and religious obscurantism.

It is certainly true that Spain was a consumer rather than a creator of new ideas, but there was a real hunger for information, especially during the thirty-year reign of King Carlos III, reflected in the increased importation of foreign books, the development of a flourishing press, and an urge to travel abroad.

The French Revolution came as a shock to Spain, and chief minister Floridablanca imposed harsh censorship and banned foreign publications, in the hope of preventing the spread of seditious ideas. The reign of Carlos IV saw the return to power of the more conservative elements in society; his father's reforming ministers were dismissed from their posts and jailed on dubious charges. The Napoleonic invasion of 1808 resulted in the elevation to the throne of Joseph Bonaparte, and liberal-minded members of the Spanish elite now found themselves with a dilemma: Joseph had been imposed on Spain by bloody foreign invasion, but he represented the best hope of continuing the political and economic reforms they regarded as essential for the prosperity of their country. The only apparent alternative was Fernando, the exiled son of Carlos IV, who was known as hostile to reformist ideas and determined to restore absolute rule.

Those reform-minded Spaniards who chose to support Joseph found themselves condemned by their fellow-citizens as *afrancesados*, or pseudo-Frenchmen, and accused of fraternising with the country's enemies. Following the defeat of Napoleon, Fernando VII returned to Spain in 1814, promptly

---

[29] Letter from Voltaire to Marqués de Miranda, 10 August 1767, in *Œuvres Complètes*, (Paris: Garnier, 1887–1882), XLV, p. 344. Cited in Jean Sarrailh, *L'Espagne Éclairée de la seconde moitié du XVIIIe Siècle* (Paris: Imprimerie Nationale, 1954), p. 289.

abolished the liberal constitution that had been adopted in his absence, and had its supporters arrested. At that point the Spanish Enlightenment was certainly over.

Even within Spain itself many people have continued to believe that ever since the Golden Age of the sixteenth century their country has been on the dark side of Europe. During the twentieth century it suited Franco to play down Spain's participation in the Enlightenment and to characterise liberalism as an alien import that was incompatible with the country's character and traditions: the official historiography presented Spain's eighteenth century as a period of decadence and failure. This is now changing: the first detailed study of Spain in the later eighteenth century was Jean Sarrailh's monumental book *L'Espagne Éclairée de la seconde moitié du XVIIIe Siècle*,[30] published in 1954, followed by Richard Herr's *The Eighteenth-Century Revolution in Spain*.[31]

More recent scholarship has begun to demonstrate the extent to which, for an all too brief period, Spain played its part in the Enlightenment in a distinctive way. Spain's reformers took from their neighbours the ideas that suited them and adapted them to their own needs. They were not interested in over-arching philosophies of existence so much as practical inventions that could help them to overcome their country's material backwardness. Carlos III may have expelled the Jesuits and reduced the power of the Inquisition, but overt anti-clerical polemic would not have been welcome: censors still had to declare that the books they approved were not in any way inconsistent with the Catholic faith. The Spanish reformers were less interested in metaphysics than in identifying a new type of plough. As Jesús Astigarraga has recently noted, by the time the first Spanish translations of works by Jean-Jacques Rousseau entered the country in 1799, Spaniards already had access to works on political economy by Adam Smith and David Hume: the Spanish desire was not principally for liberty and equality but prosperity.[32]

Sarrailh described Feijoo as 'the great precursor to whom we must always return',[33] thus identifying the Benedictine as Spain's earliest disseminator of Enlightenment ideas. Feijoo declared that it did not matter that Isaac Newton was a heretic if his ideas proved to be useful, beneficial or indeed true. He would not of course have found it necessary to state this had many of his contemporaries not taken the contrary view.

---

[30] Sarrailh, *L'Espagne Éclairée*. Translated as *La España Ilustrada de la Segunda Mitad del Siglo XVIII* (Madrid: Fondo De Cultura Económica De España, 1979).

[31] Richard Herr, *The Eighteenth-Century Revolution in Spain* (Princeton: Princeton University Press, 1958).

[32] Jesús Astigarraga, ed., *The Spanish Enlightenment Revisited* (Oxford: Oxford University Studies in the Enlightenment, Voltaire Foundation, 2015), p. 17.

[33] Sarrailh, *L'Espagne Éclairée*, p. 8.

One of the important aspects of the Spanish Enlightenment was the way it, in Astigarraga's words, 'initiated the creation of the public sphere [and] promoted the participation of women in it'.[34] This book aims to contribute towards a greater understanding of how some women exploited this opportunity.

Note on the Translations

The translation of Feijoo's *Defensa de las mugeres* is based on the fourth edition of the *Teatro Crítico Universal*, I (1731), chapter 16, 331–400.

The first volume of the *Teatro Crítico* was published sixteen times between 1726 and 1781. I have compared the 1731 edition with the online transcription of the 1778 edition (<www.filosofia.org/bjf/bjft116.htm>), and (with the exception of a small number of evident transcription errors in the online version and its use of modernised spelling) have found only one difference between the two (the exception being one extra sentence in Chapter XIII). Feijoo's practice was not to rewrite or amend his published work, but to add new arguments in subsequent volumes. Therefore, the 1731 edition has been taken as definitive.

Feijoo numbered every paragraph of his essays, but that practice is not employed here, as it seems unnecessarily distracting. However, given the multiplicity of different editions, the footnotes to the Introduction refer to chapter and paragraph numbers rather than page numbers.

In the ninth volume of the *Teatro Crítico*, published in 1740, Feijoo added a number of notes to his previous essays, including the *Defensa de las mugeres*, described as *Adiciones a este tratado*. In subsequent editions, these were distributed throughout the volumes as appendices to the relevant essays. The notes consist of sources, justifications or extra examples. Since they do not materially affect Feijoo's argument and were made subsequent to the 1731 text, they are not included here.

The translation of Josefa Amar's *Discurso in defensa del talento de las mugeres* is based on the transcription provided by the website Antología del Ensayo: <http://www.ensayistas.org/antologia/XVIII/amar-bor/>. A facsimile of the original edition of 1786 is available in López-Cordón's *Condición femenina y razon ilustrada*, and is transcribed in Negrín Fajardo's *Ilustración y educación*.

The translation of the Prologue to Josefa Amar's *Discurso sobre la educación física y moral de las mujeres* is based on the original 1790 edition (Madrid: Benito Cano). A modern edition was published by López-Cordón in 1994.

The translation of Inés Joyes' *Apologia de las mugeres* is based on the original edition of 1798, at 177–204, available online at the website Biografías de Mujeres Andaluzas: <http://www.historiamujeres.es/feminismo/Apologia_mujeres_Ines_joyes.pdf>. The text is also transcribed and edited in Bolufer Peruga,

---

[34] Astigarraga, *The Spanish Enlightenment Revisited*, p. 14.

La vida y la escritura (2008), at 273–305, and in the edition by Helena Establier Pérez (2009) of the entire 1798 volume, including the *Historia de Rasselas, príncipe de Abisinia*.

The style of all three writers is clear and concise. It has occasionally been necessary to break up sentences or paragraphs for improved readability.

Benito Jerónimo Feijoo and the
Defence Of Women

Benito Jerónimo Feijoo y Montenegro was considered an influential precursor of the Spanish Enlightenment. He was extraordinarily well-read and open-minded, and his determination to challenge error, folly and prejudice wherever he found them led to a firestorm of debate.

Feijoo's first work appeared in 1726, entitled *Theatro Critico Universal, o Discursos Varios en todo género de materias, para Desengaño de Errores Comunes* (*Universal Critical Theatre, or Various Discourses on all sorts of matters, for the Correction of Common Errors*). It consisted of sixteen essays on a variety of subjects. The final essay in the volume, running to seventy pages, was the *Defensa de las Mugeres*, or 'Defence of Women'.

Over the course of the next twelve years, Feijoo published a further seven volumes of the *Teatro Crítico*,[1] containing over one hundred more essays, and from 1742 to 1760 he brought out five volumes entitled *Cartas Eruditas*, or 'Erudite Letters'. He was a highly prolific and popular writer, and his books were frequently reprinted, running into more than twenty editions over sixty years.

The Life and Times of Benito Feijoo

Benito Jerónimo Feijoo y Montenegro was born in 1676 in Galicia in north-western Spain, the eldest of ten children. His parents were both of noble descent, and his father was a cultivated and educated man. At the age of twelve he made the unusual decision to renounce his claim as eldest son, which would have seen him succeed to the family estate, and chose a religious life. He joined the Benedictine order at the age of fourteen (along with the Jesuits, the Benedictines were considered the most intellectual of the religious orders), studied at the ancient and famous University of Salamanca, and obtained his doctorate from the University of San Vicente in Oviedo. Apart from two brief visits to Madrid, he spent most of the rest of his life in Oviedo, where he was

---

[1] The modern Spanish spelling will be adopted from this point.

professor of philosophy and theology from 1710 to 1721, with further promotions to more senior chairs in 1724 and 1739. He was elected abbot of his monastery on two occasions, in 1721 and 1729. He retired in 1739 and devoted himself to writing until his death in 1764 at the age of eighty-eight.

The moment when Feijoo started to write represented a turning point in Spain. Whilst the majority of the population was poor, illiterate and dominated by the authority of the church, the educated class eagerly took advantage of the opening to Europe to read, discuss and exploit the torrent of new ideas emerging in particular from France and England.

Feijoo was educated in a system that had changed little since the Middle Ages. As a result, he was a natural reader of Latin: in chapter seven of volume two of the *Cartas Eruditas*, in which he summarised a French book for the benefit of the monks in a monastery in Madrid, he stated that whilst he would translate the French quotations, he knew there would be no need to do so with the Latin verses, which everyone would understand.

As a priest, Feijoo was not only intimately familiar with the Bible but also with the theological commentaries of the early Fathers of the Church, such as St Augustine, St John Chrysostom and Gregory of Nazianzus. An essential part of his training was the study of the works of Aristotle, regarded as the greatest of the pagan philosophers, whose views on astronomy, medicine and the natural world were considered to be infallibly correct. The combination of the scriptures, theological commentaries and the works of Aristotle formed the basis of Scholasticism, the teaching of the major academic centres known as the 'schools'.

Like all educated men of his age, Feijoo was also well-read in the classical authors. Some of the stories in the *Defence of Women*, such as that of Portia, are clearly taken from Plutarch's *Lives of the Greeks and Romans*. His familiarity with Cicero is not surprising, since he was regarded as the greatest exponent of the art of rhetoric. However, Feijoo also quoted from Ovid's *Amores*, which was regarded as a morally risqué book, and from Lucretius' *De Rerum Natura*, which had been rejected by the church as promoting atheism.

Feijoo was a voracious reader: he enjoyed travellers' accounts, particularly of South America (e.g. Mandelslo, Muñoz Camargo, Ribadeynera), and mined dictionaries and encyclopaedias for information (e.g. Moreri, Thomas Corneille, Beyerlinck). He was a subscriber to the *Mémoires pour l'Histoire des Sciences & des Beaux Arts* (commonly known as the *Mémoires de Trévoux*), an influential literary journal published by a group of Jesuits in France, which contained summaries, reviews and commentaries on a wide range of contemporary publications in all fields of knowledge. (Feijoo stated that in 1729 he owned one hundred volumes of this journal.)[2]

---

[2]   *Teatro Crítico*, prologue to volume III.

Feijoo was clearly a French speaker, and frequently quoted and commented on writers such as La Mothe Le Vayer, Malebranche, Buffier and Descartes. Again, his reading was rather broader than might be expected, given his position: he clearly had a copy of Pierre Bayle's *Dictionnaire*, which had been banned by both the Catholic and the Protestant authorities as subversive, and referred favourably to the *Essais* of Michel de Montaigne, a work which in his day was still on the church's *Index of Prohibited Books*, and whose Spanish translation was confiscated in manuscript by the Inquisition.

Another writer regarded with suspicion by the church was René Descartes, who had rejected the closed Aristotelian system and asked questions about the nature of the universe and human existence. Feijoo's friend Father Martín Sarmiento commented that all modern philosophers had the misfortune to be accused of being Cartesians,[3] and this clearly happened to Feijoo, since he objected to being given this label, saying he had always strongly opposed the French philosopher.[4] In fact, he admired the man for his learning and imagination, but disagreed with his conclusions.[5] His particular concern was that Descartes had rejected one theoretical system and attempted to replace it with another: he found unconvincing the deductive approach that attempted to derive scientific facts by logical reasoning from first principles. He explained that he placed Descartes among the followers of Aristotle 'because no less than they [...] he wished to rule the whole of physics through imagination and ideas'.[6]

The philosopher whom Feijoo truly admired was an Englishman: Sir Francis Bacon, Baron Verulam. (There is no reason to believe Feijoo knew any English, but fortunately many English philosophical works, including Bacon's, were written in or translated into Latin.) He referred to Bacon frequently throughout the *Teatro Crítico* and the *Cartas Eruditas*,[7] and praised him for his scientific method, whereby facts were to be established by observation and tested by experiment. General principles would be derived from the accumulation of facts: the opposite of the Cartesian system. This was very much Feijoo's own approach, to the extent that his friend Martín Martínez, a Professor of Anatomy, referred to Feijoo as the 'new Spanish Verulam'.[8]

Feijoo was clearly aware of the works of other English scientists, and wrote admiringly of Boyle, Newton and Harvey, insisting that experience rather than authority was the only arbiter of truth.[9] In a chapter entitled 'The Great

---

[3]   Martín Sarmiento, *Demostración del Teatro Crítico* (Madrid: Fernandez de Arrojo, 1757).
[4]   *Teatro Crítico*, prologue to volume III. See also *Cartas Eruditas*, II, Letter 16, para. 15.
[5]   *Cartas Eruditas*, II, Letter 16, para. 17; II, Letter 23, para. 6.
[6]   *Teatro Crítico*, V, ch. 11, para. 8.
[7]   *Teatro Crítico*, III, ch. 13, para. 97; *Cartas Eruditas*, II, Letter 23, para. 5.
[8]   Martín Martínez, *Carta Defensiva*, in *Teatro Crítico*, II, para. X.
[9]   *Teatro Crítico*, III, ch. 13, paras 30 and 87; V, ch. 11, para. 42; *Cartas Eruditas*, II, Letter 23, para. 15.

Authority of Experience' he commented: 'I find more delicate ingenuity and more perspicuity in many of the experiments of the famous Boyle, than I do in all the abstractions and reduplications of the most subtle metaphysicians'.[10]

Feijoo was frustrated by the slow progress of Spain in the sciences, when compared with France, England and the Netherlands. He was embarrassed to admit that most Spaniards still refused to accept that the earth circulated round the sun,[11] and felt it necessary to point out to his countrymen that ideas should not be resisted merely because they originated from Protestants: in one of his *Cartas Eruditas* he proclaimed that 'In England Newtonian philosophy is dominant. Isaac Newton, its founder, is as much a heretic as the rest of the inhabitants of that island. Despite this, nothing has been found to date in his philosophy which is either directly or indirectly opposed to the true faith'.[12] To close the door to all new doctrines for fear that they might include some error dangerous to religion would, in Feijoo's view, be to 'condemn the soul to wretched slavery, fetter human reason with a short chain and imprison an innocent mind in a narrow cell, solely to avoid the remote contingency that it might commit some mistakes in the future'.[13] He did not, he said, wish to see ignorance awarded the glorious attribute of being necessary for the defence of faith.

The success of the *Teatro Crítico* was based on the fact that Benito Feijoo was intimately acquainted with the details of the old system, whose flaws he wished to expose, and open-minded enough to appreciate the new ways of thinking that were circulating in Europe. His arguments in favour of women's intellectual equality with men were typical of this approach.

The Works of Benito Feijoo

In the prologue to the first volume of the *Teatro Crítico*, Feijoo explains that, as his sub-title (various discourses on all sorts of matters, for the correction of common errors) suggests, he is setting out to identify and correct numerous opinions that are almost universally held by the *vulgo* or ignorant. During the course of his works it becomes clear that by *vulgo* he does not always mean the common mass of people, for he regards many so-called learned men as equally obtuse.[14] His concern is not merely to point out mistakes but to uproot and destroy beliefs and attitudes that may have been held for centuries but which he believes are foolish or dangerous. The word *desengaño* can mean to disillusion or disappoint; Feijoo knew that undermining people's long-held beliefs might

---

[10] *Teatro Crítico*, v, ch. 11, para. 36.
[11] *Cartas Eruditas*, ii, ch. 23, para. 23.
[12] *Cartas Eruditas*, ii, ch. 16, para. 23.
[13] *Cartas Eruditas*, ii, ch. 16, para. 25.
[14] *Cartas Eruditas*, ii, ch. 23, para. 29.

be unsettling and bewildering. The experience would not be pleasant, but it was for their own good.

Every eighteen months or so from 1726 until 1735, a new volume of the *Teatro Crítico* appeared, until there were eight volumes containing 117 essays in total. The subjects covered were indeed diverse, ranging from scientific matters such as the weight of air to the glories of Spanish history. His most challenging chapters focused on common superstitions, such as exorcism and possession by demons, the bad omens represented by eclipses, the practice of alchemy, or the use of magic and divination. His aim in each case was to point out how unconvincing was the so-called evidence for apparently miraculous phenomena, and to provide an alternative rational explanation. A subject he returned to on a number of occasions was contemporary medicine; he ridiculed doctors' practices such as taking the horoscope of a sick person before deciding on the appropriate treatment.

The word *crítico* was a challenging one for Feijoo's time. The Scholastic philosophy that still held sway over Spain held that all truth had already been discovered, and was set out in ancient books. Scholars were expected to expound and interpret the works of the past, not to invent new ideas or undermine accepted authorities. As Feijoo pointed out, scholars in other countries were able to disagree profoundly and argue passionately about all sorts of things to do with the human mind or the natural world without descending to personal insults, but this was not accepted practice in Spain. A critic was regarded with alarm as a potentially dangerous enemy. And indeed Feijoo showed no mercy to those he regarded as obstinate in their ignorance: in many of his essays those who cling to the philosophy of Aristotle or reject new ideas without even considering them are insulted in the roundest terms.

Feijoo claimed that his intention was to convert the *vulgo*, but it was clear he did not have in mind as his audience the general population of Spain. The vast majority of people were in any case illiterate, and books were expensive. Yet by making the deliberate choice of writing in Spanish rather than Latin, Feijoo indicated that he wanted to reach the educated population outside the university faculties. Nevertheless, his essays show astonishing erudition, and some delve into topics that require extensive prior knowledge in the reader; his analysis of Pyrrhonian scepticism is a case in point.[15]

In 1740, Feijoo published a supplement to the *Teatro Crítico*, refuting the objections of his various opponents and giving further evidence to support his arguments. Two years later he began a new series of publications, called *Erudite Letters*.[16] These were a rather different type of writing: Feijoo was responding

---

[15] *Teatro Crítico*, III, ch. 13.

[16] *Cartas eruditas, y curiosas en que, por la mayor parte, se continúa el designio del Teatro Crítico Universal, impugnando, o reduciendo a dudosas, varias opiniones comunes* (Erudite

to letters from his friends and supporters on topics of mutual interest, and was able to assume that his immediate audience at least was in sympathy with his views. In one letter he attempts to persuade a friend to learn French rather than Greek, and in another he responds to the views of another cleric on the subject of earthquakes. He writes about freemasons, obstetrics, how to get rid of thieves, and the delights of music. Five volumes containing 163 letters were published, finishing in 1760 when Feijoo was eighty-four years old.

There is no doubt that Feijoo was a devout Catholic: he insisted that the best philosophy was one that was consistent with the Christian religion,[17] and observed that the unreliability of human reason should lead us to 'be firm and steady in observing a due subjection to the sacred dogmas of faith'.[18] He nevertheless made a distinction between the articles of faith and the layers of superstition that had developed over the centuries and which in his view had to be rooted out. In this he was consistent with the principles laid down by the Council of Trent in the sixteenth century, which set out to reform the Catholic church; it is notable that despite all his challenges to Spanish theologians, and the continuing influence of the Inquisition, Feijoo was never investigated for heresy.

To those of a modernising attitude, who were ashamed of Spain's reputation as a scientific and philosophic backwater, Feijoo was a welcome champion. The influence of his works, including the *Defence of Women*, continued throughout the century.

The Woman Question

Feijoo's wide reading would have made him familiar with the *querelle des femmes*, the argument about women's nature and moral qualities that had been rumbling on for centuries. Many of the misogynistic texts based their arguments on the book of Genesis, which describes the creation of Eve from Adam's rib, and her temptation by the Devil which led her to persuade Adam to join her in eating the forbidden fruit. Eve's punishment was to be condemned by God to be subservient to her husband. Pro-women writers had to wrestle with this in order to prove that it was not as damning as it appeared; the fact that Feijoo also felt the need to address this issue demonstrates the grip this view still held on the mind of the *vulgo* in his time.

A regular feature of pro-women publications was a catalogue of illustrious women.[19] These lists often included semi-mythical characters from classical

---

and curious letters, most of which continue the objective of the Universal Critical Theatre, opposing or casting doubt on various common opinions).

[17] *Cartas Eruditas*, II, Letter 23, para. 14. See also *Teatro Crítico*, III, ch. 13, para. 92.

[18] *Teatro Crítico*, III, ch. 13, para. 88.

[19] Examples include Boccaccio, *De Claris Mulieribus* (*On Famous Women*; 1355–1359);

antiquity (Zenobia, Semiramis), historical Greek or Roman characters (Portia the wife of Brutus, Cornelia the mother of the Gracchi), women who appear in the Bible (Deborah, Judith, Esther), and female saints and martyrs. Their heroism was generally of a passive nature, and they were frequently celebrated for having killed themselves to save their husbands or defend their chastity, or for accepting martyrdom for their faith.

Feijoo chose to support his defence of women with examples of those who governed states or showed military heroism, as well as writers and painters. The women he highlighted were, however, significantly different from those admired by his predecessors. He deliberately excluded women from the Bible or Christian martyrs, on the grounds that their deeds were a reflection of divine grace rather than their personal qualities. Furthermore, his focus was not on the women of antiquity: he describes Semiramis as being 'the first woman whom history has rescued from the obscurity of fable', indicating that he did not plan to shore up his arguments with examples of women who were frankly fictional. His list of queens includes Elizabeth I of England, Catherine de Medici and Isabella of Castile: all historical characters from recent centuries whose exploits would have been familiar to his readers.

Feijoo's choice of women who showed martial valour starts with a cursory list of classical names, but again he soon turns to historically-attested characters from various wars in France, Italy and Spain. In fact, wherever possible, he uses examples who are rarely mentioned by his predecessors in the genre, drawing anecdotes from the travel writings of Mandelslo and Muñoz Camargo[20] to demonstrate that female courage and virtue are universal, and not limited to any particular time or place. He is also unusual in that he draws on his own experience: in his discussion of women who kept secrets despite being put to torture, he refers to an unnamed woman he had known personally, and also to observations made by an acquaintance.

When he turns to the question of female literary talent, Feijoo is particularly keen to showcase Spanish women, to counter the fact that 'foreigners regard Spain as having little reputation in the field of literature'. Many of these, as well as the French, Italian and other women whose biographies he summarises, were contemporary or lived in the sixteenth and seventeenth centuries. Once again, he encourages his readers not to base their view of women's abilities on the arguments of ancient writers, but by observing what they could see around them.

Henricus Cornelius Agrippa, *De nobilitate et praecellentia foeminei sexus* (1529); Lucrezia Marinella, *La nobiltà et l'eccellenza delle donne* (1600).

[20] Johan Albrecht de Mandelslo, *The voyages and travels of the ambassadors sent by Frederick, Duke of Holstein, to the great Duke of Muscovy and the King of Persia*, trans. by John Davies (London: Dring and Starkey, 1642). Diego Muñoz Camargo's *Historia de Tlaxcala* (1585) was not published in full until 1892, but the manuscript was used by other writers in Feijoo's time.

It can be seen that Feijoo took the tradition of the catalogue of illustrious women that had been around for centuries, but used it in a different way and with novel examples. When we look at his intellectual arguments in defence of women, it is similarly difficult to pinpoint any particular literary source or influence. In fact, Feijoo seems to have been unaware of some of the most important pro-women texts published in Europe during his lifetime, such as *The Equality of Men and Women* by Marie de Gournay[21] or *The Equality of the Two Sexes* by François Poulain de la Barre.[22] We are led to the conclusion that Benito Feijoo was in fact a highly original author. His voracious reading allowed him to absorb ideas from numerous sources, but he did not copy or plagiarise other writers. In arguing that women were men's intellectual equals, he used arguments from modern life, recent history, contemporary writers and his own experience.

The Controversy Over the Defence of Women[23]

Feijoo's contemporaries regarded the *Defence of Women* as an extremely radical piece of work, and — depending on their own views — either hoped or feared that it might lead to social change. Within months of the appearance of the first volume of the *Teatro Crítico*, his opponents went into print. In December 1726, Laurencio Manco de Olivares brought out his *Contradefensa crítica a favor de los hombres* (Critical counter-defence in favour of men), in which he rehearsed the usual criticisms of women, and quoted some of the many writers of antiquity whose authority Feijoo had already deprecated. He poured contempt on Feijoo's statement that modesty was a predominant quality in women, surmising that since the Reverend Father lived in isolation from society, he might not be aware that modern women were showing a shocking lack of this virtue, in their dress, ostentatious finery and excessive use of make-up. Olivares described the evidence gathered by Feijoo for equality between men and women as charming but frankly apocryphal and, using Genesis as his authority, stated firmly that reason and understanding are exclusive to men.

---

[21] Marie Le Jars de Gournay, *Égalité des Hommes et des Femmes* ([n. p.: n. pub.], 1622).

[22] François Poulain de la Barre, *L'Egalité des deux Sexes, Discours Physique et Moral, où l'on voit l'importance de se Défaire des Préjugés* (Paris: Jean du Puis, 1673).

[23] For a detailed analysis of the controversy see Sally-Ann Kitts, *The Debate on the Nature, Role and Influence of Woman in Eighteenth-Century Spain* (Lampeter: Edward Mellen, 1985), pp. 33–50. See also Mónica Bolufer Peruga, *Mujeres e Ilustración: La construcción de la feminidad en la España del siglo XVIII* (Diputació de València, 1998), pp. 29–59; Oliva Blanco Corujo, *La polémica feminista en la España ilustrada: La 'Defensa de las Mujeres' de Feijoo y sus detractores* (Almud: Ediciones De Castilla-La Mancha, 2010), pp. 91–110; Theresa Ann Smith, *The Emerging Female Citizen: Gender and Enlightenment in Spain* (Berkeley: University of California Press, 2006), pp. 35–39.

By the middle of 1727, the *Contradefensa* had spawned more pamphlets,[24] some containing diatribes against contemporary women, attacking them for their brazen self-confidence and immodest dress. Some writers expressed concern about the dangers for the institution of marriage should women become convinced of their intellectual equality with their husbands, for even without this, they were already all too inclined to break the chain of subjection to men to which God had condemned them.

It was suggested that Feijoo had no business filling women's heads with the idea that they could rival men in the field of arts and letters, as if their vanity didn't cause enough trouble already. As a theologian, he should be aware that men's superiority was decreed by God, and women's vices were confirmed in the writings of the Fathers of the Church.

Feijoo's principal opponent was Salvador José Mañer, who in 1729 published an *Anti-Theatro Crítico* attacking the first two volumes of Feijoo's work, including the *Defence of Women*. Mañer stated firmly that since the beginning of the world, God had awarded primacy and dominion to men, and to attempt to argue for equality between men and women would be to disobey God's command and to invert the law of nature.[25] Feijoo's project was therefore doomed to failure.

Over twenty works directly attacking Feijoo were published in the years following the publication of the *Defence of Women*,[26] and the controversy certainly helped to sell his books. There were twenty editions of the *Teatro Crítico* between 1726 and 1787, and the *Defence of Women* was one of its best-known texts. It has been estimated that six hundred thousand copies of Feijoo's works were sold in Spain during the eighteenth century — a colossal number at a time when an average print run might be five hundred copies.[27]

Finally, Feijoo's friends in the court petitioned King Fernando VI, who responded in 1750 with a royal decree that from then on no one was to attack

---

[24] Examples include: Juan Martínez y Salafranca, *Desagravios de la Mujer Ofendida* (*Apology for the Insults to Women*); Ricardo Basco Flancas, *Apoyo a la Defensa de las Mujeres y Crisis de la Contradefensa Critica* (*Support of the Defence of Women against the Critical Counter-Defence*); Juan Antonio Santarelli, *Estrado Crítico en defensa de las mujeres* (*Critical Platform in Defence of Women*); and *Papel en defensa de su sexo* (*Pamphlet in Defence of her Sex*), by the clearly pseudonymous Marica La Tonta ('Stupid Marica'); *La Razon con desinteres fundada, y la Verdad cortesanamente vestida* (*Well-Grounded and Disinterested Reason, and Truth Politely Clothed*); Agustín de Castejon, *Dudas y Reparos sobre que consulta a Feijóo un escrupuloso* (*Doubts and Concerns Addressed to Feijoo by a Scrupulous Man*); Jaime Ardanaz y Centellas, *Tertulia Historica y Apologetica* (*Historic and Apologetic Discussion*). All published in 1727, except Centellas (1728).

[25] Salvador José Mañer, *Anti-Theatro Critico sobre el Primero y Segundo tomo del Theatro Critico Universal* (Madrid: Juan de Moya, 1729), p. 117.

[26] Smith, *The Emerging Female Citizen*, p. 17.

[27] Source: <www.filosofia.org/feijoo/htm>.

Father Feijoo; he was consequently left to publish the last two volumes of his *Cartas Eruditas* in peace.

Reception Outside Spain

Each volume of the *Teatro Crítico* was preceded by two or three Letters of Approbation. These were required by the Spanish system of official censorship: the censors had to confirm that the work submitted for publication was not contrary to the principles of religion or the laws of the land. In practice, the Letters in the *Teatro Crítico* (many of which were written by members of Feijoo's own Benedictine order) were more in the nature of rave reviews. Martín Sarmiento went so far as to describe himself as 'a passionate disciple of the author'.

A number of these prefatory letters referred to the positive reception the *Teatro* had received in other parts of Europe.[28] This view was confirmed by Élie Fréron, editor of the Parisian *Journal Étranger*, in a review of the *Cartas Eruditas* in December 1755, on the occasion of Feijoo's eightieth birthday; this opened with the words, 'The whole of Europe knows, at least by reputation, the Spanish work entitled *Teatro Crítico* by Dom Feijoo, one of the most prolific and famous writers to honour Spain today'.

By the time of Feijoo's death in 1764, selections from the *Teatro Crítico* had been translated into French, English, Italian and Portuguese.[29] Quite often only the first, or the first two volumes were translated, including the *Defence of Women*. In addition, translations of the *Defence of Women* were published separately, which indicates that this was one of Feijoo's essays that attracted the greatest interest.

In 1742, the first volume of the *Teatro Crítico* was translated into French by Nicolas-Gabriel Vaquette d'Hermilly, and in 1743 his translation of chapter XVI was published separately as *Défense ou éloge des femmes*.[30] The *Mémoires de Trévoux*, which had provided Feijoo with much of his material, published a lengthy and complimentary review of this translation in November 1743. In May and July 1755 the *Journal Étranger* published a new translation of the *Defence of Women* by the Abbé Prévost, later to be renowned as the author of *Manon Lescaut*.[31]

---

[28] Fr Joseph Perez in *Cartas Eruditas*, II; Gregorio Moreyras (26 August 1749) and Francisco Manuel de la Huerta y Vega (3 September 1749) in *Justa Repulsa*.

[29] A Portuguese translation of the first volume appeared in 1746 and a partial Italian translation in 1744. A complete Italian translation of the *Teatro Crítico* appeared in 1777–1782.

[30] *Theâtre critique, ou discours différents sur toutes sortes de matières pour détruire les erreurs communes, par le traducteur de l'Histoire Générale d'Espagne de Jean Ferreras* (Paris: Pierre Clement, 1742-1743). Vaquette D'Hermilly's French translation was re-published by Editions Rencontres in 1962, in a collection entitled *Sommets de la Littérature Espagnole*, and incorrectly attributed to Jean de Ferreras, who was Felipe V's librarian.

[31] *Journal Étranger*, May 1755, pp. 189–226; July 1755, pp. 192–223.

In England, the *Defence of Women* was first translated anonymously in 1765[32] and re-issued nine years later under a different title.[33] In 1780 a selection of essays from the *Teatro Crítico* appeared, translated by Captain John Brett, a retired naval officer. A number of these essays, including the *Defence of Women*, had already been published during the previous three years with Brett's knowledge but without giving his name. The January 1778 issue of the *Gentleman's Magazine*[34] included an article entitled 'On the Political Abilities of the Female Sex', which was in fact a copy of Brett's translation of chapter six of the *Defence of Women*, but without attribution.

The Lady's Magazine, or Entertaining Companion for the Fair Sex, which as its name implies was a source of dress patterns and serialised romantic novels, included in its editions running from November 1810 and August 1811 a monthly column consisting of a translation by one Elener [*sic*] Irwin of the whole of the *Defence of Women*, clearly described as being 'translated from the Spanish of Geronymo Feijoo', who was at that time little known in England. There has been no subsequent English translation until the present volume.

Benito Feijoo published the last volume of his *Cartas Eruditas* in 1753 and died eleven years later in 1764, at the age of eighty-eight. A comment made by Francisco Manuel de la Herta y Vega in the Approbation to *Justa Repulsa* (1749) could be regarded as his eulogy. He described Feijoo as 'the first, and possibly the only Spaniard who has tried to direct us by opening up a new, broad and delightful road toward the sciences, strewing with flowers the arid paths left to us by antiquity'.

Perhaps the last word on the *Defence of Women* should be Abel Boyer's positive review in the *Mercure de France*,[35] saying that 'Women, and especially those who are learned and virtuous, will be obliged out of gratitude to come to his defence; for nothing is more well-researched, obliging and well-argued in the first volume than the sixteenth and last dissertation, which is entirely dedicated to the defence of the fair sex'.[36]

The Structure and Style of the Defence of Women

Feijoo starts his essay with a challenge. He knows that he is setting out to defend a cause that most people will regard as not only wrong but positively

[32] *An Essay on Woman, or Physiological and Historical Defence of Women of the Fair Sex* (London: W. Bingley, 1768).
[33] *An Essay on the Learning, Genius & Abilities of the Fair Sex, proving them not inferior to man* (London: D. Steel, 1774).
[34] *The Gentleman's & London Magazine, or Monthly Chronologer* (Dublin, 1778), XLVIII, pp. 329–30.
[35] Quoted by Sarmiento in the *Demostración*.
[36] 'Les femmes, et surtout les femmes sçavantes et vertueuses, seront obligées, par reconnaissance, de prendre sa deffense ; car rien n'est plus recherché, plus obligeant, plus étendu dans le I volume, que la XVI et dernier dissertation, qui est toute employée à la deffense du beau Sexe.'

impertinent. He explains that his main theme will be women's intellectual abilities, but first he feels he has to tackle centuries-old beliefs about their moral imperfections. His first five chapters address in turn misogynistic opinions drawn from Genesis and Aristotle, as well as ingrained assumptions such as women's inability to keep secrets. He sets up a contrast between the virtues regarded as masculine, such as courage and prudence, and those believed to be feminine, like beauty, gentleness and modesty, and attempts to demonstrate that women's virtues are at least equivalent to those of men.

Feijoo then takes up a different argument: that the qualities of men are often found also in women. He lists famous queens and rulers to show that women are capable of government, and gives examples of women who demonstrated personal courage or military valour. This is followed by stories of women who kept secrets entrusted to them even under torture.

Having dealt with these issues, he turns to his main argument about women's aptitude for learning. He condemns male writers who have stated that women are naturally intellectually inferior to men, criticising them for displaying either blind prejudice or sloppy thinking. He admits as a fact that women do not equal men in their learning, but attributes this to the deficiencies of their education and their domestic seclusion which cuts them off from intellectual exchange.

Feijoo then turns to analyse the reasons given by those who argue for female intellectual inferiority. The theological reasoning that there is a difference in their souls he dismisses with contempt, and then goes on to mock those like Aristotle who say women have smaller brains or are of a cold and moist temperament, demanding to know whether they can prove this by experimental method. Modern writers like Malebranche who claim that women's cerebral fibres are more fragile than men's are treated in the same way.

Having countered all these arguments with abstract reasoning and personal observation, Feijoo then turns to the power of example, giving brief biographies of twenty-two historical women who were known for their skill in writing or rhetorical argument, and others who were famous artists.

Feijoo was regarded by his contemporaries as having a particularly lucid style, shorn of scholastic pedantry or baroque circumlocution. His writing was simple and clear, using short sentences and paragraphs; he did not aim to show off his erudition, but to engage and persuade his audience. His arguments are set out in logical order, and he gives verbal signposts as to where he is going: 'Passing to the topic of courage', 'We have now arrived at the main battlefield', 'I shall conclude by saying'. His paragraphs frequently start with prepositions (and, but, therefore, however), which lead his reader on to the next point.

Feijoo's style is conversational and immediate. He metaphorically grabs his reader by the lapels: 'So tell me'. He writes in the first person: 'I protest', 'This gets my vote'. The very first sentence of the essay is: 'I am engaging in a risky venture'. His experience as a priest and a professor shows through, for this is a style best suited to a lecture — or a sermon.

As he approaches the end of his essay, Feijoo is conscious that, particularly in a devout country like Spain, all his arguments may be regarded as irrelevant when set against the injunction in the Book of Genesis that women should be under the power of their husbands. This is a problem which he finds difficult to resolve: he first suggests that the biblical translation may be inaccurate, then that it was a punishment for Eve's sin rather than a recognition of any innate female inferiority, and finally that in order to avoid conflict within families, it was necessary that one member of the household should be invested with authority. But why this should be the husband rather than the wife, Feijoo can only regard as one of the mysteries of God.

Benito Jerónimo Feijoo

In Defence of Women

Madrid: Viuda de Francisco del Hierro, 1731, I, chapter 16, pp. 331–400

Chapter I

I am engaging in a risky venture. I enter the lists not only against the ignorant masses: to defend all women is to offend almost all men, for there is hardly any man who does not promote his own sex by criticising the other. The general contempt for women has become so widespread that they are scarcely acknowledged to have any good qualities at all, and are assumed to be full of moral defects and physical imperfections. But the strongest attack is on the limitations of their intellect. For this reason, once I have briefly defended them against the other charges, I shall discuss more broadly their aptitude for all types of learning and sublime knowledge.

The false prophet Muhammad refused women entry to the unlikely paradise that he destined for his followers, limiting their happiness to the delight of contemplating from outside the glory enjoyed by the men. What a fine thing it would be for wives to observe the bliss, repulsive in all respects, experienced by their husbands as they recline in the arms of new consorts, created anew for the purpose by that great spinner of lies![1] If we wish to understand how far the human race can fall into error, we need only observe how this fantasy is believed in many parts of the world.[2]

But it seems that those who would refuse women happiness in the future world are not much different from those who deny them almost all merit in this one. It is frequently the most depraved of the ignorant who describe women as a horrible sink of vices, as if men were the only repository of virtue. It is true that they cite as evidence for this belief many vicious invectives in an infinite number of books, scarcely any of which can accept that a single good woman exists, saying that even the best of them combine a modest face and a lascivious soul.

---

[1] The belief was that the houris' virginity was constantly restored.
[2] It was a common misconception in Europe that Muhammad excluded women from paradise. The 1765 English translator quotes in a footnote the *Turkish Letters* of Lady Mary Wortley Montagu, who had spent time in Constantinople, saying that this was incorrect.

Aspera si visa est, rigidasque imitate Sabinas,
Velle, sed ex alto dissimulare puta.

[Though she may look as severe as the Sabines,
She wants it all the same, and it is all a mask].[3]

Against such insults, contempt and distaste are the best defence. It is not uncommon that those who describe the defects of the female sex with the greatest frequency and vehemence are the same ones who are the most anxious to gain their approval. Euripides was extraordinarily vicious about women in his tragedies, but according to Atheneus and Stobeus he was devoted to them as individuals; he despised them in the theatre and idolised them in the bedroom. Boccaccio, who was lascivious to an extreme degree, attacked women in his violent satire called *The Labyrinth of Love*. What is the mystery behind this? Perhaps by pretending to hold this opinion he wanted to hide his own propensities; perhaps in brutally sating his sordid appetite he created a bitter emptiness that he could not express without accusing the opposite sex. Perhaps he sometimes took revenge with similar insults on those who refused his advances: for there are men who are so accursed that they say a woman is not virtuous because she refuses to do evil. We have seen some relieve their feelings through the most atrocious vengeance and unjust accusations, as shown by the tragic end of the beautiful Irish lady Miss Douglas. William Leont, in a blind rage against her because she had refused to succumb to his desires, accused her of the crime of treason; and supporting this calumny with paid witnesses, he had her condemned to death. He later confessed all, as La Mothe Le Vayer describes in his *Opuscules*.[4]

I do not deny that many women do wrong. But if we look carefully at the origin of their mistakes, how often do we find that the primary cause is the determined insistence of individuals of our own sex! If you wish to make all women virtuous, you need to start by reforming the men. Women have a natural tendency to raise a wall of modesty against all the assaults of appetite, and it is very rare for a breach in this wall to be made from within the citadel.

The declamations against women that we read in parts of the scriptures should be understood as being directed against those who have gone astray, as some of them do. And even when applied to the sex in general, this proves nothing, for the doctors of the soul say about women what the doctors of the body say about food: however good, useful and attractive it may be, if you misuse it you turn it into poison. Besides, we are all aware that an orator is allowed to exaggerate a risk if his intention is to warn of a danger.

So tell me, those of you who suppose the other sex to be more vicious than

---

[3]   Ovid, *Amores*, 2.4, lines 15–16.
[4]   François de La Mothe Le Vayer (1588–1672), *Opuscules ou Petite Traictez* (Paris: Sommaville & Courbet, 1644).

our own, how do you reconcile this with the fact that the church awards to them in particular the title of 'devout'? How so, when eminent doctors say more women than men will be saved, despite there being fewer of them? They base this, as they are obliged to, on the observation that women are more inclined toward piety.

I can hear my argument being opposed by that loudly-proclaimed — and false — theory that women are the cause of all evil. Even the lowest class of men will continually insist as proof of this the idea that La Cava[5] brought about the fall of Spain, and Eve that of the whole world.

But the first of these examples is absolutely false. Count Julian was the one who brought the Moors into Spain without being persuaded by his daughter; she did nothing more than disclose to her father the outrage she had suffered. What a tragedy for women if when they were brutally assaulted, they were to be deprived of the comfort of revealing the fact to their fathers or husbands! Only those who desire to carry out such vicious attacks would wish this to be so. If sometimes the revenge that follows is unjust, that is the fault not of the innocent victim but of the man who carries out the vengeance and the one who provoked it with the insult; and so the entire fault remains with the men.

The second example, if it proved that women in general are worse than men, would similarly prove that angels in general are worse than women; for as Adam was tempted to sin by a woman, the woman was tempted by an angel. To this day it has not been decided whether Adam or Eve committed the worse sin, because the Fathers are divided on the subject. And in truth the excuse which Cajetan[6] allows to Eve, that she was tricked by a creature of far greater intelligence and cleverness, which was not the case with Adam, reduces her guilt considerably in this respect.

Chapter II

Passing from the moral to the physical, which is closer to our intention here, the superiority of the robust over the delicate sex is taken as totally proven, to the extent that many feel justified in calling the female an imperfect animal or even a monster, convincing themselves that nature's intention in the act of conception is always to create a male, and it is only a mistake or a defect in the material or the process that results in a female.[7]

---

[5]   Rodrigo, the last Visigoth king of Spain, reputedly raped Florinda, daughter of Count Julian, so Julian betrayed Rodrigo to the Moors, resulting in the Moorish domination of Spain. *La Cava* means a prostitute or seductress, an epithet which came to be applied to Florinda.
[6]   Tommaso de Vio (1469–1534), known as Cajetan or Gaetanus, was an Italian cardinal. He was a leading theologian and spokesman for Catholic opposition to the teachings of Martin Luther, known also for his extensive commentary on the *Summa Theologica* of Thomas Aquinas.
[7]   Aristotle in his *De generatione animalium* described woman as an imperfect or

Oh excellent philosophers! It would follow from this that nature is intent on its own ruin, since it cannot conserve the species without the contribution of both sexes. It would also follow that the human race fails more often than it succeeds in this, its principal activity, since in fact it produces more women than men. And how can we attribute the creation of females to insufficient strength or defective material, when we see them born of parents who are healthy, robust and in the flower of youth? Does this mean that if man had preserved his original state of innocence he would not have had these defects, no women would have been born, and there would have been no propagation of the human race?

I know the author who spread this absurd idea, to support his declared grudge against the opposite sex. It was Amalric,[8] a Parisian doctor of the thirteenth century: he was the one who, amongst other errors, said that if our state of innocence had continued, all the individuals of our species would have been male, and that God would have created them all himself as he had created Adam.

Amalric was a blind follower of Aristotle, to the extent that all, or nearly all, of his errors were consequences that he drew from the doctrines of that philosopher. For finding that in several of his works Aristotle teaches that the female is a defective animal, and her creation is an accident and alien to the intentions of Nature, Amalric inferred that there were no women before the Fall. Thus, as is often the case, a theological heresy derives from a physical error.

But the great respect which Amalric professed for Aristotle was in the end bad for both of them, for Amalric's errors were condemned by the Council of Paris in 1209; the same Council banned Aristotle's works, and this was confirmed later by the prohibition of Pope Gregory IX. Amalric died a year before his doctrines were proscribed: his bones were dug up and thrown into a pit.

We can see from this that we should give no credence to any doctor, however eminent he may otherwise be, who claims that the female sex is defective just because Aristotle said so. He still has numerous sectaries, though not all of them fall into the same error as Amalric. It is certain that Aristotle was unfair to women, for he not only made excessive claims about their physical defects but was even more vehement against their moral failures, as I shall discuss later. Who would not assume therefore that his inclinations would cause him to have an aversion to the opposite sex? But this could not be further from the truth. Not only was he passionately devoted to the two women whom he loved, but he

---

malformed creature. According to him, in the act of conception Nature would always attempt to create a male, and only some defect in the process would result in a female.

[8] Amalric of Bena. His pantheistic philosophy was condemned in 1204; in 1209 ten of his followers were burnt before the gates of Paris, and Amalric's body was exhumed and burnt, and the ashes scattered.

was so infatuated with the first, called Pythias (who some say was the daughter and others the niece of Hermias, tyrant of Atarneus),[9] that he went so far in his delirium to burn incense to her as if she were a goddess. There are also stories that he had a passionate affair with a serving-maid, though Plutarch cannot bring himself to believe them. But in this case we should give more credence to Theocritus of Chios[10] (who in a scathing epigram mocked Aristotle for his obscene behaviour), because he was contemporary with Aristotle whereas Plutarch came much later. In this example we can see that vicious criticism of women is in most if not all cases accompanied by an excessive desire for them, as we commented above.

From the same physical error which condemns woman as an imperfect animal arises another theological error condemned by St Augustine,[11] whose authors said that at the universal resurrection the imperfect work of Nature would be made perfect by transforming all women into men, and thus Grace would complete the work which Nature had left unfinished.

This error is very similar to that of the deluded alchemists who, based on the principle that when Nature creates a metal it always intends to produce gold, and only ends up with some other imperfect metal through a lack of strength, conclude that through their art they can bring this work to perfection, and turn into gold what was born as iron. But in the end this error is easier to tolerate because it does not touch on matters of faith, given that (whatever is the intention of Nature, and the imaginary capacity of their art) gold is in fact the most noble of metals and the others are of much inferior quality. But in the question we are addressing here it is all false: that Nature always tends towards the male, that the creation of a woman is a miscarriage, and far more so that this mistake must be put right at the final Resurrection.

Chapter III

Nevertheless, I do not approve of the boldness of Zacutus Lusitanus,[12] who in the introduction to his treaty *The Diseases of Women* used frivolous arguments to give women the upper hand, claiming that they are physically more perfect than men. He could have used more convincing arguments to make his case. My task is not to prove that women are superior but that they are equal.

To start by making ourselves aware of the difficulty in doing this (and leaving

9   Pythias was the adopted daughter of Hermias of Aterneus. She was Aristotle's first wife, and predeceased him.
10   Diogenes Laertius in his *Vita Aristotelis* quoted an Epigram against Aristotle by Theocritus of Chios, in which he implied that Aristotle had sexual relations with Hermias, and that Hermias was a eunuch.
11   St Augustine, *Civitas Dei*, Book 22, ch. 17.
12   Zacuto Lusitano (1575–1642) was a Portuguese physician who wrote a number of medical treatises, including *Morbis Mulierum* (*The Diseases of Women*).

aside for the moment the question of intellect, which will be argued separately, and is more important to this discourse) let us take three qualities in which men appear to have a clear advantage over women: strength, fortitude and prudence. But even if women have to cede preference to men in these aspects, they can claim superiority in three other qualities in which they excel: beauty, gentleness and candour.

Strength and beauty are physical qualities, and may be considered to balance each other. Many people would consider the latter to be more important, and they would be right if the value of these attributes were to be judged only by the pleasure they afford the eye. But if in deciding which has the advantage we put more weight on the matter of public utility, then I think we would prefer strength to beauty. The world owes to the strength of men essential advantages in the three pillars that sustain any state: war, agriculture and mechanics. I know of no important benefit we derive from the beauty of women, except by accident. Some may argue that far from being advantageous to us, it can cause great damage through inciting illicit love affairs, stirring up rivalry and causing anxiety, worry and suspicion to those responsible for them.

But this accusation is ill-founded, being based on insufficient thought. If all women were ugly, then those who had the fewest deformities would be admired just as much as beauties are today, and would cause just as much damage. The least ugly of them, if you put her in Greece, would cause the burning of Troy as Helen did; and put in the palace of King Rodrigo would bring about the ruin of Spain, as did La Cava. In countries where women are less attractive, there are no fewer illicit affairs than in those where they are the most beautiful and elegant. And in Muscovy, which has more beautiful women than all the other kingdoms of Europe, they are less abandoned to lust than in other countries, and conjugal fidelity is observed much more strictly.

In any case, it is not beauty in itself which causes the evils which are attributed to it. But in the case in question, I give my vote in favour of strength, which I judge to be a much more practical advantage than beauty. Thus as far as this is concerned, men take the credit. But women retain the right to reply, supported by the opinion of many learned men, received as truth by an entire school of philosophy,[13] that the will is nobler than the understanding. This is in their favour, for though strength may be valued more highly, as having greater influence over the understanding, beauty is more attractive and has greater sway over the will.

The quality of fortitude which ennobles men may be contrasted with gentleness which is the splendour of women. But I should make it clear that we are not talking about these and other similar qualities as virtues in the formal

---

[13] The Stoics held that training oneself to behave well was more important than acquiring knowledge for its own sake.

meaning of the term, since in this sense they are not physical aspects but are rooted and established in the temperament, which at its outset is neutral as to good or bad; and so it would be better to call them flexibility or inflexibility of character, rather than fortitude or gentleness.

You may say that gentleness in women often declines into frivolity; and I reply that constancy in men often degenerates into stubbornness. I admit that firmness in the right direction is highly beneficial, but no one can deny that obstinacy towards the bad causes great evils. If it were put to me that an invincible adherence to good or evil is exclusive to the angels, I would say that this is not so certain that certain great theologians do not deny it. Many properties which in superior natures are a mark of their excellence may in those who are inferior be a sign of imperfection. According to the doctrine of St Thomas, the more perfect the angels are the fewer their ideas, whereas for man to have few ideas is a defect. For angels to study would damage their understanding; whereas it enlightens the mind of man.

The prudence[14] of men is equivalent to the candour of women. In fact, we can say it is inferior, for in reality it is much more valuable to the human race for individuals to be candid than to be clever. No one imagines the Golden Age to have consisted of prudent men, but of sincere ones.

If someone should object that much of what in women is called candour is in fact indiscretion, I would reply that much of what men call prudence is falsity, duplicity and treachery, which is worse. Moreover, this same indiscreet frankness in women, which sometimes acts against the dictates of reason, is a good thing if it is a sign of their character. Since no one is ignorant of his own vices, whoever is aware that they are many carefully closes the recesses of his heart to spying eyes. Whoever commits crimes in his own house does not keep his door open all day so they may be observed. Caution is the bosom companion of malice. Whoever, on the other hand, finds it easy to open his heart, knows it is not so vile. From this point of view, the openness of women is always preferable: if it is regulated by good judgment it is perfection, and if not, it is still a good sign.

Chapter IV

In addition to the good qualities that have been described, there remains the one which in women is the most beautiful and transcendent of all, which is modesty:[15] a grace that is so characteristic of that sex that even their corpses

---

[14] Feijoo uses the word *prudencia*, which when used by classical writers implied the ability to think ahead and weigh the results of one's actions. (It was not limited to the modern sense of 'caution'.) He suggests that naïve honesty may be morally superior to careful consideration.

[15] The classical virtue of *modestia* implied much more than the modern sense of not

retain it, if it is true what Pliny says, that while a drowned man floats on his back, a woman floats face downwards: '*Veluti pudori defunctarum parcente natura*' (Nature spares the modesty of women, when they die in this way).[16]

Another philosopher, when asked what colour looked best on a woman's face, replied wittily and truthfully that it was the colour of modesty. In fact, I consider this to be the most important sense in which women are superior to men, for modesty puts a natural barrier between virtue and vice. A wise Frenchman called it 'the shade of beautiful souls and visible sign of virtue'. And St Bernard went further, describing it using these terms: jewel of manners, lamp of the bashful soul, sister of continence, guard of reputation, honour of life, seat of virtue, glory of Nature and emblem of all honesty.[17] Diogenes, with delicacy and accuracy, called it the colour of virtue. In fact, this is the strong bulwark which, raised against vice, protects the fortress of the soul; and once it has been conquered it is thereafter unable to resist the slightest evil, as Gregory of Nazianzus said, '*Protinus extincto subeunt mala cuncta pudore*' (the extinction of modesty opens the way to every evil).[18]

It may be said that shame is a successful defence against external actions but not against internal desires, and so leaves the way open for vice to triumph through invisible attacks that the fortress of bashfulness cannot withstand. But even if this were the case, modesty would still be a precious defence, since at least it prevents an infinite number of scandals and their disastrous consequences. But on careful reflection we can see that it also protects against most if not all of those silent attacks, so they stay within the secret recesses of the heart. For it is rare for internal impulses not to lead to external actions, which implant criminal desires in the soul, and expand and fortify vicious inclinations. In the absence of these, it is true that from time to time sin may make its way into the mind, but it does not lodge there, let alone become its mistress, but is merely a temporary visitor.

Unless the passions have something to feed on, they remain weak and timid, largely because in people who blush easily there is a direct communication between what they feel and what shows on the outside, revealing publicly on the face all that is hidden in the depths of the heart. Thus the most secret emotions are immediately painted on the cheeks: the colour of shame is the only one which allows us to guess what is invisible. And so, to counter the moral lapses caused by desire, it can be a moderating influence on women to fear that what is imprinted in their heart may be read in their face.

To this we may add that many women are so prone to shame that they blush

---

showing off, but included reserve, moderation and a heightened sense of shame.
[16] Pliny, *Naturalis Historia*, Book 7, ch. 17.
[17] Sermon 86 in St Bernard's commentary on the *Song of Songs*.
[18] Gregory of Nazianzus (360–390) was Bishop of Constantinople, and a renowned theologian of the early church.

even when alone. This heroic loveliness of modesty, which the erudite Father
Vieira[19] discusses in one of his sermons, is not merely an imaginary ideal, as
some vulgar people believe, but in those of elevated character it is a reality.
Demetrius of Phaleron[20] was aware of this when he instructed the young people
of Athens that when at home they should show respect to their parents, when
in public they should show respect to all those who saw them, and when alone,
they should respect themselves.

Chapter V

I think I have pointed out enough advantages in women to equal or perhaps
outweigh those qualities in which men excel. Who will give judgment in this
case? If I had the authority to do so, perhaps my verdict would be that women's
superior qualities make them better as individuals, whereas the talents in which
men excel make them better, that is more useful, in public life.[21] But since I am
playing the role not of judge but of advocate, the case will have to remain for
the moment undecided.

And even if I had the necessary authority, I would have to suspend the
sentence, for it may be argued in favour of men that the good qualities that are
attributed to women are common to both sexes. I confess this is true, but in
the same way that the good qualities of men are also common to both sexes.
So as not to cause confusion, I have tried to indicate those perfections which
it is more common to find in the individuals of one sex than in the other. I
concede, therefore, that one can find men who are gentle, candid and shy, and
furthermore that if blushing is a good sign in women, it is even more so in men,
for in a generous character it denotes acute sensitivity. John Barclay[22] said so
more than once in his *Satyricon* (and his erudition is such that his opinion must
be admitted as particularly important), and though it is not an infallible sign,
it is my own observation that I no longer expect much good from a boy who
shows signs of bold effrontery.

I state therefore that various members of our sex demonstrate — though not

---

[19] Father António Vieira (1608–1697) was a Portuguese Jesuit scholar who published
fifteen volumes of sermons, which were translated into several different languages. He also
produced a report on the Inquisition in Portugal which led the Pope to suspend its operation
for seven years.
[20] Demetrius of Phaleron (born *c.* 350 BC) ruled Athens for ten years, and wrote extensively
on history, rhetoric and literature.
[21] This theory became popular in the eighteenth century: that men and women had
different qualities, perfectly designed by Nature to suit men to public life and women to
domesticity. Neither was superior to the other: they were just different. However, for women
to try to play a part in public life would be going against Nature.
[22] John Barclay (1582–1621) was a Scottish writer and neo-Latin poet. His *Satyricon* was a
satire against the Jesuits.

with the same degree of frequency — the good qualities which give nobility to the other. But this in no way inclines the balance in our favour, for weighing equally on the other side, the perfections of which men boast are also found in many women.

Chapter VI

We can find a thousand examples of princesses who displayed political expertise. No age will forget the first woman whom history has rescued from the obscurity of fable: I mean *Semiramis*, Queen of Assyria, who was nursed in her childhood by doves, and later soared higher than eagles. Not only did she maintain the blind obedience of those subjects left to her by her husband, but she also subdued all the surrounding peoples, and made neighbours of the most distant countries by extending her conquests to Ethiopia on the one side and to India on the other.

Neither should we forget *Artemisia*, Queen of Caria, who not only retained throughout her long widowhood the devotion of that kingdom, but when it was attacked by the army of Rhodes, with two remarkable stratagems and in two strikes she destroyed the invading troops and passing swiftly from defence to offence, conquered and triumphed over the Island of Rhodes.

Nor must we overlook the two *Aspasias*, to whose admirable management Pericles, husband of the one, and Cyrus, son of Darius Nothus and lover of the other, entirely entrusted the government of their states, with great success. Nor the wise *Phila*,[23] daughter of Antipater, whose father consulted her about the government of Macedonia while she was still a girl, and who later skilfully extricated her husband, the rash and fickle Demetrius, from a thousand difficulties. Nor the crafty *Livia*, whose subtle cunning seems to have exceeded the perception of Augustus; for he would not have given her such power over him had he understood her better. Nor the wily *Agrippina*, whose schemes were fatal for her and for the world, when she used them to promote her son Nero to the throne. Nor the learned *Amalasuntha*,[24] whose knowledge of the languages of all the subject nations of the Roman Empire was reckoned to be less important than her skill in governing the state during the minority of her son Athalaric.

Leaving aside many others, and coming nearer to our own times, we shall never forget *Elizabeth of England*, a woman whose character was influenced equally by the three Graces and the three Furies; whose conduct as a monarch would always invite the admiration of Europe, if her vices had not been so mingled with her maxims of government that they became integral to it; and

---

[23] The story of Phila (d.287 BC) appears in Plutarch's *Life of Demetrius*.

[24] Amalasuntha was the wife of Eutharic, king of the Ostrogoths. Her son Athalaric (516–534) became king at the age of ten, and his mother ruled as regent.

whose political reputation will always in the eyes of posterity be coloured (I should say stained) with the blood of the innocent Mary Stuart, Queen of Scots. Nor *Catherine de Medici*, Queen of France, whose astuteness in maintaining in equilibrium the two opposing parties of Catholics and Protestants, in order to prevent the fall of the crown, seemed like the skill of a tightrope-walker who above the crowd handles two opposing weights with extreme finesse to prevent himself from falling, and delights the spectators as he flirts with risk and keeps himself from danger.[25]

Our Catholic Queen *Isabella* would have been in no way inferior to any of these examples in the administration of government, if she had been a reigning queen and not a queen consort. Despite this she did not lack opportunities to display her consummate wisdom. And Lawrence Beyerlinck[26] in his eulogy says that during her time no great action took place for which she was not partly or wholly responsible: '*Quid magni in regno, sine illa, imo nisi per illam fere gestum est?*' At least it is certain that the discovery of the New World, which was Spain's most glorious achievement in many centuries, would not have happened if the magnanimity of Isabella had not overcome the fear and indolence of Ferdinand.

Finally (and most important of all) it appears — although I am not absolutely sure of the numbers — that among the queens who reigned for a long time in their own right, the majority have been celebrated in history as excellent rulers. But women are so unfortunate that people always bring up in opposition to so many illustrious examples a Brunhilda, a Fredegunda,[27] the two Joannas of Naples,[28] and a few others; despite the fact that although the first two may have been outstandingly wicked, they were not lacking in cleverness.

The conviction that the crown does not sit well on the head of a woman is not as universally held in the world as people think, for in Meroe, an island formed by the Nile in Ethiopia (or a peninsula, as people think today) women reigned for many centuries, according to Pliny. Father Cornelius van Lapide[29] wrote about one of them, the Queen of Sheba, and thought her empire extended

---

[25] This is not a view that would have been shared by many French commentators, who attributed the prolongation of the bloodthirsty religious wars to Catherine's indecisive and devious behaviour.

[26] Lawrence Beyerlinck (1578–1627) was a theologian based in Antwerp who wrote one of the first encyclopaedias, the *Magnum Theatrum Vitae Humanae* (Cologne, 1631).

[27] Brunhilda (*c.* 543–613) was a Visigothic princess from Toledo, notorious for her cruelty and avarice. Fredegunda (*c.* 545–597) was a Frankish queen who conspired to murder Brunhilda's sister in order to marry her husband Chilperic. They detested each other and persuaded their husbands to go to war.

[28] Joanna I of Naples (1326–1382), who reigned for nearly 40 years, was accused of complicity in the murder of her first husband. Joanna II (1373–1435) ruled for nearly 20 years, and was known for having numerous lovers. Both were powerful queens, but were disapproved of for their 'unvirtuous' behaviour.

[29] Cornelius van Lapide (1597–1637) was a Flemish Jesuit priest who was Professor of Scripture in Leuven and later in Rome, and a writer of biblical commentaries.

far beyond the limit of Meroe, and may have covered the whole of Ethiopia. He based this on the fact that our Saviour called her the Queen of the South, a title which suggests a vast dominion in this part of the world. So much so that, as can be seen with Thomas Corneille,[30] there is no shortage of writers who insist that the island, or peninsula, of Meroe, was larger than Great Britain; and thus these queens reigned over a large area even if it did not extend beyond the limits of Meroe. Aristotle[31] says that among the Lacedaemonians women played a great role in government, and this was consistent with the laws handed down to them by Lycurgus.

Moreover, in Borneo, a large island in the Indian Ocean, according to Mandelslo's[32] account which can be found in Olearius's second volume, women reign as queens without granting their husbands any prerogative other than to be their senior vassals. And on the island of Formosa, situated in the South China Sea, the idolaters there have such a respect for the prudent conduct of their women that they alone are entrusted with the priestly function and all that pertains to religion; and in politics they occupy a position superior to the Senators, being seen as the interpreters of the will of their gods.

Nevertheless, the common practice of all nations is more in line with the rules of reason and in conformity with the divine command made to our first mother in Paradise and to all her daughters in her name, namely that they would be subject to the men. We should only correct the impatience which many peoples display towards female government when the laws command them to obey; and also that excessive admiration for our own sex which at times has made them prefer to be governed by an incompetent child than an experienced woman. The ancient Persians took this to such a ridiculous extreme that when the widow of one of their kings was with child and they were advised by their priests that the child was male, they laid the crown on his mother's belly and proclaimed the foetus their king, giving him the name Shapur even before he was born.[33]

Chapter VII

So far we have restricted ourselves to a small number of examples of political skill, and ignored many others. It is pointless to discuss economic skill, when every day we see households that are extremely well managed by women, and very badly managed by men.

And passing to the topic of courage, a quality which men consider peculiar

---

[30] Thomas Corneille (1625–1709), brother of the playwright Pierre Corneille, published in 1708 a *Dictionnaire Universel Géographique et Historique*.
[31] Aristotle, *Politics*, Book 2, ch. 7.
[32] Johan Albrecht de Mandelslo (1616–1644) wrote a book about his travels in India and the Far East which was translated into Dutch, English and French, and remained popular into the eighteenth century. Its first editor was Adam Olearius, who accompanied Mandelslo on his travels.
[33] This legend refers to Shapur II, who ruled the Persian Empire from AD 309 to 379.

to their sex, I grant that heaven has given them a portion of this that is three or four times greater; but not that it has been handed down to them as a birthright in an unbroken chain, or that it is never shared with the other sex.

There is no age that has not been enriched by valiant women. Leaving aside the examples of heroines in scripture, and the holy martyrs of the Law of Grace[34] (since deeds that are provoked by the special intervention of divine aid are a credit to the power of God and not to the natural qualities of the sex), there are so many women of heroic valour and bold actions that they crowd into the theatre of our memory. After Semiramis, Artemisia, Thomiris and Zenobia appears *Aretaphila*, wife of Nicotratus, king of Cyrene and Libya, whose generous spirit combined an ardent love for her country, great courage and the most subtle eloquence. To free her country from her husband's violent tyranny and to avenge his murder of his first wife in order to marry her, she made herself leader of a conspiracy and deprived Nicotratus of both his throne and his life. And when Leander, brother of Nicotratus, succeeded to the throne and displayed the same cruelty, she had the courage and skill to rid the world of this second tyrant, crowning her illustrious deeds by refusing the crown which the Cyrenes offered her out of gratitude for her many good deeds.

There was *Dripetina*, daughter of the great Mithridates and her father's inseparable partner in many dangerous undertakings, who displayed a strength of body and soul for which she had seemed destined since her infancy, having been born with two sets of teeth. Following the destruction of her father by Pompey the Great, besieged in a castle by Manlius Priscus and finding it impossible to defend, she took her own life so as not to suffer the humiliation of slavery.[35] There was *Clelia*, a Roman who was taken prisoner by Lars Porsena, King of the Etruscans, but overcoming immense difficulties she broke out of prison and rode through the Tiber on a horse (or as some say, swam across), arriving safely in Rome.[36] There was *Arria*, wife of Cecina Petus, whose husband was involved in Camillus' conspiracy against the Emperor Claudius and condemned to death for his crime, and who resolved not to outlive her husband. Having tried without success to smash her head against a wall, she managed to get inside Cecina's prison and persuaded him to cheat the executioner by taking his own life, and was the first to thrust a dagger into her own breast.[37] And there was *Eponina*, whose husband Julius Sabinus claimed the title of Caesar in Gaul, and who suffered unspeakable tortures with rare

[34] The period since the coming of Christ was seen as the time when the grace of God had been substituted for the law laid down in the Old Testament.
[35] Dripetina was included in Boccaccio's *De Claris Mulieribus*. Legend had it that she never lost her milk teeth, and therefore had two sets. Feijoo's even more bizarre version is she was born with two sets of teeth, which would mark her out as an extraordinary being.
[36] The source for this story is Livy's *Ab Urbe Condita*, 2.13.
[37] This story is found in Pliny the Younger's *Letters*, 3.16.

fortitude; when she was finally condemned to death by Vespasian, she bravely told him that she would die content, since that would save her from the disgust of seeing such an evil emperor seated on the throne.[38]

And so we do not imagine there are fewer courageous women in the modern era than in antiquity, let us behold the armed figure of *Joan of Arc*, a pillar that supported the tottering French monarchy in its time of greatest affliction, to such effect that when they heard about her the English attributed her exploits to a pact with the Devil and the French to divine inspiration. It seems the English pretended the first out of hatred, and those who managed affairs in France invented the second for political reasons; for it was essential to raise the spirits of their discouraged army and people by persuading them that Heaven had declared for their side, and for this purpose they introduced into the field of war a valiant and spirited maid as a suitable instrument for their miraculous rescue.[39]

Margaret of Denmark in the fourteenth century personally conquered the Kingdom of Sweden and captured its King Albert; the writers of her time called her the second Semiramis.[40] There was *Marulla*, a native of Lemnos, an island in the Greek archipelago, who during the siege of the fortress of Coccino by the Turks, seeing her father die, seized his sword and shield, and inspiring the whole garrison by her example, put herself at their head and bore down with such force against the enemy that she not only succeeded in her attack, but forced Suleiman Pasha to raise the siege. Her deed was rewarded by General Loredano of Venice, whose town this was: he promised her as a husband her choice of the most valiant captains in his army, and offered her a suitable dowry in the name of the Republic.[41]

There was *Blanca de Rossi*, wife of Battista Porta, an officer from Padua, who courageously defended the town of Bassano in the Marches of Treviso from its walls, but the place was lost through treachery and her husband taken prisoner and murdered by the tyrant Ezzelino. She could find no other way to resist the brutal assaults of this ruthless man, who was enamoured of her beauty, but to throw herself out of a window; she was nursed back to health (no doubt against her will) and suffering the shame of being forcibly raped by this brute, she

---

[38] This story is told by Plutarch's *Moralia*.

[39] In *Teatro Crítico*, IV, ch. 8, para. 36, Feijoo revisits this idea, and relates further evidence that Joan's apparently miraculous actions had rational explanations. He concludes that she should nevertheless continue to be regarded as a heroine.

[40] Margaret of Denmark (1353–1412) ruled Denmark, Norway and Sweden as regent for her infant son and later for her great-nephew. She was the effective ruler of the whole of Scandinavia until her death.

[41] The source for this tale is one of the novellas of Matteo Bandello (c. 1480–1562) (IV, p. 18). He claimed that many of his stories were recounted to him by eyewitnesses. An English translation of his work by William Paynter provided Shakespeare with episodes in *Much Ado about Nothing*, *Cymbeline*, *Romeo and Juliet* and *Twelfth Night*.

put an end to her bitter grief and demonstrated the constancy of her conjugal fidelity by taking her own life in the tomb of her husband, which she caused to be re-opened for this purpose.[42]

A girl named *Bonne*, a humble peasant from Valtellina, was met on a march by Pedro Brunoro, a famous captain from Parma, when as a young girl she was watching her sheep in the fields. He was taken by her vivacity and abducted her to be his mistress, but she shared not only his shame but his glory, for putting an end to her dishonest life through the sacrament of marriage, she not only fought fiercely as a soldier in numerous battles, but became so skilled in the art of warfare that she was put in charge of several actions, in particular the taking of the castle of Pavono from the Venetians for Francesco Sforza, Duke of Milan. In this exploit she assumed the office of general and went into the assault at the head of her troops.

Maria Pita, a Galician heroine, was in Corunna when it was besieged by the English in 1589, and when the enemy had breached the walls and the garrison was on the point of surrender, she berated her compatriots for their cowardice in vivid and vulgar terms, seized a sword and shield from the hands of a soldier, crying that whoever was a man of honour should follow her; inspired with courage, she threw herself into the breach with martial fury, striking such sparks in the hearts of the soldiers and onlookers that it was like a match to a powder keg, and they closed on their enemies with such ferocity that they killed fifteen hundred of them (one being the brother of General Henry Norris, commander of the army) and forced them to lift the siege. Philip II rewarded Pita for her valour, giving her the rank and pay of an ensign during her life, and Philip III settled the same rank and pay on her descendants.

Maria de Estrada, wife of Pedro Sanchez Farsan, a soldier in the army of Hernan Cortés, is worthy of particular memory for her extraordinary exploits, which are described by Fray Juan de Torquemada in the first volume of his book *Indian Monarchies*.[43] Writing of the tragic withdrawal of Cortés from Mexico after the death of Montezuma, he describes her as follows: 'Maria de Estrada showed great valour in this dangerous conflict; taking a sword and shield in her hands she performed marvellous deeds, and opposed the enemy with courage and spirit, as if she were one of the most valiant men in the world, forgetting that she was a woman, and displaying a degree of valour which in such cases is usually seen only in the most noble of men. She performed such marvels that

---

[42] This story first appears in Giuseppe Betussi's 1547 translation of Boccaccio's *De Claris Mulieribus* (*On Famous Women*). Betussi (who came from Bassano) updated Boccaccio's work by adding more recent stories. It was also related by Ludovico Domenichi in his *La Nobiltà delle donne* (*The Nobility of Women*), published in 1551.

[43] Juan de Torquemada (*c*. 1562–1624), a Franciscan friar, was a missionary and historian in Mexico. His three-volume history of the Spanish conquest was first published in 1615 and reprinted in Madrid in 1723, shortly before the first volume of Feijoo's *Teatro Crítico*.

all who saw her were struck with awe and terror'. Referring in the following chapter to the battle that took place between the Spanish and the Mexicans in the valley of Otumpa (or Otumba, according to Don Antonio de Solís),[44] he recalls the memory of this illustrious woman in the following words: 'In this battle,' says Diego Muñoz Camargo[45] in his *Memoir of Tlaxcala*, 'Maria de Estrada fought on horseback with a lance in her hand with such virile courage that you would have thought her one of the most valiant men in the army, and she prevailed over many opponents'. The author does not say where our heroine came from, but her name suggests she was from Asturias.

And *Anna de Baux*, a brave Flemish woman from Aldea near Lille, in the wars of the last century, with the sole motive of guarding her honour against the insults of the soldiers, disguised her sex in male attire and joined the army, where she served for a long time and showed great courage in many engagements, and was promoted to be lieutenant of her company. When she was taken prisoner by the French and her sex discovered, the Marshal of Senneterre invited her to command a company in the service of France; but she refused to fight against her own prince, and returning to her country, became a nun.[46]

If so far I have not mentioned the Amazons, who are relevant to my topic, it is because I plan to discuss them separately. Some authors deny they existed, while others assure us they did. What we can be sure of is that the story of the Amazons is mingled with a great deal of fable: for example that they killed all their male children, or that they lived completely apart from the other sex and sought them out only once a year in order to conceive. In the same strain are their supposed encounters with Hercules and Theseus, the support given by the fierce Penthisilea to the troubled city of Troy, and maybe also the visit of Queen Thalestris to Alexander. But it would be rash to deny the testimony of so many ancient authors that there was a formidable body of warlike women in Asia who were given the name of Amazons.

If even this were to be denied and we had to give up the idea of Amazons in Asia, then for the glory of women Amazons have been found in the other three continents: America, Africa and Europe. In the Americas the Spaniards discovered armed women on the banks of the longest river in the world, the Marañón, and for this reason gave it the name it still has today, the River Amazon. In Africa there are some in a province of the Empire of Monomotapa, and they are said to be the best warriors the prince has in all his territories

---

[44] Antonio de Solís y Ribadeneyra (1610–1686) was a Spanish dramatist and historian. His *Historia de la conquista de México* was published in 1684.

[45] Diego Muñoz Camargo (*c.* 1529–1599) was born in Mexico and was the son of a Spanish conquistador. His *Historia de Tlaxcala* was an important source of information on Spanish colonial Mexico.

[46] The story of Anne de Vaux appears in Louis Moreri's *Grand Dictionnaire Historique*, published in 1725.

(though there is one geographer who puts this state inhabited by warlike women in a different part of the country).

In Europe, although there is no country where women follow the military profession, we may give the name of Amazons to those who on specific occasions formed a company and defeated the enemies of their country. Such were the French women of Belovaco, or Beauvais, whose city was besieged by the Burgundians in 1472, and who joined together under the leadership of *Jeanne Hachette* on the day of the attack and vigorously repulsed the enemy, with Hachette herself throwing their captain from the wall when he attempted to raise his standard there. In memory of these exploits they hold an annual holiday in the city to this day, granting the women the unique privilege of going in procession before the men.

Of the same stamp were the women of the Echinada Islands, now called Cur-Solares, made famous in the victory of Lepanto, which was fought in the surrounding sea. The year before this famous battle, the Turks had attacked the main island, and the Venetian governor Antonio Balbo and all the male inhabitants were so terrified that they fled during the night; but the women were persuaded by a priest named Antonio Rosoneo to stay and defend the town, which they did to the great honour of their sex, and the equal disgrace of our own.

Note: The resolution of women who kill themselves should not be taken as an example of virtue but of courage taken to excess, which is what we are demonstrating here.

Chapter VIII

Let us move on from these reminiscences of courageous women to say something about the subject on which men make the most frequent accusation against women, and treat as their greatest weakness or defect, which is their inability to keep a secret. Cato the Censor would not admit any exception to this rule, and held it to be one of the greatest errors a man could commit to confide a secret to a woman. But Cato's own descendant *Portia* proved him wrong: for the daughter of Cato the Younger and wife of Marcus Brutus compelled her husband to tell her the great secret of the conspiracy against Caesar, giving him the extraordinary proof of her valour and constancy by wounding herself with a knife in her thigh.[47]

Pliny says, in the name of the Magi, that the heart of a particular bird, if

---

[47] Marcus Porcius Cato 'the Elder' (234–149 BC) was a Roman statesman known for his rigid discipline and resistance to what he saw as the increasing decadence of society. His great-grandson Marcius Porcius Cato 'the Younger' (95–45 BC) was a statesman in the latter years of the Republic, known for his stern morality and opposition to the accumulation of power by Julius Caesar. The story of Portia is related in Plutarch's *Lives of the Romans*.

placed on the breast of a sleeping woman, would make her reveal all her secrets. He says the same elsewhere of the tongue of a particular insect. It cannot be that easy to break into a woman's thoughts if magicians have to go around looking in the most obscure parts of nature for keys to open the gates of their hearts. We can laugh at Pliny's inventions and admit that there are very few women who keep secrets; but on the other hand, the most skilled statesmen would admit that it is also extremely rare to find a man to whom one may confide a secret of any importance. In truth, if these jewels were not so rare, princes would not value them so highly, thinking them of greater worth than their most treasured possessions.

It is not difficult to find examples of women who showed unshakeable constancy in the keeping of secrets. Pythagoras, being close to death, entrusted all his writings, containing the most hidden mysteries of his philosophy, to the learned *Damo*, his daughter, with the command that they should never be published; she obeyed this so rigorously that even when she was reduced to the direst poverty and could have sold the books for a large sum of money, she preferred to be loyal to her father's trust than to escape from her misery.

The noble *Aretaphila* whom we have already mentioned, planned to kill her husband Nicotratus with a poisonous draught (before she tried this by means of an armed conspiracy) but her plan was discovered and she was tortured to make her reveal everything she knew. But the agonies she suffered could not overwhelm her mind and spirit, and even under the extremities of the rack not only did she conceal her objective, but she had the skill to persuade the tyrant that the potion she had prepared was a love philtre designed to increase his love for her. And indeed this clever fiction was as effective as a philtre, since Nicotratus loved her much more afterwards, in the belief that someone who wanted to elicit extreme passion from him would love him with the same ardour.

In Aristogeiton's conspiracy against Hippias, tyrant of Athens, which began with the death of Hipparchus, Hippias' brother, a courtesan who knew of the plot was put to torture, but to demonstrate to the tyrant the impossibility of drawing the secret from her, she bit off her own tongue in his presence.

In Piso's conspiracy against Nero, many of the most celebrated Roman citizens yielded at the first sign of the instruments of torture, with Lucan accusing his own mother of being complicit in the plot, and others betraying their closest friends; but *Epicharis*, a woman of the people who knew everything, was the only one from whom neither lashes nor fire nor any other torment could draw the slightest information.

And I myself knew one woman who was put on the rack to make her reveal an atrocious crime that had been committed by her employers, and resisted the agonies of this cruel examination not to save herself but solely to save her masters; she was so little to blame, not being aware of the gravity of the crime, and having been commanded to carry it out, and for other reasons, that she would never have been condemned to suffer a punishment anything like as great as the agony of this torture.

There are numerous examples of women who cannot be prevailed upon to speak even by the harshest of beatings. I heard from someone who had been present at several of these events that many women confess when required to strip naked to be thrashed, but it is rare for any, once they have suffered this martyrdom of their modesty, to surrender to the violence of the whip. Truly this is an excellent quality in their sex, that their own modesty affects them more than all the force of the executioner!

No doubt some people will accuse me of flattery in making this parallel between men and women. But I would point them to Seneca, whose Stoicism spared no one, and whose severity sets him far from any suspicion of aiming to please; yet he drew a comparison that was no less favourable to women, for he held them to be absolutely equal to men in all their qualities and natural faculties. These were his words:

> Quis autem dicat naturam maligne cum mulieribus ingeniis egisse, & virtutes illarum in arctum retraxisse? Par illus, mihi credi, vigor, par ad honesta (libeat) facultas est. Laborem doloremque ex aequo si consuevere patiuntur. (In *Consolatory Letter to Martius*)

> [Who shall say that Nature has dealt unkindly with women, and endowed them with only a slender share of virtue? No, they have equal strength of mind, equal disposition and ability for virtue and decorous actions; and with a little practice, bear toil and pain as well as we do.]

Chapter IX

We have now arrived at the main battlefield, which is the question of their intellectual capacity. I admit that on this subject if I could not rely on reason, I would not get much help from authority; for the authors who write about it (save the odd one or two) are so much on the side of the opinion of the ignorant masses that they almost without exception speak of women's understanding with contempt.

In truth, one could well reply to the authority of these writings with a story the Sicilian writer Carducci[48] used for another purpose in his *Dialogues on Painting*. A man and a lion were walking along the road and arguing about

---

[48] Vincenzo Carducci (1568–1638) was born in Florence but worked in Spain for most of his life. He and his brother Bartolommeo produced paintings for Philip II at the palace of Escorial. His book *Diálogos de la Pintura* was published in 1633. It is not clear why Feijoo thought he was Sicilian.

which were more courageous, men or lions. Each of them claimed that his own species was superior, until they came across a beautiful fountain, and the man pointed out that on the top was the marble statue of a man treading a lion underfoot. Turning to his opponent he said in the triumphant tone of one who had found the conclusive proof, 'Here I have succeeded in making you see that men are more valiant than lions, for you can see a lion in agony, expiring under the attack of a man'. 'A fine argument that is,' said the lion with a smile, 'for this statue was made by a man, and it is hardly surprising that he carved it in a way to make his own species look good. I assure you that if a lion had made it, he would have reversed it and planted the lion on top of the man, making a meal of him.'

It is the same thing here: men wrote the books which condemned women's intellect as inferior. If women had written them, we would be the ones who found ourselves put down. And there was one who actually did this, for Lucrezia Marinella,[49] a learned Venetian lady, wrote a number of books, one of which was called *The Excellence of Women compared with the Defects & Vices of Men*, in which she set out to prove the superiority of her sex over ours. The learned Jesuit Juan de Cartagena says that he saw and read this book in Rome with great pleasure, and I myself have seen it in the Royal Library in Madrid. We can truthfully assert that neither they nor we are in a position to judge, for we are parties in the case; and we shall have to leave the decision to the angels who, being of no sex, can be objective.

And first, those who reduce women's understanding almost to the level of pure instinct are unworthy to be admitted to the dispute. They are the kind who assert that the most a woman is capable of is to rule a henhouse.

They are like that priest quoted by Don Francisco Manuel in his *Guide for Husbands*, who said that the summit of female knowledge is being able to fold a pile of laundry. However respectable the men who say such things may be for other reasons, they will not earn respect with such phrases, since the kindest interpretation is to recognise them as deliberate hyperbole. It is a well-known fact that there have been women who were capable of governing and ruling religious communities, and even women who were capable of governing and ruling entire countries.

These attacks on women come from superficial men. They see that in general women know nothing beyond those domestic employments to which they are destined, and conclude from this (without realising this is why they draw the conclusion, since they don't reflect on the question at all) that they are incapable

---

[49] Lucrezia Marinella (1571–1653) published *La Nobiltà et l'eccellenza delle donne, co' difetti et mancamenti degli uomini* in 1600. In his *Anti-Theatro Critico*, Salvador José Mañer denied that such a book existed, which led to an angry justification by Feijoo in his *Suplemento de el Theatro Critico*.

of anything else. The most basic logician could work out that lack of knowledge is not the same as lack of ability; and thus the fact that women have limited knowledge does not imply that they have no talent to learn.

No one knows anything other than the subjects he has studied, but it would be wrong to conclude and offensive to suggest that he could achieve nothing other than what he has practised. If all men were dedicated to agriculture (as the famous Thomas More imagined in his *Utopia*), would this be a good reason to argue that men are incapable of anything else? Among the Druze, a Palestinian tribe, women are the only ones who learn, for nearly all of them can read and write; and whatever literature these people have is stored in the minds of the women and hidden from all the men, who are solely dedicated to farming, war and business. If this custom prevailed across the world, no doubt women would believe men to be incapable of learning, just as today men judge women to be incapable. And as this belief would be incorrect, so in the same way is the one which prevails today, being based on the same foundation.

Chapter X

Perhaps on the same principle, though he is more sympathetic to women, Father Malebranche in his book *The Search for Truth*[50] conceded their superiority over men in their ability to perceive things through the senses, but viewed them as much inferior in their capacity for abstract thought. He ascribed this to the softness of their brains, but it is obvious that everyone looks for these physical causes and interprets them in his own way in order to prove what experience has persuaded him to be their effects. This being the case, the author fell into the same intellectual defect he wanted to cure in the whole of mankind: that is, the error caused by common prejudices and ill thought-out ideas; for there is no doubt he came to this conclusion either because he was carried away by the common flow or because he observed that women who are regarded as intelligent speak more fluently and perceptively than men on matters to do with the senses, and much less (if at all) on abstract topics. But even if this is so, it indicates a disparity not in talent but in practice and application. Women are occupied with cookery and embroidering clothes and other things of this nature, and think much more about them than men do, and so they can talk about them with more acuity and fluency. By contrast, very few women think about theoretical questions or abstract ideas, and then only rarely; so it is not surprising if they encounter obstacles when they speak about such subjects.

---

[50] Nicolas Malebranche (1638–1715) was a French Oratorian priest who argued that all human ideas and perceptions are put into our minds by God. His book *De la Recherche de la Vérité* (also published in Latin as *De Inquirenda Veritate*) was first published in 1674; his theory of the softness of women's brains is found in Part II, ch. 1, 'De l'imagination des femmes'.

Furthermore, we may observe that knowledgeable women of a lively disposition who enjoy conversing about the subtleties of Platonic love can, when they come to analysing this subject, leave the most learned man far behind, if he has not spent his time exploring these trivial fantasies.

Generally speaking, however intelligent someone is, he will appear incompetent or useless if he tries to do things that he is not familiar with. An agricultural labourer whom God has gifted with a clever wit (which is sometimes the case), but who has never thought about anything but his own occupation, will appear far inferior to the most ignorant courtier whenever he tries to talk about politics. The most ingenious politician, if this is all he is, who is rash enough to talk about how to draw up regiments and order a battle, will say a thousand foolish things; and if an experienced military man were to hear him, he would take him for a fool. In this way it is said that Hannibal laughed at a certain great Asian orator when he tried to lecture him and King Antiochus on military matters.

The case in question is exactly the same: a woman of superior intelligence spends her time at home and is occupied all day long in thinking about domestic tasks, without ever hearing (or if hearing, not concentrating) if from time to time someone discusses more significant matters in front of her. Her husband, though his talents may be much inferior to hers, often has business outside the house with wise churchmen or clever politicians, and by communicating with them he picks up different kinds of information, becomes familiar with public affairs and broadens the range of his knowledge. Being educated in this way, if some day he talks in the company of his wife of these subjects on which he has picked up some information, and she says what comes into her mind, then however intelligent she may be, since she is deprived of all education, there is no doubt she will say something silly and make her husband and any other men who may hear her think she is a fool, and give her husband the satisfaction of believing that he, on the other hand, is a clever fellow.

What happens to this woman happens to an infinite number of them who, despite having far greater ability than the men they are up against, are despised as being incapable of talking about any important matter. We can see that if they cannot discuss them, or do so badly, this is a result not of lack of talent but lack of information, without which not even someone with the intelligence of the angels could be sure of being right about anything. Men, on the other hand, even if they are of more limited ability, always triumph and shine in comparison, since they are provided with the necessary information.

Apart from the advantage of being better-informed there is a more significant one, which is that men are used to analysing, arguing and reasoning about these subjects, which are relevant to their lives, whereas women very rarely think about them: for this reason it may be said that when the opportunity arises, men's speech is premeditated but women's is extempore.

Lastly, men discuss these matters between themselves and can learn from each other's insights, so when they are talking about them they are not just expressing their own ideas, but taking advantage of those they have acquired elsewhere; so sometimes what comes from the mouth of one man is not the result of his thoughts alone, but of many others. But women in their conversations do not talk of these superior subjects but only of their tasks and other domestic matters, so they do not share each other's observations; and if they are called upon to talk about these things they have to think on their feet, and lacking information they can only rely on their own thoughts.

These advantages that enable a man of limited intelligence to talk longer and more knowledgably about important topics than the most perceptive woman, are so significant that in an argument between a sensible woman and a foolish man, it is likely that anyone who has not made the reflections written here would consider him to be the clever one and her to be the fool.

It is the failure to reflect on this that persuades so many men (including some who are otherwise reasonable and thoughtful) to regard women's intelligence with great contempt; and the irony is that they have exclaimed so often that all women are stupid, that they have persuaded many — if not most — of them to believe it.

Chapter XI

It seems that even those men who get closer to the truth still claim — though much less aggressively — that men are more intelligent than women, though they admit that there are some women who display good sense and native wit. But I affirm that even they would not, in my opinion, have insisted on this inequality between the two sexes, had they taken account of the circumstances described above, which cause even women of remarkable capacity to appear inferior on many occasions.

And I do not know what this supposed inequality can be founded on other than the arguments I have mentioned, and whose inaccuracy I have exposed. If I am told it is proved by experience, then I have already demonstrated that the experience which is quoted is an illusion, and pointed out its many errors. Moreover, if we are to talk of experience I shall quote two important witnesses in favour of women. The first is the excellent Portuguese writer Don Francisco Manuel[51] in his *Advice for Husbands*. The qualities combined in this gentleman make him an outstanding authority on the subject under discussion, for beside

---

[51] Francisco Manuel de Mello (1608–1666) spent much of his life as a soldier in the Portuguese wars against Spain and France. He travelled to England in 1640 and visited the court of Charles II, to whose queen, Catherine of Braganza, he was distantly related. He was imprisoned for nine years on trumped-up charges and then exiled to Brazil. The *Carta de Guia de Casados* was written during his imprisonment.

his remarkable talents, he travelled to many countries, was regularly involved in public affairs; as a result of this, and of his courtier's grace and elegance, he was frequently in the company of ladies, as can be seen in his writings.

It appears that this writer was not content to assert that women are equal to men in intellect, but claimed that in some respects they are superior. For example, on page 73 of the book I mentioned, having referred to views against women, he says: 'My opinion is very different, and I believe there are many women of profound judgment. I met and conversed with women like this in Spain and other countries. For this reason I think their acuteness in observation and conversation, which is superior to ours, should be tempered with great circumspection'. And further on: 'Since we are not allowed to deprive women of that subtle metal with which Nature has endowed them, we may perhaps avoid giving them the opportunity to sharpen it in a way that endangers them and damages us'. The testimony of this author, as I have said, is of great weight, since in addition to his wide experience and intelligence is the fact that in his book he does not generally take the side of women, and at the end he frankly accuses himself of being too severe towards them.

The second witness is the learned Frenchman the Abbé de Bellegarde,[52] who was also a courtier and well connected in that great theatre that is Paris. He published a book called *Curious Letters on Literature and Morality*, which claimed that women's minds are in no respect inferior to men's for any of the sciences, arts or employments. (I have not read this book, but it is cited on this subject in the April 1702 issue of the *Mémoires de Trévoux*.) The author of *A Journey by Coach from Madrid to Alcalá*[53] (whoever he is, he is clearly a man of some note) is of the same opinion. And Father Buffier, the famous French Jesuit writer, proves it formally in his book *An Examination of Common Prejudices*.[54]

Chapter XII

Leaving aside, therefore, the argument of experience, the only remaining way to prove this supposed intellectual inequality is to find some physical reason for

---

[52] Jean-Baptiste Morvan de Bellegarde (1648–1734) was a Salesian priest who wrote numerous works on religious and moral subjects. His *Lettres Curieuses de Littérature et de Morale* (1707) was largely based on Poulain de La Barre's *L'Égalité des Deux Sexes* (see volume introduction).

[53] *Jornada de coches de Madrid a Alcala, o Satisfacion al Palacio de Momo, y a las Apuntaciones a la Carta del maestro de niños* (Zaragoza, 1714), whose author has never been identified, was written in response to a work entitled *Carta del maestro de niños a don Gabriel Alvarez de Toledo*.

[54] Claude Buffier (1661–1737) was a prolific writer, best-known for his *Traité des vérités premières* (1717), in which he aimed to discover the ultimate principle of knowledge. The *Examen des Prejugés Vulgaires* was published in 1704.

it. But I affirm there is no such thing, for the only way of proving it would be to assume it lies in an inequality of souls, or in the different physical organisation and temperament of the two sexes.

As for inequality of souls, this is not a subject for debate, for it is the general conclusion of philosophers that all rational souls are equal in physical perfection. I know that some people will try to prove the contrary by quoting St Augustine,[55] but I cannot find that St Augustine even touched on this point in this chapter. I am also aware that the Faculty of Paris condemned a proposition claiming that the soul of our Lord Jesus Christ was not more perfect than the soul of the traitor Judas. The noble Scotist Mastri replied that since this condemnation was not confirmed by the Holy See, it is of no effect.[56] And so it is; but I do agree that such a proposition should be deleted from any book where it appears since it is offensive and to the minds of the simple, who cannot distinguish between the physical and the moral, it is scandalous. But this does not in any away affect the truth of the common opinion, which affirms the complete physical equality of souls.

Even if some were to argue that souls are different, how would they prove, or persuade us to believe, that God selected the best for men and left the inferior ones for women? We would rather believe that the soul of the Blessed Virgin Mary was above that of any other mere creature, and indeed the erudite Suárez[57] has confirmed that as regards her physical nature she was absolute perfection. And so those women who claim that the soul is neither male nor female may hold to their belief, for they speak the truth.

On the subject of the physical organism, I am ready to believe that its variety may have an impact on the operation of the soul, but until now we do not know what kind of physique is most beneficial to the mind. Aristotle claimed that people with small heads are the most intelligent. (I expect that before writing this, he measured his own!) Others vote in favour of large heads; one assumes these were not the ones whose own heads were small, or else they would have sided with Aristotle. Cardinal Sfrondati[58] says in his *Course of Philosophy* that Cardinal de Richelieu had two brains, and this was why he had such perspicacity and mental agility. I take this as meaning not that he really had two brains, which would have made him a monster, but that his brain was very large, which is consistent with the common view that larger brains think better;

---

[55] St Augustine, *De Trinitas*, Book 15, ch. 13.

[56] Bartolomeo Mastri (1602–1673) was a Scholastic philosopher who followed the teachings of John Duns Scotus (*c.* 1266–1308), a mediaeval theologian who wrote highly complex commentaries on the nature of God and the angels.

[57] Francisco Suárez (1548–1617) was a Spanish Jesuit, regarded as one of the most eminent and prolific neo-Scholastic theologians. His Latin works ran to 26 volumes.

[58] Celestino Sfrondati (1644–1696) was Abbot of the Benedictine monastery of St Gallen in Switzerland. His two-volume *Cursus Philosophicus* was published in 1686 and 1695.

they draw this conclusion from the observation that the human brain is larger than that of animals. Others (like Martínez in his *Anatomy*)[59] exclude both large and small heads, and claim that those of average size are the best for the operation of the intellect. Whatever may be said by those who measure the parts of the body in order to compute the excellence of the soul, actual experience shows that among men with large heads some are clever and others stupid; and the same thing is true of small heads. If the different size of the head or the brain implied a difference in the operation of the intellect, we would find that men of different stature would be very unequal in intelligence, since the size of their skulls (and thus their brains) is proportional to their height — but this is not what we observe at all.

Therefore, even if Pliny were right when he said that the substance of the brain is larger in men than in women (on which subject I suspend judgment until I know the opinion of expert anatomists), no conclusion could be drawn from this, for if intellectual advantage were determined by an excess of cerebral matter, it would be essential for a sharp-witted man to have a brain forty or fifty times the size of an idiot's, and tall men would always be cleverer than short ones, since their brains would be proportionately larger. And since this writer is a big man, he would be much obliged to them if they could persuade him that this is true.

I agree, therefore, that greater or lesser clarity and facility in understanding is in large part dependent on a physiological difference; not in our major organs, but in those minute aspects such as the different texture or rigidity of tiny fibres,[60] and the shape, purity and smoothness of the delicate channels through which our spirits flow. And we have no way of knowing whether these are different in men and women, since anatomical instruments have not been able to identify them; just as the Cartesians, however good their microscopes, could not tell whether the pineal gland, which they identified as the seat of the

---

[59] Martín Martínez (1684–1734) was Professor of Anatomy in the General Hospital of Madrid, and the King's personal physician. His work *Noches anatomicas, o Anatomia compendiosa* was published in Madrid in 1716. Martínez was similar to Feijoo in his insistence on the value of observation and experience over ancient authority, and was bitterly attacked for his 1722 work *Medicina Sceptica*, since scepticism was associated with religious heresy. Feijoo defended Martínez in an *Aprobación Apologetica* which was published in the 1727 second edition, and Martínez returned the compliment by publishing a *Carta Defensiva* in 1727, in which he supported Feijoo by stating that as a Professor of Anatomy he could confirm that men's and women's brains were physically identical.

[60] The theory that thought was transmitted by the oscillation of fibres in the brain was discussed by Malebranche, to whom Feijoo refers in chapters X and XIV, and by Antonio Conti (1677–1749), who in a letter dated 2 August 1721 insisted that since women's bodies were full of fluid, their cerebral fibres were soft and they were therefore universally incapable of sustained or analytical thought. (This letter was published in his *Prose e Poesie* in Venice in 1756, well after Feijoo's essay was published.)

soul, has a different texture in men and in women.[61]

That our different physical organisation has no effect on our mental operations (unless it is excessively abnormal) is obvious from the fact that there are men who are physically different but equally clever, and men who look the same but whose mental abilities are very different. Aesop the Phrygian had such a deformed body and was so misshapen that he appeared scarcely human; for this reason he was remembered in later ages as the very definition of ugliness; yet he is known to have had the most delicate and penetrating mind. Socrates was little different from Aesop in the irregularity of his appearance, but a finer mind could not be found in all antiquity. Even if we were to concede that different physical characteristics could indicate different intellectual ability, what would we conclude from this? Nothing, for women are no different from men in the organs which are used for thinking, but only in those which are to do with the reproduction of the species.

Chapter XIII

No more could we find the imagined inferiority of female understanding to be due to a difference of temperament.[62] Not that I deny that temperament affects the normal or abnormal use of our mental capacities. Indeed, I am convinced that difference in temperament creates more variety in the way we think than physical build; anyone can try the experiment on himself, seeing that changes in his constitution, without disturbing his organs, will affect his ability to carry out all sorts of activity; and there is hardly an illness that upsets the body which does not at the same time disturb the mind. But what kind of temperament or temperature is conducive to thinking or understanding better, it is not easy to tell.

If we are to take Aristotle's word for it, we would conclude that the female temperament is more suited to this. This philosopher derived all the varieties that appear in the broad field of nature from his four principal humours, saying that men with a cold temperament are more intellectual, while those

---

[61] René Descartes (1596–1650) speculated in his *Treatise on Man* (written before 1637 but not published until 1662) that the pineal gland, a small organ at the centre of the brain, was responsible for thought and sensation, being the source of 'animal spirits' which flowed through the nerves of the body.

[62] The theory of the four temperaments was originally expounded by Hippocrates and developed by Galen. The varying combinations of blood, yellow bile, black bile and phlegm would result in a personality that was either sanguine, melancholic, choleric or phlegmatic. It was connected to the theory of the four humours, whereby the combination of heat or dryness determined physical and mental characteristics; an imbalance could also cause disease. Women were believed to be cold and moist. These views had already been largely discredited by philosophers in Feijoo's time, but were still popular.

with a warm temperament are more creative.[63] However, he based this on the supposition that men in hot climates are more ingenious than those in cold (which I do not believe, since it would follow that the Africans would be cleverer than the English or the Dutch). For following his opinion on the intensity of these qualities, from the force of *antiperistasis*,[64] he claims that the coldest men live in the hottest climates, and the hottest in the coldest.

> Etenim, qui sedes frigidas habent, frigore loci obsistente, longe calidiores, quam sua sint natura, redduntur.

> [In the inhabitants of cold countries, the contrast of the ambient cold increases their natural heat.]

And he believes hotter men to be so inferior in mental ability to those of colder temperament that he does not hesitate to compare them to men whose heads have been addled by too much drink. So this quotation follows immediately afterwards:

> Itaque vinolentis admodum similes esse videntur, nec ingenio valent quo prospiciant, rerumque rationes inquirant.

> [They seem like so many drunkards, quite incapable of thinking ahead or examining the reason of things.]

This philosopher must have forgotten his disciple Alexander when he classed men of heat as stupid, or maybe not forgotten but resented him, since it is certain that he wrote most of his works after Alexander dismissed him out of suspicion that he was disloyal; and after he retired to Athens he was again mortified to see the Prince send thirty talents of gold as a gift to his competitor and fellow-student Zenocrates, without remembering Aristotle. However, it is doubtful that his resentment pushed him as far as to conspire with Antipater against Alexander's life, and to discuss with him how to poison him. But let us return to our subject.

Aristotle taught (and all the physicians and doctors agree with him) that the difference in temperament between the two sexes is that the man is hot and dry, and the woman is cold and moist: '*Est autem vir calidus, & sicus, mulier frigida, humidaque*'. Since in Aristotle's view, the cold temperament (as opposed to the hot) is more suited to thought, and since women are cold and men are hot, it follows that the female temperament is more adapted to intellectual activity than the male.

This proof is conclusive for those who believe in what Aristotle said; but I protest that it does not convince me, for I neither believe there are more clever

---

[63] Aristotle, *Problems*, Section 14, question 15.

[64] This theory, derived from Aristotelian philosophy, held that a quality could be increased by its opposite: for example, cold could increase a body's heat. Feijoo wrote a refutation of this theory in chapter 13 of volume II of the *Teatro Crítico*.

people in hot countries than in cold, nor that cold men are cleverer than hot; and far less that fiery temperaments are practically incapable of thought. And as for the theory of *antiperistasis*, we may continue to doubt its veracity.

Moisture and dryness are the other distinctive qualities of the two temperaments. If we look at them we shall also conclude from Aristotle's doctrine that women are more intelligent than men. Those who agree that having a larger brain implies superior understanding base their belief on the fact that man, the most skilled of all the animals, has a larger brain than all the others. Now they argue as follows: Aristotle says that man has a moister temperament than the other animals: '*Homo omnium animantium maxime humidus natura est*'. So the fact that man has a larger brain than beasts implies that a larger brain means greater intelligence, and the fact that a man is moister than the beasts indicates that greater moisture means better reasoning. Woman is moister than man: so she is the more intelligent of the two.

But this argument is not convincing either, or only by taking the opposite side; for the principles on which it is based are, when considered properly, dubious and uncertain. Who told Pliny that man had a bigger brain than all the other animals? Did he by some chance have an assistant who was so meticulous that he had opened the skulls of every living species in order to weigh their brains? And who told Aristotle that man is moister than all the beasts? Did the philosopher put them all in a press to see how much liquid they contained? In fact, it seems that several domestic animals, as well as insects and nearly all fish, contain more water than man. And even if it were true that the human brain were bigger than the others, this would imply that within our own species having a larger brain would make you cleverer; but many other parts of the body distinguish men from beasts without the size of certain individuals arguing for greater understanding. It would be necessary to observe that amongst the beasts themselves, those with larger brains had a superior instinct, which I believe would not be the case, for if it were so, an organism that had no brain would be completely incapable of perception, which is false: according to Pliny, many creatures which lack blood or a brain nevertheless possess instinct.

Chapter XIV

Let us now leave aside these proofs, which are derived from Aristotelian doctrines that are either untrue or uncertain, and are of use to women only in arguing with closed-minded devotees of Aristotle who believe whatever their master said. Let us examine whether this issue of women having more moisture than men implies anything to the detriment of their intellectual ability. This is the handle that is often grasped by those who wish to prove the inferiority of women's minds on the basis of some physical difference, and it appears likely that excessive moisture, either in itself or through some exhalation of vapours, may tend to limit the course of the animal spirits by blocking the narrow ducts through which these minute elements flow.

Nevertheless, it is obvious that this argument is fallacious; for if it were not, it would prove not that women's understanding is less perceptive and profound, but that their reasoning is slower and more sluggish. This is false, since many men concede that women are more quick-witted than they are.

Furthermore, many men who are quick, acute and profound suffer from regular catarrhal discharges, caused by excessive humidity in the membranes round the brain, which are apparently of the same substance as the brain, as we can read in Ribeiro's chapter on *Catarrh*.[65] Therefore the excessive humidity of the brain does not hinder the quick and correct use of the mind. And if excess humidity does not hinder it, then much less so would normal humidity.

And since natural humidity does not disturb it, we may add that according to Pliny's doctrine, the brain of man is more humid than that of all other living creatures: '*Sed homo portione maximum & humidissimum*'. And it is not credible that Nature would put into the organ which serves for the most perfect understanding, a temperament capable of making the mind damaged or defective. If it be said that the natural humidity which man has in greater abundance than the beasts is given in proportion to the better use of reason, and that women have even more of it, then I would reply that if natural humidity is no impediment, nobody knows what is the quantity or proportion the brain requires to carry out its functions; and consequently it is pointless to claim that either men or women have more of it.

Many will nevertheless argue that wet and foggy countries produce dull-witted minds; and by contrast, sunny, clear and dry lands give birth to quicker spirits. But however many people hold to this belief, they hold it on no better basis than to imagine the clouds on the horizon transferred inside the brain; as if in rainy countries the mists of the atmosphere cast a shadow on the soul, or in those which benefit from clear skies, the brighter light of day illuminates the mind. It would be more probable to suggest that in clear and sunny regions, since objects are more visible, they distract the mind more through the windows of the eyes, and thus leave people less fit for speculation and mental exercise; since for this reason we observe that in the darkness of night our train of thought is less often interrupted, and follows more easily a sequence of ideas, than in the light of day.

---

[65] Antonio Ribeiro Sanches (1699–1783) was a Portuguese converted Jew who received his doctorate at the University of Salamanca in 1724 but was denounced to the Inquisition and spent the rest of his life in exile. He became a member of the Royal Society of London, and was for sixteen years physician to the Russian court. He spent the last 36 years of his life in Paris, and left 27 volumes of unpublished manuscripts. As a young man he wrote *A Memoir on the Waters of Penha Garcia* (published 1725), which is presumably the work to which Feijoo refers.

Those who believe that wet regions are unsuitable for producing clever men should turn their eyes to the Dutch and the Venetians, who are among the most skilled peoples in Europe; for the former live surrounded by lakes and the latter may be said to have stolen part of their empire from the fishes. Even here in Spain we have the example of the Asturians who, despite living in a province that suffers from more fog and rain than any other in the Peninsula, are generally reputed to be clever, observant and mentally agile.

But why should this surprise us? Dolphins live in conditions so wet that they are often beneath the waves, yet Nature has not produced any beast with such a noble instinct, nor one that is so close to man either through affection or a similarity in customs. As we can read in Conrad Gesner,[66] they take especial care of their older relatives, have been known to guide men across the sea and help them when fishing; they have even been observed to look after the bodies of their dead, protecting the corpses of their species even when at risk of being devoured by other marine animals.

By contrast, the birds, which for most of the time have the advantage of the clearest air, rising above the vapours, soaring on the winds and perching on the highest mountains, should be the wisest of all the beasts on earth — but this is not the case.

For the same reason the Egyptians should be the cleverest people in the world, since they benefit from the clearest skies on the whole globe. Egypt hardly sees a cloud during the whole year, and its soil would be completely infertile if it were not irrigated by the Nile. And although this country was venerated in antiquity as the great seat of learning, as is demonstrated by the visits made there by Pythagoras, Homer, Plato and other Greek philosophers, in order to pursue their studies in philosophy and mathematics, this does not prove they were cleverer than other mortals, but that learning has wandered about the earth; in one century residing in one region, and in the next another.[67]

We can say the same of the Valley of Lima, whose sky is so clear that the people in that country do not know what rain is, and owes its fertility entirely to a light dew and a balmy temperature well balanced between cold and hot. They are not for all that particularly clever: in fact the Pizarro brothers who conquered them said they were easier to trick than were the Mexicans who were conquered by Cortés.

I am not unaware that the inhabitants of Boeotia were in antiquity held to be so dull that people would quote the proverbs 'Boeoticum ingenium' (a Boeotian mind), or 'Boeotica sus' (you're a Boeotian) to mean a man was stupid,

---

[66] Conrad Gesner (1516–1565) published his *Historiae Animalium* in Zurich between 1551 and 1558; it became the most popular Renaissance natural history.
[67] The 1778 edition adds here: 'Furthermore, the singular extravagance of the ancient Egyptians in matters of religion demonstrates their lack of intellectual ability.'

and that this was attributed to the damp and heavy climate that dominated this province. For this reason, Horace in one of his Epistles says, 'Boeotum in crasso jurares aere natum' (you could have sworn he was born in the foggy air of Boeotia). Yet I believe the ancients quoted above did not do justice to this country, taking their ignorance which was due to a lack of application to be instead a lack of ability. One may add that Boeotia bordered on Attica, where literature flourished, and by comparison with a province that was seen as the seat of wisdom, its neighbour looked like a land of ignorance. Moreover, it is certain that Boeotia did produce certain first-rate minds, such as Pindar, prince of lyric poets, and the great Plutarch who, in the opinion of Bacon, Lord Verulam, was the greatest man of antiquity.

I even suspect that going back to an earlier era, there was a time when the Boeotians were superior to all their neighbours and to the rest of Europe in cultivating the arts and sciences; for Cadmus of Phoenicia, who was the first to introduce the letters of the alphabet to Greece, and invented writing and history, settled in Boeotia, where he founded the city of Thebes. Furthermore, in Boeotia is Mount Helicon, dedicated to the Muses (who as a result are called Heliconides); and from this mountain flows the famous spring of Aganipe, sacred to the same imaginary goddesses, whose water was believed to be the wine of the poets, who on drinking it were raised to a state of rapture which fired their minds with furious imaginings. All these fictions would seem to have their origin in the fact that at some time poetry flourished in this region.

But even if we accept that the Boeotians were naturally dull, how does this prove that it was caused by the humidity of the country, and not by other unknown causes, especially when we consider other wet countries which are not similarly despised? Let us then excuse humidity from the false claim that it is incompatible with intellect, and agree that this argument cannot be used to prove that women are less intelligent than men.

Chapter XV

Father Malebranche argues from a different direction, and denies women equal understanding with men as resulting from the greater softness or pliability of their cerebral fibres.[68] I truly do not know if his assumptions about this softness are correct or not; I have read two anatomical treatises which do not say a word about it. Even assuming greater moistness, this does not necessarily imply greater softness, for ice is wet but not soft, and heated metal is soft but not wet. Perhaps from the greater gentleness or docility of women's character they conclude that their entire material composition must be similarly impressionable; there are men who think in such a superficial way that they

---

[68] See note 50 to the *Defence*.

form their ideas from analogies of this sort, and then for lack of reflection they spread even to the most thoughtful.

But even if we accept this, what is the connection between a softer brain and an imperfect intellect? For if this means it more readily accepts the impression of ideas, it would be better suited to mental activity. Such an argument could be supported by Malebranche's own doctrine, for he says elsewhere that the vestiges left in the brain by the movement of the animal spirits are the lines with which the imagination forms images of objects; and when these vestiges or impressions are stronger and more distinct, the mind will similarly perceive objects with greater force and clarity.

> Cum igitur imaginatio consistat in sola virtute, qua mens sibi imagines objectorum efformare potest, eas imprimendo, ut ita loquar, fibris cerebri, certe quo vestigial spirituum animalium, quae sunt veluti imaginum illarum lineamenta, erunt distinctiora, & grandiora, eo fortius, & distintius mens objecta illa imaginabitur.

[*De Inquirenda Veritate*, Book 2, Part I, ch. 1][69]

Now it is clear that if the brain is softer, and its fibres more flexible, it will receive impressions more easily, and the vestiges left by the spirits will be greater and more distinct. More easily because the material is less resistant, and more distinct because if the fibres are rigid, their elasticity will make them attempt to return to their former position, and thus restrict the pathway that the spirits have opened as they pass through. Therefore, since the fibres of the brain are more flexible in women than in men, they will form better and more distinct images, and will consequently perceive objects more clearly.

However, it should not be concluded from this that I believe women are more intelligent than men; I am merely arguing against Father Malebranche by showing that this advantage could be deduced from his doctrine, instead of the opposite conclusion that he reached in another part of his work. What I believe is that nothing is proved, or indeed could be proved, from this type of philosophical discourse. Each one philosophises in his own way, and if I were to write from a desire for fame or out of amusement, or to show off my wit, I would find it easy to draw conclusions from generally received principles that would prove the understanding of women to be several degrees above our own. But this is not my style, since I merely wish to give my sincere point of view. I therefore state that neither Father Malebranche nor any other person until now has known the precise method or specific mechanism by which thought arises in our brains. We do not know how fire burns or snow freezes, and these are things which we can see and touch: yet Father Malebranche and the

---

[69] It appears that Feijoo had read Malebranche's work in its Latin translation, published in Geneva in 1685. He conveys the sense of the quotation in the preceding paragraph.

other Cartesians wish to persuade us that they have identified the most secret workings of the rational soul.

Neither do I believe those maxims are well-founded that reduce everything to a mechanical process, imagining that the spirit stamps the images of objects on the brain like etching on to copperplate. I am not ignorant of the enormous problems that arise from Aristotle's 'intentional species',[70] but the conclusion we reach from this is that none of us has done more than touch the outward garb of nature. We all grope in the dark, and there are none so blind as those who think they see clearly; as in the story of Harpacta, Seneca's maidservant, who was so misguided that when she lost her sight she was convinced she could still see. It is certain that those who are most satisfied with their ability to understand nature are the most prone to dangerous error; for he who walks with great confidence but little illumination is the most likely to fall, whilst he who best protects himself from this danger is the one who knows the path is dark, and proceeds with caution.

But if we concede to Father Malebranche and the other Cartesians that objects present themselves on the mind through the medium of material images, which the spirit impresses on the brain, what follows from this is that if the female brain is softer because of the malleability of its material, it will receive images more strongly. And what then should we conclude? Two alternatives arise from Father Malebranche's doctrine: that women understand better than men, or that they understand just as well. The first is derived from the point discussed earlier, and the second from the fact that when he is arguing against women, he claims that the vivid imagination which results from these stronger images impedes the correct interpretation of the objects:

> Cum enim tenuiora objecta ingentes in delicates cerebri fibris excitant motus, in mente protinus etiam excitant sensationes ita vividas, ut iis tota occupetur.
>
> [*De Inquirenda Veritate*, Book 2, part 2, ch. 1]
>
> [Since the smallest objects cause large movements in the delicate fibres of their brains, they necessarily excite in their minds sentiments that are strong enough to occupy them completely.]

Chapter XVI

The time has come for us to leave the thorny paths of philosophy for the pleasant ones of history, and to persuade by example that the intellect of women is in no way inferior to that of men, even for the most difficult areas of knowledge. This

---

[70] The theory of 'intentional species' was part of Aristotle's attempt to explain how the images of material objects are transmitted via the eyes to the brain.

is a better way to convince the ignorant, who are usually more impressed by examples than by reasoning. To make a list of all those who have existed would be very tedious, so I shall refer only to the women who in recent centuries were most distinguished for their learning in Spain and in neighbouring countries.

Foreigners regard Spain as having little reputation in the field of literature, but we have produced many women who were skilled in all fields of writing. The main ones were as follows.

Ana de Cervaton, lady-in-waiting to Queen Germana de Fox, second wife of King Ferdinand the Catholic, was even more famous for her elegant writing and outstanding talents than for her extraordinary beauty, which was such that she was regarded as the most beautiful woman in the court. In the works of Lucio Marineo Sículo we find the Latin letters which he wrote to this lady, and her replies in the same language.

Isabel de Joya,[71] in the sixteenth century, was extremely learned. It is said that she preached in the cathedral in Barcelona, to the astonishment of the enormous crowd who heard her. (I assume that the bishop who permitted this took the view that the rule laid down by the Apostle Paul in his first epistle to the Corinthians,[72] that women are not allowed to speak in church, admitted certain exceptions, as did the prohibition against women teaching in the first epistle of Timothy;[73] for it is a fact that Priscilla, a companion of the Apostle, taught and instructed Apollos Ponticus[74] in the doctrine of the gospel, as we read in the Acts of the Apostles.) And later she went to Rome during the pontificate of Paul III, and to the great satisfaction of the cardinals she interpreted before them many difficult aspects of the books of the subtle Scotus.[75] But the noblest of her acts, while in that capital of the globe, was to convert many Jews to the Catholic religion.

Luisa Sigéa, resident in Toledo but originally from France, as well as being erudite in philosophy and literature, was remarkable for her grasp of languages, for she knew Latin, Greek, Hebrew, Arabic and Syriac; and it is said that she

---

[71] Her name was in fact Isabel de Josa y Cardona (1508–1575). She was a Catalan noblewoman and a member of a group of female devotees of St Ignatius Loyola, founder of the Jesuit order. She travelled to Rome in 1539 and ended her days in a convent in Lérida.

[72] 1 Corinthians 14. 34–35: 'the women should keep silence in the churches. For they are not permitted to speak, but should be subordinate, as even the law says. If there is anything they desire to know, let them ask their husbands at home. For it is shameful for a woman to speak in church' (Revised Standard Version).

[73] 1 Timothy 2. 11–12: 'Let a woman learn in silence with all submissiveness. I permit no woman to teach or have authority over men; she is to keep silent' (RSV).

[74] Acts 18. 24: 'Now a Jew named Apollos, a native of Alexandria, came to Ephesus. He was an eloquent man, well versed in the scriptures'. Acts 18. 26: 'He began to speak boldly in the synagogue: but when Aquila and Priscilla heard him, they took him and expounded to him the way of God more accurately' (RSV).

[75] John Duns Scotus (see note 56 to the *Defence*) was known as the 'Subtle Doctor' for the complexity of his thought.

wrote a letter in these five languages to Pope Paul III. When her father Diego Sigéo was summoned to the Court of Lisbon to be tutor to Teodosio of Portugal, Duke of Braganza, the Infanta Maria of Portugal, daughter of King Manuel and his third wife Leonora of Austria, who was a great lover of literature, took the learned Luisa into her entourage. She married Francisco de Cuevas, Lord of Villanasur, a knight from Burgos, and (according to Don Luis de Salazar in his 'History of the House of Farnese') many of her descendants are living in Castile to this day.

Oliva Sabuco de Nantes, a native of Alcaráz, was a great genius, and particularly inspired in physical, medical, moral and political matters, as we can see from her writings. But the most outstanding thing about her was her new physiological and medical theory which, against all the beliefs of antiquity, established that it is not the blood that nourishes our bodies but the white substance which travels from the brain to our nervous system; and she attributed almost all illnesses to a disorder of this vital liquid. This theory was ignored in Spain but embraced with enthusiasm in England, and now it is returned to us by foreigners as being their invention, when in fact it was our own. What a disastrous habit we have in Spain, that for us to accept something that is born in our own country, it must be developed and sold to us by foreigners!

It also appears that this remarkable lady was ahead of René Descartes in her belief that the brain was the seat of the thinking soul, though she extended this to the whole of the brain and not just the pineal gland, like Descartes.

The confidence that Doña Oliva had in her ability to defend her opinions was so great that in the dedication addressed to the Count of Barajas, President of Castile, she begged him to use his authority to organise a meeting with the most distinguished physicians and doctors in Spain, offering to convince them that all the physic and medicine taught in the schools was wrong. She flourished in the time of Philip II.[76]

Bernarda Ferreyra, a Portuguese lady who was the daughter of Ignacio Ferreyra, a knight of the order of Santiago, as well as being adept at various languages, was skilled in poetry, rhetoric, philosophy and mathematics. She left a collection of her poems. Our famous Lope de Vega was so impressed by the merit of this extraordinary lady that he dedicated to her his elegy 'Phyllis'.

Juliana Morell, from Barcelona, was a prodigy of learning. Her father

---

[76] Oliva Sabuco de Nantes Barrera (1562–c. 1622) wrote a collection of medical treatises, analysing the theories of ancient philosophers. She coined the term 'chilo' for a white liquid which she believed maintained the body in its proper balance. The 1744 English translation of *In Defence of Women* uses the word 'lymph', but this was not strictly what Sabuco meant; the lymphatic system was not identified until 1652 by Olaus Rudbeck and Thomas Bartholin, who were respectively Swedish and Danish. Feijoo may be referring to William Harvey (1578–1657), an Englishman who was the first to describe the circulation of the blood.

had committed a murder and had to flee, taking her with him to Lyon in France, where this extraordinary little girl made such rapid progress that at twelve years old (this was in 1607) she made a public defence of her thesis in philosophy, which she dedicated to Margaret of Austria, Queen of Spain. At the age of seventeen (according to a contemporary report by Guy Patin), she participated in a formal disputation in the Jesuit College in Lyon. She was well-versed in philosophy, theology, music and jurisprudence. They say she could speak fourteen languages. She became a nun in the Convent of St Praxedis in Avignon.

The famous Mexican nun Sister *Juana Inés de la Cruz* is known to everyone for her erudite and incisive poetry, so I have no need to speak in her praise. I shall only say that poetry was the least of her talents, though it is the one for which she is best known. There have been many Spanish poets who showed greater inspiration, but none is her equal in the variety and extent of her knowledge. Her style was natural but lacking in force. Her criticism of Father Vieira's[77] sermon shows her wit, but to be fair it is much inferior to that of the incomparable Jesuit whom she criticised. And who can be surprised if a woman were inferior to that man, whom no preacher has to this day equalled in sublime thought, perceptive argument and clear expression?

It would be pointless to make a panegyric of the deceased *Duchess of Aveyro*,[78] for there has been recent news of her in the court and in the whole of Spain.

Chapter XVII

There are many learned French women, since they have more opportunity in France, and I believe women there have greater freedom to study. I shall reduce their number to the most famous.

Susanne Habert, wife of Charles de Jardin, an officer of King Henri III, understood philosophy and theology and was well-versed in the doctrines of the Fathers of the Church. She learned Spanish, Italian, Latin, Greek and Hebrew. But her true glory came from the Christian piety for which she was famed, rather than from her vast learning.

Marie de Gournay, a Parisian of noble family, to whom the wise Dominicus Baudius[79] gave the epithet of 'the French Siren', achieved such fame and glory

---

[77] See note 19 to the *Defence*.

[78] Maria de Guadalupe de Lencastre (1630–1715) came from the Portuguese nobility but went into exile in Madrid, where she married the Duke of Los Arcos, Manuel Ponce de León. It was agreed that the two houses should remain separate, so on the death of her uncle she was recognized as the sixth Duchess of Aveiro on condition she returned to Portugal. Her husband objected to this, so she divorced him. King Carlos II of Spain conferred on her the Spanish title of Duchess of Aveyro. Feijoo uses the Spanish spelling.

[79] Dominicus Baudius, or Dominique Baudier (1561–1613), was a Flemish Calvinist and neo-Latin poet, who taught for ten years at the University of Leiden.

from her intellect and her writings that there was scarcely a great man of her time who did not think it an honour to correspond with her. Thus at her death were found in her collection letters from Cardinals Richelieu, Bentivoglio and Perron, from St Francis de Sales and other eminent prelates, from Charles the first Duke of Mantua, from the Count d'Alais, Henri du Puy, Justus Lipsius, Balzac, Maynard, Heinsius, César Cappaccio, Carlos Pinto and many other outstanding minds of her generation.[80]

Madeleine de Scudéry was appropriately known as the 'Sappho of her age', since she equalled that famous Greek poetess in the delicacy of her compositions, and excelled her in the purity of her morals. Her great knowledge was exceeded by her unmatched intelligence, as can be seen in her many excellent works. Her *Artamène, or the Grand Cyrus* and her *Clélie*, which behind the veil of fiction concealed many true stories (in the manner of Barclay's *Argenis*), are exquisite compositions which, in my opinion, are superior to anything of their type written in France or in other countries (with the sole exception of *Argenis*).[81] For the nobility of their observations, the harmonious texture of the stories, the effective pathos of their arguments, their lively descriptions and the natural purity, majesty and boldness of their style, adds up to an admirable whole. They have the added lustre of the perfect decency with which they treat the topic of love, representing the moral virtues in their highest beauty, and the heroic virtues with the most brilliant splendour.

In recognition of this lady's prodigious achievements, she was awarded the singular honour of being admitted as an honorary member by all the academies which accept members of her sex. In 1671 the Académie Française presented her with the prize for eloquence, which effectively meant that this august body declared her to be the most eloquent person in France. King Louis XIV, from whom no superior merit was ever hidden, settled on her a pension of two hundred livres. Cardinal Mazarin had long before left her a legacy in his will, and she received another through the generosity of that prudent Chancellor of France, Louis de Boucherat. Thus her lengthy and respectable life ended full of glory in the year 1701.

Antoinette de la Garde[82] was a noble French lady whose body and soul were

---

[80] Marie de Gournay (1565–1645) was most famous as the editor of the *Essais* of Michel de Montaigne. She wrote a number of original works, including *L'Égalité des Hommes et des Femmes* (*The Equality of Men and Women*). This would have been much more relevant to Feijoo's argument than the list of famous men and eminent scholars who wrote letters to her, but he seems to have been unaware of it.

[81] Feijoo's preference for Barclay's *Argenis* over the works of Scudéry is extraordinary. Her works were enormously popular during her lifetime, whereas Barclay was a very minor writer.

[82] Antoinette de la Garde (1638–1694), better known as Madame Deshoulières, wrote a large number of poems in a range of styles. She was admired by her contemporaries, and elected an honorary member of the Academy of Ricovrati in Padua.

of equal beauty; it was said of her that Nature had been pleased to blend all the graces of body and spirit in one woman. She was such an outstanding poet that, in an age when that art was better cultivated and respected in France, there was no man in that extensive kingdom who could match her. Her works are collected in two volumes, which I have not seen. She died in 1694, leaving a daughter who inherited her genius and inspiration, and who won the Académie Française's prize for poetry.

Marie Madeleine Gabrielle de Mortemart, daughter of the Duke of Mortemart, was a Benedictine nun, and was born with all the skills necessary to study the most difficult and abstract science, being endowed with a sure memory, subtle understanding and correct judgment. In her youth she learned Spanish, Italian, Latin and Greek. At the age of fifteen she was presented to the Queen of France, Maria Teresa of Austria, on her entry into the kingdom, and immediately attracted the admiration of the court, who heard her speak Spanish correctly and elegantly. She was familiar with all that was then known of the ancient and the modern philosophy, and absorbed herself in studying scholastic, dogmatic, expositive and mystical theology. She produced a number of translations, the most highly regarded being the opening books of the *Iliad*, and wrote on different matters such as morality, criticism and academic subjects.

Her letters were so highly respected that even Louis XIV received them with great pleasure. She composed exquisite verses, but they were few in number and once read, she condemned them to the fire: a sacrifice her humility compelled her to make of many of her works, and which she would have made of them all had the decision depended on her. Her piety and gift for organisation were as outstanding as her learning. In consideration of her many great talents, she was chosen as Abbess General of the Community of Fontévraud, of the Order of St Benedict, which was unusual in that it consisted of a large number of communities of both sexes, spread over four provinces, and all recognizing as their single authority the Abbess of Fontévraud, a famous monastery and one renowned for nobility as much as for virtue, since among its superiors were fourteen princesses, five of them from the royal House of Bourbon.

There was a time when the jurisdiction of the Abbey of Fontévraud extended beyond France, and it is certain, as the chronicler Yepes[83] assures us, that the two convents of Santa Maria de la Vega in Oviedo in the principality of Asturias, and Santa Maria de la Vega de la Serrana, in the Campos region, came under the diocese of Fontévraud before they were united with the Congregation of St Benedict in Valladolid.[84]

---

[83] Antonio Yepes was a Spanish chronicler of the Benedictine order. His *Cronica General de la Orden de San Benito* was published in 7 volumes in 1609–1621.
[84] Brett and the 1765/1774 English translation both skip this paragraph, which is of interest only to Spanish ecclesiastics.

The Abbess Mortemart fulfilled this exalted role to universal satisfaction, increasing the size and edification of her community: a woman who ruled men with dignity and whose combination of talents was such that if she was not superior to all the men of her age, at the very least, in the opinion of those who had dealings with her, there was none who outshone her. She died full of merit in the year 1704.

Marie-Jacqueline de Blémur, a Benedictine nun, according to the erudite Mabillon, compiled the Benedictine year, in seven quarto volumes, and also eulogies of many famous members of the order, in two quarto volumes.

Anne Le Fèvre, better known under the name of *Madame Dacier*, was the daughter of a learned father, Tanneguy Le Fèvre; she was his equal in erudition and his superior in eloquence and in her ability to write with delicacy and elegance in her own language. She was a critic of such eminence that in the field of secular literature there was no man who could equal her, either in France or in other countries. She made many translations of Greek authors, which she illustrated with a variety of commentaries. Her passion for Homer embroiled her in various controversies, in which she demonstrated quick intellect as well as acute judgment. She defended her preference for Homer over Virgil against the critics who attacked her, and particularly against Monsieur de La Motte of the Académie Française, and did this so well that though some supporters of the Latin poet took the side of Monsieur de La Motte, they could not deny that his views carried little weight, since he was unfamiliar with the Greek language in which Homer wrote, whereas his learned opponent understood it perfectly. For any impartial judge it is significant that only a few Latin authors, and no Greeks, gave Virgil precedence over or even equality with Homer; whereas Homer has the support of all the Greek and many Latin authors, among them the notable historian Velleius Paterculus, who praised him saying that no one had or ever would be able to imitate him. I believe Anne Le Fèvre died three or four years ago.[85]

Chapter XVIII

Italy is France's equal in the number of its learned women; but for the same reason that we restricted ourselves to a small number of Frenchwomen, we shall do the same with the Italians.

Dorotea Bucca,[86] a native of Bologna, was destined from a young age for

---

[85] In fact Anne Dacier died in 1720.

[86] Dorotea Bucca or Bocchi (1360–1436) held a chair in medicine and philosophy at the University of Bologna for nearly forty years; it had previously been held by her father. She was generally forgotten by the time Feijoo was writing, and the honour of being the first woman to receive a doctorate was usually attributed to Elena Cornara Piscopia, whom Feijoo mentions later.

literature, and made such great strides in this that her famous university conferred on her the then unprecedented distinction of a doctor's hood, and she was a professor there for a long time. She flourished in the fifteenth century.

Isotta Nogarola, a native of Bologna, was the oracle of her age; to her knowledge of philosophy and theology she added the ornament of various languages, extensive reading of the Fathers of the Church, and an eloquence which was in no way inferior to that of the greatest orators of her time. The proofs of her extensive talents were exceptional, for she discoursed several times before the Popes Nicholas V and Pius II and in the Council of Mantua which the latter pontiff convoked in order to unite all the Christian princes against the Turks. Cardinal Besarion, an illustrious patron of literature, having read some of Isotta's works, travelled from Rome to Verona specifically to meet her. This lady died in 1466 at the age of thirty-eight.

Laura Cereta,[87] a native of Brescia, gave public lectures in philosophy to general applause from the age of eighteen, at the beginning of the sixteenth century.

Cassandra Fedele,[88] from Venice, was so famous for her knowledge of Greek, philosophy, theology and history that there was scarcely a noble prince of her time who did not publicly acknowledge his respect for her. Amongst her admirers were Popes Julius II and Leon X, King Louis XI of France, and our Catholic monarchs Ferdinand and Isabella. She wrote various works, and died in 1567 at the age of 102.

Caterina de Cibo, duchess of Camerino in the Anconian Marches, understood Latin, Greek and Hebrew, philosophy, and theology. Her virtue added lustre to her erudition. She built the first ever Capuchin convent and died in 1557.

Marta Marchina, from Naples, was of humble birth but her genius was so great that she overcame the disadvantages of her limited fortune and learned with greet speed the Latin, Greek and Hebrew languages, and was a poetess of no mean ability. But her exalted talents were insufficient to lift her from the state into which she was born, and stood in contrast to the malign influence of the stars; for it is known that after she moved to Rome she supported herself and her family by making soap. We may imagine that if someone with this kind of mind had enjoyed the same opportunity to study as other women, she would have been a prodigy amongst women and men alike. She died in 1646 at the age of forty-six.

Elena Lucrezia Cornaro, of the illustrious Cornaro family in Venice, may be the last in this series of learned Italian women, since she is the most recent, but

---

[87] There was a tradition that Laura Cereta (1469–1499) taught philosophy at the University of Padua, but no records have been found to verify this. She died before the sixteenth century began, so Feijoo's dating is incorrect.

[88] Cassandra Fedele's date of birth is uncertain but is believed to have been around 1465. She died in 1558, which would have made her 93 years old.

we may regard her as the first in eminence without doing any of the others an injustice. This lady, an honour to her sex, was born in 1646. Since her earliest infancy she displayed a keen interest in letters, and this led to her astonishingly rapid progress, for not only did she learn with rare facility the Latin, Greek and Hebrew languages, but also almost all the modern European languages. She showed such distinction in philosophy, mathematics and theology that the University of Padua decided to make her a Doctor of Divinity, and this would have happened were it not for the opposition of Cardinal Barbarigo, bishop of the city, out of respect for the maxim of St Paul which excludes women from the ministry of teaching in church. Therefore, so as not to violate this aspect of canon law but to continue to respect Elena's singular merit, they decided instead to make her a Doctor of Philosophy, and the ceremony was graced with the presence of many princes and princesses from different parts of Italy.

Since her learning was so eminent, it could be exceeded only by her outstanding piety. At the age of twelve she made a vow of perpetual virginity, and though later on a German prince came to ask urgently for her hand in marriage, and offered to ask the Pope for a dispensation to release her from her vow, and was supported by the arguments of her parents, she refused to give up her resolve. In order to end the hopes of many other persistent suitors, she decided to become a Benedictine nun, but since her father prevented this, she did what she could, which was to renew her vow of virginity and add the religious vows of an oblate of the Rule of St Benedict, before the Abbot of the Monastery of San Giorgio.

This sacrifice of her liberty was followed by a life, spent in her father's house, of such exemplary piety that it would have been admired by the most austere of nuns. Such was her love of retirement and reluctance to appear in public that, although she sometimes complied with her father's wishes by allowing herself to be seen occasionally, it was so distressing to her that she used to say that such obedience would be the death of her. And her life was indeed short, since she passed on to a better one at the age of thirty-eight, to the joy of the angels and the grief of men. She left behind many works which will guarantee her eternal fame. Many writers have written in praise of this extraordinary woman; among them Gregorio Leti in his *Raguallos Historicos* calls her 'heroine of literature' and 'prodigy of learning', and also 'an angel of beauty and purity'.[89]

---

[89] The 1765/1774 English translator added in a footnote to this chapter a brief biography of Maria Gaetana Agnesi (1718–1799), who in a later generation had a similar career as a child prodigy, was given an honorary chair in mathematics at the University of Milan, but tired of being brought out to perform for her father's guests, refused to marry and devoted herself to good works.

Chapter XIX

Amid the snows of Germany Apollo may influence minds more easily than he can melt icicles, but one spark of the sun existed in a woman of that country.

She was the famous *Anna Maria van Schurman*, the glory of both upper and lower Germany; for although she was born in Cologne, her parents and grandparents came from the Low Countries. To this day no greater genius has been seen in either sex. All the sciences and all the arts submitted with the same obedience to the power of her mind, and none could resist when this heroine took it upon herself to conquer them. At the age of six she could make exquisite and delicate paper cuttings without following a pattern. At eight she learned in a few days to make lovely flower paintings which were much admired. At ten she needed only three hours of practice to produce beautiful embroidery. But her talent for more advanced studies was hidden until the age of twelve, and was discovered in this way. Her younger brothers used to study at home, and it was noticed several times that when they were having their lessons, if they could not remember the answers their sister would remind them, without having made any study other than listening in the background when they were at their lessons. This and other signs which indicated a completely extraordinary understanding, led her father to decide to permit his daughter to follow a course of studies of her choice. But her rapid progress meant this course was not so much a race[90] as a flight, as Schurman journeyed through the broad expanse of sacred and profane erudition, in time achieving a grasp of almost all the humanist subjects,[91] together with theology and a wide understanding of scripture. She had a perfect understanding of German, Dutch, English, French, Italian, Latin, Greek, Hebrew, Syriac, Chaldean, Arabic and Ethiopian.[92] She also had the gift of poetry, and composed many modest poetical works. She received as much applause in the liberal arts as in sciences and languages. She understood the technicalities of music, and played various instruments skilfully. She excelled at painting, sculpture and in the art of engraving on glass. It is said that she made her own portrait in wax, decorated with pearls which appeared so natural that no one could believe they were made of wax until they were pricked with a needle.

Her letters made her so famous and respected, not just for the elegance of their style but also for the beauty of her handwriting, that many who read them judged them to be unequalled; the smallest example of her penmanship was sought after as if it were a rare artefact. There was scarcely a great man

---

[90] Feijoo is playing on the two senses of the word 'carrera', as a course of studies and as a race.

[91] These subjects were grammar, rhetoric, moral philosophy, history and poetry.

[92] In fact Schurman did not speak or write English, but she was proficient in all the other languages Feijoo mentions, and produced the first Ethiopian grammar.

of the time who did not declare his admiration, and seek to enter into literary correspondence with her. The illustrious Queen of Poland, Louise-Marie de Gonzague, on her journey to that kingdom following her marriage by proxy in Paris to King Ladislas, did Schurman the honour of visiting her in her own home. She never married, despite receiving many advantageous offers, especially from Jacob Cats,[93] the Dutch pensionary and famous poet, who had written verses in her praise when Anna Maria was only fourteen years old. At last this lady, who deserved to be immortal, died in 1678 at the age of seventy-one.

Chapter XX

I will not mention the many learned women who did honour to Germany and other European countries, but will finish with a recent example from Asia, to prove that female literary glory is not restricted to Europe.

This is the story of the beautiful, wise and generous *Sitti Maani*, wife of the famous traveller Pedro de la Valle, a Knight of Rome. Maani was born in Mesopotamia, and thus that happy province (within whose boundaries certain commentators believe the garden of Paradise was situated) had the honour of being the fatherland of two Rachels; for it is certain that Haran, birthplace of Jacob's beloved wife, was located in Mesopotamia. Since her earliest youth she had demonstrated a noble intellect, quick understanding and matchless beauty, news of which excited the curiosity of Pedro de la Valle and gave him the desire to see her. The experience of doing so inspired him with such love that he desired to make her his wife.

After their marriage, not only did Maani give up the Chaldean religion and embrace the Church of Rome, but she persuaded her relatives to do the same. It seems incredible what this charming Asian lady achieved in such a short time (for she did not live long), for not only did she acquire a knowledge of all the learning available in those regions which today are still strangers to the sciences, but she also learned twelve different languages. Moreover, the number and perfection of her virtues increased, including that shining virtue of courage which is most unusual in her sex, for two or three times she took up arms to defend her husband. This lady, so outstanding for her talents, lost her life near Ormuz on one of her many travels, dying of a malignant fever at twenty-three years of age. Thus died, to the grief of all who knew her, this new Rachel, so similar to the original that it would seem as if Nature and Fortune had deliberately created them in parallel to each other. For both were exceedingly beautiful, both married foreigners of great merit, and both chose to give up the religion of their fathers for that of her their husbands. And finally, both died in

---

[93] Feijoo calls him 'Monsieur Catec' and the English translator 'M. Catoe'.

the flower of their youth, whilst on a journey.

But in this final aspect the two husbands appeared very different, for Pedro de la Valle outshone even the Patriarch Jacob in refinement. Jacob buried his Rachel on the road where she died; later he believed that his wife's merits were such that he should show to her body the same respect as to his own, and urged his son Joseph to transfer it to the sepulchre of his ancestors in Hebron. This seems like a lesser degree of care than we might expect, given the Patriarch's love for his wife (though we may assume that he had some important, mysterious or natural reason for it), and may be contrasted with the shining delicacy of Pedro de la Valle; for he had the body of his adored Maani embalmed and placed in a costly casket, and carried it with him during the entire four years he spent travelling in Asia, thus keeping in his sight her remains, her heart and the memory of her virtues. This continued until he arrived in Rome, where he placed the remains of his beloved in his family vault in the chapel of St Paul in the church of Santa Maria de Ara Coeli, with an elaborate funeral the like of which had rarely been seen. Pedro de la Valle pronounced the eulogy himself, and his eyes were more eloquent than his lips, for at length he could not speak for tears. When his throat was choked by distress, he abandoned the unfinished eulogy; and failing to pronounce his eloquent phrases, was overcome with bitter tears, the true voices of grief which echoed the groans of the assembled throng.

Note: Sitti is an honorific title among the Persians, the equivalent of Señora.

Chapter XXI

We have omitted from this catalogue of learned women many modern ladies, for lack of space, and all those of antiquity, since they can be found in an infinite number of books. It is enough to say (indeed it seems to be the key point) that almost all those women who have dedicated themselves to letters have demonstrated considerable achievements, whilst out of a hundred men who are put to study, only three of four turn out to be real scholars.

But since this observation might give women a chance to consider themselves greatly superior in ability to men, it is only fair to check this supposition by pointing out that the inequality of outcome derives from the fact that the opportunity to study is given only to those women who are recognised either by those who are in charge of their education, or by the women themselves, as having a particular disposition towards learning. Men, on the other hand, have no such choice: parents wishing to enhance their prospects destine them for a literary career without consideration for whether they are clever or stupid; and since most men are of limited ability, it is likely that they will emerge with little advantage from their studies.

It is my opinion, therefore, that there is no inequality in the capacities of either sex. But if women have to defend themselves against attacks on their aptitude for the arts and sciences, they may if they wish pass from defence to offence by using the above arguments as a way of claiming superiority over men; for we have shown that the same physical maxims used to deprecate women's ability may be used to show a greater likelihood that they are superior to us.

To this I would add the authority of Aristotle, who in various places teaches us that in all species of animal, expressly including the human race, the females are cleverer and more astute than the males:

> In omnibus vero, quorum procreatio est, foeminam, & marem simili fere modo natura distinxit moribus, quibus mas differt a foemina, quod praecipue tum in homine, tum etiam in iis, quae magnitudine praestent, & quadrupedes viviparae sint, percipitur: sunt enim foeminae moribus mollioribus, mitescunt celerius & malum facilius patiuntur, discunt etiam, imitanturque ingeniosius.

> (*Historia Animalium*, Book 9, ch. 1)

> [Nature has in all species, especially the human and viviparous quadrupeds, distinguished male and female by particular qualities; the females being of a softer disposition and more patient and docile, they are quicker at observation and more skilled at imitation.]

This authoritative statement by Aristotle, which concedes to women not only greater docility and mental receptiveness but also greater acuteness than men, should carry great weight with the devotees of this philosopher, whom they call the 'penetrating genius of nature' and the height of human intelligence. But I must warn women not to rely too much on Aristotle, for though in the passage cited above he ennobles them with superior perception, a little later he degrades them with an accusation of greater malice: '*Verum malitiosores, astutiores, insidiores foeminae sunt*' (Women are truly more malicious, sly and treacherous). And although later on he concedes that they show more than men the noble attribute of pity, he then stains them with the blots of envy, slander, spitefulness and other vices: '*Ita quod mulier misericors magis, & ad lacrymas propensior, quam vir est: invida iter magis, & querula, & maledicentior, & mordacior*' (Thus woman is much more prone to pity and tears than man, but is also much more querulous, slanderous and spiteful). I therefore question whether women would wish to accept at the price of such disadvantages the concession of mental superiority that Aristotle offers them. They may nevertheless consider that if someone who thought so badly of them agreed to their being cleverer than men, this must have been based on some sure foundation.

Chapter XXII

Here it is appropriate to say something about the aptitude for women in those arts in which they rarely participate, such as painting and sculpture. Very few women have dedicated themselves to these arts, but from these few have emerged some excellent practitioners. I have already described above how the admirable Anna Maria van Schurman was outstanding in painting, sculpture and etching.

In Italy three sisters were celebrated as painters: *Sofonisba*,[94] *Lucia* and *Europa Anguissola*. Queen Elizabeth of Spain, wife of Philip II, took the first of these into her service, and she had such a great reputation that Pope Pius IV commissioned a portrait of the Queen by Sofonisba.

Irene di Spilimbergo,[95] from Venice, was so skilful in this art that her paintings were often taken to be by Titian, her contemporary. Her life was snatched away at the age of seventeen, to universal grief and lamentation, even from her competitor.

Teresa del Po[96] lives in Naples (if she is still alive) and is highly regarded for her painting; some of her splendid canvases may be seen in the collection of the Marquisa de Villena, who had them made when the Marquis was Viceroy of Naples.

Italy has also produced famous women sculptors. *Properzia de' Rossi*[97] was widely applauded for her beautifully-designed and well-executed marble statues. But above her, and indeed above all others, was the famous *Lavinia Fontana*.[98]

I know of only one woman painter in France, but she was of the first rank. This was *Élisabeth Sophie Chéron*, better known as Madame Le Hay, who in addition to her greater than average talents for poetry and music, was a leading

---

[94] Sofonisba Anguissola, or Anguisciola (c. 1532–1625) was born in Cremona and was one of five sisters, all of whom were painters. At the age of 26 she went to Madrid to be tutor to Elizabeth of Valois, Queen of Philip II, and, remarkably for a woman, became official court painter. She married twice and died in Palermo at the age of 93. About fifty works have been attributed to her, including a portrait of Philip II of Spain in the Museo del Prado in Madrid. Her sister Elena died young, and Europa abandoned painting upon her marriage.

[95] Irene di Spilimbergo (c. 1540–1559) studied under Titian. Few of her works are known.

[96] Teresa del Po was born in Palermo. She became a member of the Accademia di San Luca in Rome, and died in Naples in 1716, ten years before Feijoo's work was published.

[97] Properzia de' Rossi (1490–1530) was the only woman included in Giorgio Vasari's book *Lives of the Most Eminent Architects, Painters, and Sculptors of Italy* (1550). The best-known of her surviving works is a panel on the west façade of the church of San Petronio in Bologna depicting Joseph and Potiphar's wife.

[98] Lavinia Fontana (1552–1614) was born in Bologna and taught by her father Prospero Fontana. She painted portraits, which was a traditional genre for women, but also religious and mythological subjects. Her husband Paolo Zappi became her assistant, and she moved to Rome at the invitation of Pope Clement VIII. There are records of over 100 of her works, of which more than half survive; this is the largest oeuvre of any female artist prior to 1700.

painter and so much admired that the Dauphin, son of Louis XIV, had her make a portrait of him and his sons. The same was done by Casimir V, King of Poland, who lived in Paris after his voluntary abdication of the crown; and many of the leading noblemen of France honoured her with their visits, as did the Prince de Condé on numerous occasions. The Emperor Josef offered her a significant pension if she would move to Vienna, and when he could not persuade her to do so, he sent her models of his face and those of his sons, so she could paint their portraits. She was equally outstanding in design and in the use of colour, and her marvellous facility was shown by the fact that she was able to make conversation without interruption to her brushwork. But her generous Christian actions and her pious spirit made her even more admirable than her handiwork. She died as she had lived in 1711.[99]

The area where we can most easily judge the equality of men and women in their aptitude for the noble arts is in music (which is a faculty found indifferently in men and women). For those women who apply themselves to it can measure their progress according to their length of study, just as we can; and the masters of this art find girls no more difficult to teach than boys. I knew one girl in this profession who was a composer before she reached the age of fifteen.

In this list of so many excellent women, I have deliberately not mentioned the outstanding talents of our illustrious Queen Elizabeth Farnese,[100] since my respect for her does not allow me to touch this sublime subject with so coarse a pen, and also because another writer much more knowledgeable than I of the glories of her royal house has sketched an outline of her radiant personage.

Chapter XXIII

I can imagine that some may refute everything I have said in this way: if women are men's equals in their aptitude for the arts and sciences, for the government and the economy, then why did God establish the dominion and superiority of men over women in the sentence of Genesis, chapter three: '*Sub viri potestate eris*' (thou shalt be under the power of thy husband)? For we may expect that he would grant power to the sex which could be seen to be more capable.

My first response is this: that no one can be sure of the specific meaning of this text, because of the many different versions. The Septuagint says: '*Ad virum conversio tua*' (thou shalt turn to thy husband). Aquila says: '*Ad virum societas*

---

[99] Elisabeth Sophie Chéron (1648–1711) was the fourth woman to be admitted to the Académie Royal de Peinture et de Sculpture in 1672, being sponsored by Charles Le Brun. She was also admitted in 1699 to the Academy of the Ricovrati in Padua under the name of Erato, but for her writing rather than her painting. She was married for the first time at the age of 63, to Jacques Le Hay. Very few of her works survive.

[100] Elizabeth Farnese (1692–1766) was the second wife of Philippe de Bourbon (grandson of Louis XIV of France), who took the Spanish throne in 1700 as Felipe V, and mother of the future King Carlos III.

tua' (thou shalt be in the company of thy husband). Simmachus says: 'Ad virum appetitus, vel impetus tuus' (thy desire shalt be to thy husband). And the learned Benedictine Pereira says that, if you translate the Hebrew word for word, the sentence comes out like this: 'Ad virum desiderium, vel concupiscentia tua' (to man, as thy husband, shall be thy desire).

My second response would be that the subjection of the woman was a direct punishment for her sin, and therefore did not exist in the state of innocence. The text does not contradict this, for if the woman had been obliged to obey the man before the Fall, then God would have had to make this clear to her when he created her. This being so, we may conclude that God did not give man the preference because he was superior to the woman in understanding, but because she was the first to fall into sin.

My third argument is that even if God had given the man power over the woman from the beginning, this would not necessarily imply that he had superior talent. The reason is that, even though their talents may be the same, it is necessary that one of the two should take the lead in governing the family and household; otherwise there would be confusion and disorder. All the moral philosophers agree with Aristotle that among the different types of political system, the worst is democracy, in which all the individuals in the republic share equally in government, or hold equal votes. Now between a husband and wife, this model of domestic government would not only be imperfect, it would be impossible; for whilst the population of a city can settle their differences through a plurality of votes, this could not happen between husband and wife, since there are only two of them, and if they have opposite opinions, they cannot choose which of them is better. But if one of them had to be superior, and their talents are equal, why did God choose the man? One may imagine he had various reasons based on different characteristics such as constancy or courage, for these virtues are required to take necessary decisions and carry them out, sweeping aside the vain or trivial fears of one or the other that may stand in their way. But it is better to say that in most cases we are ignorant of the reasons behind the judgments of God.

Chapter XXIV

I shall conclude this essay by dealing with an objection that could be made to its argument; that is, that persuading the human race of the equality of both sexes in intellectual talents does not appear useful to the public, and could indeed be harmful if it encouraged women in pride or presumption.

This doubt may be removed simply by saying that whatever the subject under discussion, it is useful to seek truth and reject error. A correct understanding of things is important in itself, without considering any other result. Truth has an intrinsic value, and expanding or enriching the understanding cannot be measured in money. Some truths are more precious than others, but none of them is useless. And the truth which we have proved here would not increase the vanity or presumption of women. If they are truly equal to us in the qualities of their souls, there can be no harm at all in their knowing and understanding this. St Thomas, when discussing vainglory, says that this is not a sin if each person is able to assess correctly his own qualities: '*Quod autem aliquis bonum suum cognoscat, & approbet, non est peccatum*'. And elsewhere, speaking of presumption, he says this is only a vice if it is founded on erroneous understanding: '*Praesumptio autem est motus appetitivus, quia importat quamdam spem inrdinatuam, habet autem se conformiter intellectui falso*'. If women come to understand what they truly are, they will not think more of their talents than they should, and cannot be vainglorious or presumptuous. On the contrary, careful consideration of the explanations given in this discourse would not make women more proud, but would lessen the pride of men.

But I would go even further, and claim that the maxim which we have established here is not only incapable of causing any moral evil, but can be the source of great advantage. Let us consider how many have been emboldened by their imagined superiority to make criminal assaults on the opposite sex. In any contest, having or lacking confidence in one's own strength has a major impact on winning or losing the battle. The man who believes in his superiority will speak boldly; the woman, judging herself inferior, listens to him with respect. Who can deny that this makes it far more likely that he will prevail and she will submit?

So let women know that they are not inferior to men in judgment; secure in this knowledge, they will be confident in refuting men's sophisms, which hide their wiles behind a veil of reason. If a woman is persuaded that man is an oracle compared to her, she will pay attention to the most indecent proposal, and will revere the most notorious lie as an infallible truth. It is well known to what indignities those heretics which we call Molinists[101] have reduced many formerly virtuous women. What caused this perversion, if not the fact that they imagined them to be men of superior judgment, and failed to have confidence in their own understanding, when the falsity of those poisonous dogmas was presented to them?

There is another consideration that is very important in this matter. It is certain that any woman would surrender more easily to someone who offers her some clear advantage. A man will happily serve another who is his social

---

[101] Miguel de Molinos (*c.* 1628–1697) was a Spanish mystic who developed the doctrine of Quietism, which held that individuals could through meditation develop a direct spiritual relationship with God without the mediation of the church or the necessity to follow a particular ritual. His doctrines were very popular, but were condemned by the Holy Office and he spent the last ten years of his life in a pontifical prison. He was accused of sexual misconduct with some of his female penitents.

superior, but will be extremely reluctant to do so if he is similar in status. The same thing happens here. If a woman holds the error that the male sex is much nobler, and she is in comparison an imperfect animal and of little value, she will not hold it a crime to surrender to him; and if he adds to this a little flattery and kindness, she will judge a shameful act to be glorious. Let women, therefore, be aware of their own dignity, as St Leo wished men to be. May they know that our sex has not the slightest advantage over them, and it would therefore always be vile and shameful for them to grant a man ownership of their bodies unless sanctioned by the state of holy matrimony.

I have not said all there is to say about the moral advantages of removing men and women from this erroneous belief in the inequality of the sexes. I firmly believe that this error causes an infinite number of marriage-beds to be sullied by the stain of adultery. It may seem that I am entangling myself in a strange paradox, but this is an absolute truth. Now pay attention.

Once a few months have passed after the bond of marriage has joined a couple together, the woman loses the respect which she previously enjoyed as a newly-acquired treasure. The man turns from tenderness to coldness, and coldness often declines into derision and actual contempt. When the husband reaches this vicious extreme, he starts to mock and insult his wife, confident in the advantages which he imagines he is afforded by his sex. Encouraged by the common belief that the most knowledgeable of women knows less than a fourteen-year old boy, that it is pointless to expect a woman to have brains or good sense, and other nonsense like this, he despises everything about her. Once it reaches this state, everything the poor woman does is treated as absurd: every statement is folly and every action a blunder. If she has beauty, it no longer helps her, since the confidence of possession reduces the value of the object. Her charm has already faded. All the husband thinks is that woman is an imperfect animal, and he despises her so much that he will tell even the most beautiful to her face that she is vile and disgusting.

While the unfortunate woman is in this state of humiliation, it is often the case that an admirer starts to pay court to her. To someone who is tired of being scowled at every hour of the day, it is natural that a smiling face will be most appealing. This is enough to make her listen to him, and she hears nothing that is not designed to please her. Before she heard nothing but contempt; now she hears only adoration. Before she was treated as less than a woman; now she sees herself elevated to the status of a goddess. Before she was told she was stupid; now she hears that she has a divine understanding. In the mouth of her husband there was nothing good about her; to the lover she is grace personified. One acted like a tyrant; the other offers to make himself her slave. And even though the lover, if he is married, may act the same in his own home, this does not prevent the sorry wife from seeing the two as being as different as an angel is from a beast. She sees in her husband a heart full of thorns, and in the lover one that is garlanded with flowers. Here is a bed of nails and there a bed of gold; here is slavery and there is power; here is a dungeon and there is a throne.

In this situation, what would even the most strong-minded of women do? How is she to resist two forces directed to the same end, one pushing and the other pulling? If she is not firmly held back by the hand of God, she is bound to fall. And if she falls, who could deny that her own husband is to blame? If he had not treated her with such abuse, she would not have fallen into the lover's trap. The ill treatment of the one enforced the surrender of the other. All these evils frequently arise from the low opinion that husbands hold of the other sex. If they rejected these false maxims, they could keep their wives more faithful. They should remember that God has commanded them to love their wives, and I cannot see how love and contempt for the same person can exist together in one heart.

Josefa Amar y Borbón, A Woman of Erudition

A generation after the death of Benito Feijoo, the argument about women was renewed with even greater vigour in Spain. The reforming ministers of King Carlos III encouraged the participation of volunteer groups in their mission to make the country more prosperous, and a number of societies were established to debate policy and encourage best practice, the most prestigious being the Madrid Royal Economic Society of Friends of the Nation. This was set up by royal decree in 1775, and immediately a group of ladies began to lobby for the right to become members, leading to an impassioned public debate about whether it was appropriate for women to fill public positions.

One of the most outspoken proponents of the female cause was Josefa Amar y Borbón.[1] Amar was born in Zaragoza in 1749, the fifth of eleven children. Her father was an eminent doctor who had been appointed to the chair of anatomy at the University of Zaragoza at the early age of twenty-four, and moved to Madrid to become court physician when Amar was five years old. He later became vice-president of the Royal Academy of Medicine in Madrid, and a member of the Royal Society of Sciences in both Seville and Oporto.

The young Amar was given a high-quality education and benefited from the attentions of two important tutors: Rafael Casalbón, the royal librarian, and Antonio Berdejo, a member of the Aragonese Economic Society. She learned Latin and Greek from them, and it is clear from her later works that she was also fluent in French, Italian and English. Furthermore, she had the opportunity to study in the royal libraries.

In 1772, at the age of twenty-three, she married Joaquín Fuertes Piquer, a forty-seven-year-old lawyer, and moved with him back to Zaragoza. There her husband also became an active member of the Aragonese Economic Society, and would become its second director. Three years later their only child, Felipe, was born, and in 1782 Amar published her first work. This was the first volume of a translation from Italian of a defence of Spanish literature written by Francisco Javier Lampillas, a Spanish Jesuit based in Genoa, and

---

[1] For Amar's biographical details, see Maria Victoria López-Cordón Cortezo, *Condición Femenina y Razón Ilustrada* (Zaragoza: Prensas Universitarias de Zaragoza, 2005).

was entitled *Ensayo histórico-apologético de la literatura Española*. The timing of the publication was perfect, since it coincided with an outcry of indignation by Spaniards against an article written by Nicolas Masson de Morvilliers and published in France in the *Encyclopédie Méthodique* (a revised and expanded version of Diderot's *Encyclopédie*), which sneeringly suggested that Spain had contributed nothing of significance to the arts, sciences or commerce, and declared it to be the most ignorant nation in Europe.[2]

During the next two years, Amar published five more volumes of the translation, and in 1786 produced a translation of a second response by Lampillas to the same controversy. A seven-volume second edition of the *Ensayo* was published in Madrid in 1789.

Amar became something of a local heroine in her city of Zaragoza, for having produced (albeit as a translation of someone else's book) a work that enabled Spaniards to reassure themselves that their literature could stand alongside the output of other European nations. In gratitude, in 1783 they elected her to full membership of the Aragonese Economic Society, a distinction of which she was enormously proud.

The Society proceeded to commission another translation from Amar, this time of an Italian work by Francisco Griselini on the subject of how parish clergy could help to train farm labourers in better agricultural techniques. This was published in 1783, with her name in full and her membership of the Society proudly indicated on the title page. However, tragedy struck three years later when her husband had a stroke. He lived for another thirteen years, but his health during this time was very poor, and much of Amar's time was taken up in nursing him.

This did not prevent her from continuing to write and to engage in political debate. It was in 1786 that she published her first original work, an essay entitled *Discurso en defensa del talento de las mujeres, y de su aptitud para el gobierno, y otros cargos en que se emplean los hombres* (*Discourse in Defence of the Talents of Women, and their Aptitude for Government and Other Positions in which Men are Employed*). The purpose of this essay was to demand that women should be admitted to membership of the Madrid Economic Society, and the fact that a woman was able to publish such a work under her own name is itself a sign of how far things had come in the sixty years since Feijoo's *Defence of Women*. When Amar and her supporters were admitted to the Society in 1787, she wrote the expected *Congratulatory Oration*, but expressed disappointment that they had been restricted to a separate 'Ladies' Section'.[3]

---

[2] Nicolas Masson de Morvilliers, 'L'Espagne' in *Encyclopédie Méthodique*, I (Paris: Panckoucke, 1782). Translated in *Enlightenment Spain and the Encyclopédie Méthodique*, ed. by Clorinda Donato and Ricardo López (Oxford: Oxford University Studies in the Enlightenment, Voltaire Foundation, 2015), pp. 27–93.

[3] 'Oración Gratulatoria que la Señora Doña Josepha Amar y Borbón, elegida socia de

Three years later, Amar published a more substantial work, a lengthy treatise on female education entitled *Discourse on the Physical and Moral Education of Women*. In 1798 her husband finally succumbed to his long illness, and died at the age of seventy-two.

The question of female education was taken up in a serious way by the Madrid Economic Society. In February 1795 the Countess of Trúllas proposed a list of topics to be considered, and two subcommittees were set up to discuss them and put forward recommendations. Josefa Amar submitted a treatise on the subject of parents helping their daughters to choose between marriage and the religious life, which was one of the issues she had covered in her 1790 book. In her absence the Countess of Montijo, as secretary of the Ladies' Committee, read her paper to the assembled company at their meeting on 18 December 1795.[4] The following year the Council of the Society asked the Ladies' Section to submit a selection of their work for publication, and they proposed seven papers, all on the subject of education. These were approved by the censor in 1801, but do not appear to have been published, and the originals have disappeared.

Amar continued to produce translations during the 1790s, but they do not appear to have been published, and are now lost. The two that have been recorded were both English works: Captain Henry Boyde's 1736 travel journal *Several Letters from Barbary*, and a work by Vicesimus Knox, the headmaster of Tonbridge School; this is assumed to be his *Liberal Education*, which she referred to in her own book.[5]

The French writer Alexandre de Laborde, who travelled extensively in Spain during the early years of the new century, was highly impressed by the efforts of the Aragonese Economic Society to revive and develop agriculture and industry in their province, and spoke in glowing terms of the free school in Zaragoza established for the education of young girls. The school taught spinning, and distributed prizes to the most diligent, including equipment and materials so they might work to earn money on their own account, and a cash sum to be paid to them as a marriage portion. In 1804 twenty-six of these valuable prizes were awarded.[6] Josefa Amar was one of two ladies who had been commissioned in 1784 to take over the management of this school, and we may assume that she

---

honor y mérito, dirigió a la junta de Señoras de la Real Sociedad Económica de Madrid', in *Memorial Literario*, 12 (1787), pp. 588–92. See López-Cordon, *Condición Femenina y Razón Ilustrada*, pp. 311–15.

[4]   Smith, *The Emerging Female Citizen*, p. 150. For the remarkable life of the Countess of Montijo, see Paula Demerson, *Maria Francisca de Sales y Portocarrero, Condesa de Montijo: Una figura de la Ilustración* (Madrid: Editora Nacional, 1975), and the same author's *La Condesa de Montijo, una mujer al servicio de las luces* (Madrid: Fundación Universitaria Española, 1976).

[5]   López-Cordón, *Condición Femenina y Razón Ilustrada*, p. 84; Fernández-Quintanilla, *La mujer ilustrada*, p. 130.

[6]   Alexandre de Laborde, *A View of Spain* (trans.), II (London: Longman, 1809), p. 268.

had continued to contribute to an institution so close to her heart.[7]

But all of this was to come to an end in the year 1808, when Spain was invaded by Napoleon's army. During the summer, the French laid siege to Zaragoza, but were unable to take the city. They returned in December with larger forces, and finally forced it to surrender after two months of heavy bombardment and brutal hand-to-hand fighting which left 54,000 people dead. Amar survived, but her beloved city was left in ruins.

An English traveller, Sir John Carr, visited Zaragoza a year later, and reported that he had heard numerous stories of female heroism during the siege, as 'women, many of them of the highest orders of life, and of elegant habits, without respect to rank, formed themselves into corps, to carry provisions, to bear away the wounded to the hospitals, and to fight in the streets'.[8] Josefa Amar was one of these: the director of the Hospital of Nuestra Señora de Gracia recorded her name among the women who had transported the patients to safety, showing more care for their lives than for her own.[9]

In 1810, Amar was struck by a further loss, as her son Felipe was killed in an uprising in Quito in Ecuador, where he was a magistrate. The subjugation of Spain by Napoleon, who took the royal family into captivity in France and put his brother Joseph Bonaparte on the throne, led to instability throughout Spain's possessions in South America. A number of Quito's prominent citizens rebelled against the colonial government and set up a junta which ruled briefly in the name of the exiled Spanish King Fernando VII, but this was not supported by the rest of the country and was easily crushed by troops sent from Lima and Bogota. Felipe was a friend of the junta's leader, but appears to have changed allegiance and was accused of duplicity.

Josefa Amar lived for a further twenty-three years following this tragedy, as the new king, once restored to his throne in 1814, reversed the liberal reforms of his predecessors and returned Spain to a state of religious and monarchical absolutism. The only place for women in his society was in the home, and the works and the reputation of Josefa Amar y Borbón sank into obscurity for nearly two hundred years.

The Debate over the Admission of Women to the Madrid Economic Society[10]

The late eighteenth century saw a flowering of salons, known as *tertulias*, in

---

[7] López-Cordón, *Condición Femenina y Razón Ilustrada*, p. 66.
[8] Sir John Carr, *Descriptive Travels in the Southern & Eastern Parts of Spain & the Balearic Isles in the Year 1809* (London: Sherwood, Neely & Jones, 1811), p. 155.
[9] López-Cordón, *Condición Femenina y Razón Ilustrada*, p. 55.
[10] See Olegario Negrín Fajardo, *Ilustración y Educación: La sociedad económica matritense* (Madrid: Editora Nacional, 1984) and López-Cordón, *Condición Femenina y Razón Ilustrada*, pp. 68–71 (these include facsimiles or transcriptions of a number of the key documents). The debate is also discussed in Fernández-Quintanilla, *La mujer ilustrada*,

Spanish urban society. These were modelled on the Parisian salons, and, like them, were usually hosted by women in their homes. Both men and women were among the guests, thus permitting the sexes to mingle on terms of familiarity that represented a novelty in a society that had traditionally practised a far greater degree of segregation. The *salonnières* were invariably women of high status, such as the Duchess of Osuna, the Duchess of Lemos, the Countess of Montijo and the Marquesa of Fuerte-Híjar. Their discussions included politics, art and literature, and they acted as patrons, providing financial support and social approval for writers and artists.

During this time, official institutions were founded to promote the economic and cultural regeneration of Spain, often under royal patronage. These included academies based on French models, such as the Royal Academy of Sciences, which admitted scholars and experts to their membership. The majority of the educated population, however, and those who lived outside Madrid, were unable to participate in these academies, leaving a gap that was filled by a network of Economic Societies of Friends of the Nation. As the name implies, any man who was keen to contribute in some way to the improvement of the arts, sciences, commerce or manufacture, would be a candidate for membership. The first of the Economic Societies was founded in the Basque Country in 1764, and they spread rapidly to fifty-four towns and cities in Spain; they held meetings, commissioned inquiries, sponsored competitions and wrote reports. In a state where the power of the king remained absolute, censorship of books and journals was strict, and the church had an overwhelming influence over daily life, they provided a rare forum for public debate.

The different Societies had their own statutes and were able to set their own qualifications for membership. As already mentioned, Josefa Amar was admitted to full membership of the Aragonese Economic Society, which was a rare honour, but when the Madrid Society was set up in 1775, its members were exclusively male. This led to a controversy that was to last for twelve years.

In October 1775, Manuel José Marín presented to the newly-established Society a paper in which he recommended that women should be allowed to join. He cited examples of women who had participated in public assemblies in Spain in the past and, pointing to the success of French ladies in stimulating literary production through the interest they took in writers and artists, expressed a wish that reading and appreciation of literature could in time substitute for women's frivolous and costly diversions. Nevertheless, he reassured potential women members that they would not be required to employ themselves in 'occupations

---

pp. 43–77; Kitts, *The Debate on the Nature, Role and Influence of Woman in Eighteenth-Century Spain*, pp. 139–72; Smith, *The Emerging Female Citizen*, pp. 74–107; and Elizabeth Franklin Lewis, *Women Writers in the Spanish Enlightenment: The Pursuit of Happiness* (Aldershot: Ashgate, 2004), pp. 23–38.

inappropriate to their sex'. Such inappropriate occupations apparently included attending the assemblies, taking positions of responsibility within the Society or even paying the membership fee. It appeared that the female members were not actually expected to do anything, but merely through their appearance on the membership list to inspire industry in other women, and spur on the male members to greater achievements.

Two further papers were submitted on this subject, one from Count Pedro Rodríguez Campomanes and the other by Luís de Imbille. Campomanes (1723–1802) was a lawyer and a great admirer of Feijoo. He moved into politics and joined the government of the reforming king, Carlos III, holding numerous posts including Minister of the Interior. He was the author of numerous works, including two treatises which claimed that the idleness of women was harming the nation, and suggested they should become economically active citizens. It was generally accepted that women led empty and useless lives, and their greedy consumption of luxury goods, particularly those imported from other countries, was wasting the national patrimony. Campomanes calculated that if all four million able-bodied women in Spain were to spend their days spinning, they could produce enough yarn to add a billion *reales* a year to the nation's wealth. He somehow overlooked the fact that outside the confines of the aristocracy and high bourgeoisie, women spent most of their days working in the fields or in their husbands' workshops, and carrying out essential domestic tasks.

In his speech, Campomanes was the only man who went beyond the utilitarian arguments and stated that there should be no debate over permitting women to join the Society, since they had an equal right to do so. However, he supported Marín's suggestion that they should form a separate class of members and not attend the meetings. He assured his colleagues that he did not propose that women should act against their delicate nature, and turn into militant Amazons.

Marín and Campomanes disagreed over whether women should be required to pay the annual membership fee, and this issue was taken up by Luís Imbille, who worried that if there were no financial barrier to membership, it would no longer be limited to the wealthy elite, and women from the lower classes would want to join. On the other hand, given that the objective was to entice women away from their frivolous pastimes and put them to work at spinning, weaving and embroidery, charging them money as well might make membership an entirely unattractive proposition. His own idea was to create three tiers of membership for women: wealthy benefactresses who supported the Society with their money, useful citizens who promoted productive industry, and women who taught in schools established by the Society and could be awarded prizes for their achievements.

The members could not reach agreement on this vexed topic, and the argument was shelved for ten years, until in January 1786 the President of the Society, the Duke of Osuna, proposed that María Isidra Quintina de Guzmán should be admitted to membership. Guzmán (1768–1803) was a member of one of the highest noble families, had received an exceptionally good education and was regarded as unusually erudite. In 1784, when she was only seventeen years old, she was made an honorary member of the Royal Spanish Academy and the Royal Academy of History, and a year later was awarded a doctorate by the University of Alcalá and given the title of Professor of Philosophy. This was, however, an honorary position, since as a woman, a teenager and a member of the nobility, she was not actually expected to teach classes.

Guzmán's membership of the Economic Society was intended to be similarly decorative, and the Society graciously responded by offering to admit Osuna's own wife, María Josefa Pimentel, one of the leading *salonnières*, on the same basis. Like Guzmán, the Duchess of Osuna was a grandee in her own right; it was clear that in the case of these two ladies their high birth was considered to outweigh the obstacle of their gender. Nevertheless, the Society's censor, José de Guevara Vasconcelos, immediately suggested they be informed that their membership did not entitle them to attend meetings.

Somewhat to the surprise of the members of the Economic Society, this precedent was taken by other women and their male supporters as a signal for them to revive their demand that women should be admitted to membership. In February 1786, Francisco Cabarrús presented a paper on the subject, and over the next six months, three further contributions to the dispute were published, by Gaspar de Jovellanos, Ignacio López de Ayala, and Josefa Amar y Borbón.

Cabarrús (1752–1810) was completely opposed to the admission of women to the Society. A Frenchman by origin, he had become a wealthy banker and a member of the Financial Council. His paper urged that, now the Society had admitted Isidra de Guzmán and the Duchess of Osuna, the door should be shut for ever to all others of their sex. Admitting women to their assemblies would, he asserted, invert the age-old order that in all times and places had excluded them from public affairs. How could a group of men who were accustomed to spending their time in profound contemplation suffer the petulance, caprice and frivolity of women, and the small-mindedness that was a necessary characteristic of their sex? If young unmarried women were to attend, they would be a distraction and a temptation to the men, leading to adultery, corruption and the loss of all decency. If married women became members, this would be contrary to Nature, which requires women to remain subject to their husbands, care for their children, and live a life of retired domesticity. To admit women who, by their very presence, were neglecting their duties as wives and mothers was a disgusting thought.

The presence of women would, according to Cabarrús, damage the status of the Society and reduce its influence in the eyes of the public. How could women vote on subjects of which they knew nothing, and which it might even be indecent for them to learn about? The more he thought about it, the more he concluded that there was not a single way in which women could be useful to the Society. On the contrary, if they were admitted, within five years the place would be overrun with women, and they would be the ruin of it.

We may be sure that Cabarrús was not the only one to hold these opinions, given the anxiety of the supporters of women's membership to reassure their colleagues about the consequences of such a move. The first to speak up in opposition to Cabarrús was Gaspar Melchor de Jovellanos (1744–1811), a reformist lawyer who was a member of the Royal Council.

Jovellanos argued that the principle of whether women should be admitted to the Society had already been resolved by its unanimous approval of Isidra de Guzmán and the Duchess of Osuna. The only decision that remained was whether women should be permitted to attend the general assemblies and vote alongside the men, and on this point Jovellanos was clear that it would be unacceptable and insulting to invite women to join the Society and then shut the door in their faces. However, he then explained reassuringly that although it was true that if women were to come to the meetings frequently and in large numbers, they would be a disruptive influence, this was in fact highly unlikely to happen. Only a small number of women of distinction would be invited to join the Society, and they would be chosen not for their noble birth, wealth or beauty, but because they had demonstrated good behaviour and philanthropic spirit. What is more, it was unlikely they would all turn up to meetings at the same time, so no harm would be done.

It became clear that Jovellanos did not expect the women to do anything active in the Society; the main advantage of their presence would be to spur the men on to greater achievements, in order to win merit in the eyes of the ladies. The women could also benefit by learning from men the spirit of patriotism and spreading this amongst the rest of their sex. Jovellanos' view of women in general was not very different from Cabarrús': all over the country they could be seen abandoning their domestic duties, showing contempt for modesty and decorum, wallowing in luxury and corrupting manners. By admitting to the Society a few illustrious matrons who had 'preserved themselves from this contagion' and publicly honouring their virtuous conduct and devotion to their domestic duties, men could help to return the mass of women to the path of virtue.

In case anyone was still worried, Jovellanos triumphantly concluded that in fact no women would ever attend the Society's meetings, for their natural modesty, shyness and reserve would prevent them from exposing themselves to the rough-and-tumble of public debate. If they ever emerged into the public space, it would be to award prizes to those whom the Society wished to honour for their hard work and application.

Jovellanos' objection to the formation of a separate class of membership for women was based not on any sense that women should be treated equally with men but on his belief in their inability to run any sort of sensible organization. It would be inappropriate for men to attend their meetings, but without them, how would women know how to chair a meeting, set an agenda or take minutes? No, the ladies should not meet together but work alone; they could be made governors of schools for spinning, embroidery and lace-making, where they could demonstrate skills appropriate to their sex.

Ignacio López de Ayala (d.1789) was a professor of poetry who hosted a celebrated literary salon in Madrid, attended by the most famous writers of the day, where the only permitted subjects of conversation were poetry, love and bullfighting. His paper in favour of women's membership was, like Jovellanos', based on a less than glowing opinion of the sex in general. The female half of Spain, he claimed, was completely useless: the question was whether it was possible to extract some utility from them, or whether they would have to be abandoned to idleness and caprice. He believed that women's brains were the same as men's (a view that continued to be contradicted by contemporary writers), and they could benefit from education; in fact, women's folly was the fault of men who had taken care to keep them in ignorance. Women of antiquity had played a part in public life, but in contemporary Spain they were shut up like sheep or chickens.

The arguments used by López were principally utilitarian: Spain was falling behind in the economic race, particularly in the textile industry, and needed all the hands it could get. The seclusion of women and their lack of education were, he claimed, relics of the country's Moorish past that had no place in the modern age. Men had come to see that it was better to promote the prosperity of the state by improving the state of factories and schools, rather than fighting battles and conquering provinces; women, on the other hand, had no concept of patriotism, and needed to be taught that the money they spent on imported goods was destroying Spanish industry and reducing its artisans to penury. López wanted to encourage women of the labouring classes to work beside their men in the fields rather than sitting around doing nothing; he seems to have had little understanding of what the lives of these women were really like.

López did not expect women to make any contribution to the Economic Society, but to learn passively from the men. It was not surprising they were frivolous, petulant and capricious, since men had deprived them of anything useful to do in their lives. By attending the Society's meetings, they could learn to be prudent and thrifty wives; if they were not already happy with their domestic duties, they would learn to become so.

It was a royal decree that finally closed the argument. In March 1787, the Economic Society wrote to the king to say it was minded to admit women, but to a separate section. On 27 August, the Prime Minister, the Count of Floridablanca, communicated to the Society the king's approval for a *Junta de Damas*, or Ladies' Section 'of honour and merit'. This took place without delay; fourteen ladies, most of them members of the nobility, were invited to join, and on 5 October they held their first meeting, at which they nominated five more members. Three of these were royal princesses, one was a marquise, and the fifth was Josefa Amar y Borbón.

Amar wrote a letter of thanks in which, after the usual courtesies, she made some pointed remarks. If she were to attend the meetings of the Society (which was unlikely, since she would have to travel from Zaragoza), she would come to observe how the royal ladies would defend the group against 'the shafts of envy and malignity' she expected it to suffer. She would come to praise the men of the Society who had graciously delegated part of their authority 'in order to benefit from the intelligence provided by women equally with men, since nature bestows this without distinction'. The men had, of course, not permitted the women to enter on equal terms with men, and were far from conceding that men and women were equally enlightened.

Amar noted that the matters that would be entrusted to the ladies, including the improvement of education, were serious and important, and would require time, hard work, sensitivity and unusual fortitude, particularly since the public would expect them to fail. The men, she assumed, were exempt from this 'agreeable temptation', but the trouble was that when they decided to reform something, they rushed into it without anticipating the opposition or indifference they would meet. The women, she hoped, would show more patience, and prefer to establish something that would last for generations, rather than seeking for present glory. She expressed her hope that the whole of Spain would greet the foundation of the Ladies' Committee not with indifference or contempt, but as a new and glorious epoch in its history; though it appears from the tone of her letter that she was not entirely convinced this would be the case.

The Ladies' Committee[11]

Amar's cynicism about the way the Ladies' Committee would be treated

---

[11] The activities of the Ladies' Committee are discussed in Fernández-Quintanilla, *La mujer ilustrada*, pp. 79–99, and in the same author's 'La junta de damas de honor y mérito' in *Historia*, 16, 54 (1980), 65–73. See also Smith, *The Emerging Female Citizen*, pp. 129–49. The Committee's activities in the field of education are analysed in Olegario Negrín's *La educación popular en la España de la segunda mitad del siglo XVIII: Las actividades educativas de la Sociedad Económica Matritense de Amigos del País* (Madrid: Universidad

seemed to be justified when, one year later, it received a letter from the Count of Floridablanca, enclosing a paper which he asked the ladies to review and, if they saw fit, endorse. This anonymous proposal was entitled *Discourse on Luxury and Proposal for a National Uniform*,[12] and purported to be written by a woman, although many readers thought its author was more likely to be male, and some suspected it to be Floridablanca himself.[13]

It was common not only in Spain but across Europe for social reformers to speak out against 'luxury', defined as the excessive consumption of expensive goods, particularly those imported from abroad. The negative results of this practice were held to include the decline of local manufacturers, depletion of the national treasury and ruin of individual families. All commentators agreed that the main culprits were women, whose insistence on wearing French silks and fine jewellery and competing with each other to display their wealth and taste was driving the luxury trades. It was even suggested that the decline in the birth rate (which was a matter of great concern) could be ascribed to a reluctance among men to marry, for fear that their fortunes would be absorbed by their wives' exorbitant expenditure. And more subtly, the hierarchical order of society was breaking down, as the wives and daughters of men who had made money through trade were able to ape the lifestyle of the nobility.

The author of the *Discourse on Luxury* had come up with a brilliantly simple solution for this problem: all women above the labouring classes should be required by law to dress in a prescribed style. Women would have to wear the dress indicated by the status of their husbands if they were married, or their fathers, brothers or sons if they were not. All the dresses would be made from materials manufactured in Spain. Three main designs were put forward but, like a military uniform, more subtle gradations could be indicated by different ribbons and trims, and as a result it would be immediately apparent to any observer to which of eight defined classes their wearers belonged.

The Countess of Montijo, Secretary to the Ladies' Section, wrote a letter to Floridablanca on behalf of her colleagues that could barely contain their distaste and indignation.[14] There had been 'sumptuary laws' in Spain in the past that prescribed what people of different status could wear and outlawed the use of expensive materials — in fact the latest had been promulgated as recently as 1723 — but they were of limited effect, and had always applied to both men and women. Never before had it been suggested that the sole cause of all social problems was the uncontrolled vanity of women, and that it could be prevented

---

Nacional de Educación a Distancia, 1987).

[12] *Discurso sobre el lujo y proyecto de un traje nacional* (Madrid: Imprenta Real, 1788). *Prologue* transcribed in Fernández-Quintanilla, *La mujer ilustrada*, pp. 149–50.

[13] See Fernández-Quintanilla, *La mujer ilustrada*, pp. 101–08; Bolufer, *Mujeres*, pp. 169–74; Smith, *The Emerging Female Citizen*, pp. 80–86.

[14] The letter is transcribed in Fernández-Quintanilla, *La mujer ilustrada*, pp. 147–49.

by law. In an age when the Enlightenment ideas espoused by the reformers tended towards increased freedom and self-determination, such a proposal was nothing less than insulting.

Montijo's letter, and the minutes of the meeting of the Ladies' Section at which it was discussed, demonstrated a reluctance to enforce precise social distinctions, and a sort of female solidarity that prevailed over the differences of class. Some of the ladies present were from the highest aristocracy whilst others, like Josefa Amar, were the wives and daughters of professional men, and they were hardly likely to wish to be forced to wear different 'uniforms' to their meetings. They also expressed sympathy with other women who might be less privileged but still enjoyed dressing well, and would not tolerate being compelled to demonstrate their social inferiority in public. What is more, they were outraged that women should be singled out in this way, and turned the argument by stating that:

> If it would be a difficult thing to force men to wear a single uniform, when they are considered to be less influenced by vanity over their outward appearance, how much more difficult would it be to impose a similar distinction on the ladies? For this reason, it would be impossible to make women adopt such a reform unless they were following the men's example.[15]

When Floridablanca received Montijo's letter, the proposal was quietly dropped. This was an early example of how the ladies turned to their advantage the fact that they constituted a separate section of the Society. Whereas they would have represented a small minority within the general assembly, as a Committee they were able to make their own decisions. This was an unforeseen consequence of the decision the Society had taken, and the men were rather taken aback by their female colleagues' unexpected independence.

The Ladies' Committee diligently applied themselves to activities where they could benefit society, and particularly other women and their children. They took over the management of the newly-founded 'Patriotic Schools' where girls were given an elementary education and taught useful trades, and the running of a foundling hospital.

There is no evidence that Josefa Amar attended the meetings of the Ladies' Committee: she was, after all, living in Zaragoza and looking after a sick husband. Her most important contribution was the paper she had written in response to Cabarrús and Jovellanos in June 1786, demanding that women be admitted to the Economic Society. Two months later, when the *Memorial Literario* published the various papers that had contributed to the debate, this was printed in full under the title *Discourse on the Talents of Women*.

---

[15]   Bolufer, *Mujeres*, p. 173.

The Discourse on the Talents of Women

The *Discourse* is succinct, running to only thirty pages, and often sarcastic in tone. At times Amar uses the vocabulary of a true battle of the sexes, accusing men of tyranny and injustice and describing women as being kept in a state of cruel subjection. It is notable that she does not include any of the modest disclaimers often used by women to excuse their temerity for stating their opinions publicly and in print. In fact, she boldly sets out her credentials, pointing out that she is already a member of the Aragonese Economic Society, and says it is necessary for women to speak up in their own cause, or men will assume they are indifferent to the issue.

Amar begins the *Discourse* in a weary tone, expressing her surprise that it is yet again necessary to write a defence of the intelligence of women. She objects to men's duplicity, observing that whilst they praise women publicly, they secretly despise them. Women are left unsure of their own purpose, since men refuse them any opportunity to play a role in public life. Even worse, by denying them a proper education, they deprive them 'even of the satisfaction that comes from having an enlightened mind'.

She draws a comparison between the life of women in Western Europe and in the Muslim world, and suggests that beneath the surface, there is little difference between them. Europeans were fascinated by stories of women kept as slaves in the harem of the Turkish Sultan, and assumed that the lives of all women in the Muslim world were the same. Amar ascribes this state of slavery to the tyranny of men, and warns her readers not to assume that such subjugation implies that women are naturally inferior, for 'violence cannot establish universal laws'.

In Europe, it at first appears that women are entirely free; in fact, men do not revile them as inferior but address them in terms suggestive of extreme admiration. However, warns Amar, if you look more closely, you see that the difference is only one of degree. Women may not be legal slaves, but they are kept in a state of dependence on men, who find that 'to command is delightful'. They enforce this dependence by keeping women in a state of ignorance.

Amar goes on to discuss whether people are justified in believing that men are intellectually superior to women. Like Feijoo, she analyses the story of Adam and Eve, but comes to the original conclusion that Eve's sin in eating the apple was a result of curiosity, which is itself a sign of intelligence. She then gives a brief catalogue of women of the past and present who were known for their intellect, ruled over nations, and carried out heroic deeds. She concludes from these examples that if women were given the same education as men, they would achieve as much if not more.

It is education that is the problem. Women receive a basic training in literacy, but are then taught nothing but to work with their hands. Boys know that they may aspire to go to university or obtain public appointments, and their efforts to succeed are rewarded with public praise and acknowledgment. Women can have no such ambitions, and have little incentive to make the effort to learn.

This brings Amar to her main topic. Women may have become inured to the humiliation of being excluded from public life, but they have just received another shocking rebuff in the suggestion that they should be excluded from the Madrid Economic Society of Friends of the Nation. This is an ironic title, she suggests, since excluding women is not only an unfriendly act, but a matter of fundamental significance, since what is now under discussion is nothing less than the equality of men and women.

Amar pours scorn on Cabarrús, who had argued that once the principle of female membership was accepted, this would mean all women would be able to join the Society. She observes that the governing committee is perfectly capable of distinguishing between women of 'constancy and discretion' and those who are 'petulant, capricious or frivolous'. In fact, she says that if they failed to do so, this would be a sign of injustice and tyranny, and would reinforce the general attitude of contempt for women's abilities.

She is particularly sarcastic about Cabarrús' objection that women would be incapable of keeping the Society's proceedings confidential. How is it, she asks, that so many secrets of the court, government councils, academies and societies are divulged? These are all-male bodies, so you cannot blame women for such indiscretions — it seems that men must be just as bad. She also mocks the suggestion that mixing of the sexes would lead to immoral behaviour, and observes that in the days when women were kept locked away at home, this did not mean there were no rapes or murders. It is insulting to the men who have joined the Society from the best of motives to suggest that the sight of women in their meetings will instantly transform them into libertines. There may be people who still think men and women should live entirely separate lives, but this is not the custom of today's society, and letting women into the Economic Society is not going to 'lead to the destruction of the human race'.

Next she deals with the complaint that women will not be able to make a useful contribution to the Society because of their ignorance of the subjects under discussion. The men are not all geniuses either, she suggests, and any woman of 'normal talent' would be able to understand what was going on as long as things were properly explained.

Women are believed by men to be part of the national problem, since their love of luxury leads to the importation of expensive goods that the country cannot afford, and the failure of domestic industry to develop. Well, says Amar, why not engage women in finding the solution? Shouting at them from the pulpit has not changed their behaviour, but if they could join the Economic Society and observe at first hand the reforms necessary to generate national prosperity, they would have a new motivation, and would participate with enthusiasm in the common cause. What is more, they could bring an understanding of spinning, weaving and lace-making that is far greater than could be expected from men, who are ignorant of such activities.

In conclusion, Amar reiterates that women have all the necessary natural talents and attributes, and need only education and opportunity to apply themselves to things that will benefit the state. She ends with the ringing statement that admitting women to the Society 'can and must be the right thing to do'.

Josefa Amar y Borbón

Discourse in Defence of the Talents of Women, and their Aptitude for Government and Other Positions in which Men are Employed

Member of The Royal Aragonese Society of
Friends of The Nation

Memorial Literario, 8, August 1786, pp. 399–430

When God handed over the earth for men to argue about, he made sure there would be an infinite number of things for them to dispute for ever and never come to an agreement. It seems that one of these was destined to be the question of the intelligence of women. On the one hand, men seek their approval and pay them compliments in a way that never happens between themselves; they permit women no public authority but concede absolute power to them in secret; they deny them education and then complain that they are ignorant. I say they deny it, since there exists no public institution designed for the education of women, nor is there any kind of prize that could encourage them in this vocation.

What is more, they attribute to women almost all the evils in the world. If the courage of heroes fails them, if ignorance reigns throughout society, if manners are corrupt, if luxury and profligacy ruin families, it is women who are the cause of all these failings, or so they proclaim. Women themselves do not agree about their true purpose. They take pleasure in fine words and flattery; they have for many years become used to both of these, but have never managed to turn them into something solid that they could truly deserve, which would happen if they could combine external and fleeting graces with something more intrinsic and durable.

In truth, the applause and flattery of men, as much as the tasks they impose on women, are a tacit admission of their intelligence; for otherwise they would not seek their approval and admiration nor suffer any distress on their account.

If one being can influence another, whether for good or evil, this change must of necessity imply an element of virtue and power; for a weaker agent could not alter or attract a stronger. Consequently, if the vices of women can exert such a hold over men, then we are bound to agree on their physical equality, without of course denying the exceptions which are specific to each sex.

Yet despite these reasonable assumptions, it seems that we continue to argue over the talents and capacities of women as if this were a phenomenon newly discovered in nature, or a problem that is difficult to solve. But what kind of phenomenon can this be, when woman goes back as far as man, and both can count so many thousands of years of existence on earth? And why is it a problem when so many outstanding proofs have demonstrated women's suitability for everything? How is it possible that we are hearing new challenges to this truth? For it is certain that we do hear them, and that they are of such a kind that we must not ignore them, for they are gaining in influence, and the question is not yet settled.

Men are not content with having reserved to themselves all positions, honours and benefits — in a word, everything that provides a motive for hard work and application — but have deprived women even of the satisfaction that comes from having an enlightened mind. Women are born and raised in absolute ignorance; for this reason men despise them and women persuade themselves they are incapable of anything else, and as if their talent resided in their hands, they cultivate only manual activities. See how influential is public opinion in such matters! If instead of pronouncing that the principal value of all women is beauty and grace, it promoted wisdom, we would immediately see them just as anxious to acquire this as they are now to appear beautiful and charming. Let men first apply their admiration in the right way — that is, let them appreciate those talents that are truly deserving — and there is no doubt they would reform the vices they complain about. Until this happens, women should not be criticised if they are interested only in adorning their bodies, for they can see that this is the idol before which men burn their incense.

How can we hope for such a necessary change to take place if men themselves treat women with such unfairness? In one part of the world women are slaves, in the rest they are dependants. Let us consider the first. What progress can they make when they are surrounded by tyrants instead of companions? In such a situation it is right for them to remain in total ignorance, so their chains may weigh less heavily. If they could desire one thing, or make one effort, it would be to educate and civilise those men, in the hope that the use of reason would break the bars which are now kept in place by ignorance. If ignorance were destroyed, slavery would be destroyed as well. How shall we reconcile the contempt in which they hold women, whom they keep as slaves, with the effort they put into acquiring the largest number they can maintain, and with the care they put into pleasing them? Why does Muhammad exclude women from the paradise he promises to his followers?[1] Is this not to assimilate them to brute beasts, which perish and are extinguished at death? If such fantasies are not worth refuting, since it would do them too much honour, how much less may our opponents cite them in order to deduce from the slavery in which certain women languish, that their talents are inferior! If this argument had any basis, it could be turned against men also, since some of them are slaves of others, and we do not conclude from this that the former must be irrational beings. We say instead that force destroys the equality and effaces the resemblance between individuals. It is of little use for a slave to have the same ability as his master if the oppression under which he suffers prevents him from using his reason and his rights. Put the two on the same level, and then you may judge correctly. Violence cannot establish universal laws: let those women who are born and raised in a land of tyranny and ignorance be subjugated, since for the time being they are obliged by necessity, but do not pretend to degrade the sex as a whole.

The situation of those living in the other major part of the world offers a different aspect. Far from being called slaves, these women are entirely free, and benefit from privileges which approach extreme veneration. Both religion and the law prohibit men from possessing more than one woman; in this way the conditions are created for the greatest conformity between the sexes, so they may look upon each other with mutual appreciation and respect. Men have done even more in our favour, for they have offered everything in tribute to women, retaining hardly more than the name of authority they obtain from their positions and their riches. What generosity, what nobility, we may exclaim, but at the same time, what a contradiction! Here we observe the state of dependence which we indicated above. Men who are educated and cultured do not dare to oppress the other half of the human race so openly, for they have not discovered the institution of slavery to be an intrinsic law of creation. But since to command is delightful, they have managed to appropriate to themselves a certain superiority in talent, or what I would call understanding, which makes women, who do not possess it, appear to be their inferiors. There are few men who, on achieving the height of ability and intellectual aptitude, concede to women what they need in order to enlighten their understanding.

Women know they cannot aspire to any employment or public position, and that their imagination cannot extend beyond the walls of a house or a convent. If this is not enough to suffocate the greatest talent in the world, I know not what other shackles we should seek. What is sure is that it would be better to be totally ignorant and lack any kind of understanding, than to suffer this state of

---

[1] It was widely and erroneously believed in Europe that Muhammad had said that women did not have souls. Feijoo makes a similar comment in chapter 1 of *In Defence of Women*.

slavery or dependence. The latter is almost more painful, since it sets up a clear opposition between adulation and contempt, elevation and abasement, love and indifference; these attitudes are combined in the way men conduct themselves towards women.

What if women were to reject the alternating admiration and rejection, adulation and disdain, they experience every day? Are they not judges today and prisoners tomorrow? Are they not treated as goddesses one minute and brute beasts the next? Do they not at times receive adoration and homage: their wish becomes law, and their approbation is required to satisfy the desires of an author, adorn the laurels of a conqueror or crown the glory of a hero? But women are diminished all the same, for the men who treat them like this afterwards complain in public assemblies that they have no true discernment, are incapable of judging what is true and real, and allow themselves to be carried away by vain and frivolous appearances.

Such a profound contradiction has often made me wonder on what foundation men base their pretensions of superiority, particularly in the gifts of the mind. Perhaps we may seek enlightenment in the original creation of men and women. But what do we find? That God created Adam and once this was done, soon afterwards made him a companion of the same nature, and the companion he gave him was woman. Could we wish for any more convincing proof of the equality and similarity of the two in their primal state? Is there the slightest suggestion here of subjection or dependence of one on the other? It is true that man was created first, and created alone, but it was not long before it was understood that he could not live without a companion: this was the first pattern of matrimony and also of a perfect society.

If we proceed to consider what happened in the Fall of our first parents, we shall not discover anything that shows woman's rational faculties to be inferior. The way she abused them was her sin, and also Adam's and that of their entire posterity. But without excusing this event, who could deny that woman was ahead of man in her desire for knowledge? The forbidden fruit contained the knowledge of good and evil. Eve could not resist this temptation, then she persuaded her husband, who committed through acquiescence the sin she committed out of curiosity. This curiosity was doubtless detestable, but curiosity is generally an indication of talent, for without it no one would undertake the delightful effort of learning.

Neither does the just penalty imposed on them both detract in any way from woman's intellectual faculties. If man could labour without as a result losing his aptitude for knowledge, then the subjection of woman was the same. Man should limit himself to being head of the family and controlling his servants, without pretending to extend his authority any further. For even if we accept it in this case, it is never conclusive proof of superior talent. Men themselves are not, and never can be, equal. It is necessary for some to be in command over others, and not infrequently those of greater ability have the misfortune to serve and obey those who have less. Thus women may in certain cases be subject to men, without for all that losing their intellectual equality.

If this equality is clearly demonstrated in the story of Creation, it can be even better proved by evidence from women themselves. It is clear that talent, or intelligence, which is the highest part of our being, is also the part that is incomprehensible, and can be known only by its effects. In this instance, if men demonstrate their ability through the works they perform and the theories they expound, then as there are women who can do the same, it would not be rash to consider them as equal, deducing that similar effects must presuppose identical causes. If the examples of this are not as numerous in women as in men, it is clear that the cause lies in the fact that they study less, and that men permit them fewer opportunities to display their talents.

No one with a basic level of knowledge will deny that in all ages and all countries there have been women who have progressed to the summit of the most abstract sciences. Their literary history may always be judged alongside that of men, for whenever men have flourished in letters, they have had companions and imitators from the other sex. In the age when Greece was wise, it contained among other eminent women Theano, who wrote a commentary on Pythagoras, Hipparchia, who in philosophy and mathematics excelled even Theon, her father and master, and Diotima, whose disciple Socrates confessed to being. It is said that Nicostrata of Latium invented Latin letters, later cultivated by various women including Fabiola, Marcella and Eustechia.

In France the catalogue of eminent female writers is a lengthy one, and even if no other names existed, those of the Marquise de Sevigné, the Countess de La Fayette and Madame Dacier would be sufficient to demonstrate that they have distinguished themselves just as much as their famous countrymen. Today there are still ladies who honour their sex through their writing, as we can see in the *Década Epistolar* of Don Francisco María de Silva.[2]

Today in Russia literature is flourishing, and although this glorious revolution is due to the efforts of the Czar Peter the Great, they are continued by the present Czarina Catherine II, who wrote the *Legal Code*, a work which cannot be too highly praised, and a wise and moral novel designed for the instruction of her nephews; she wrote both works in French, a language in which she showed a grace and finesse which the French themselves rarely achieve. This eminent woman would be unjust if, knowing through her own experience

---

[2]   Pseudonym of Pedro Jimenez de Góngora y Luján, Duque de Almodóvar del Río (1727–1794). The *Década Epistolar sobre el Estado de las Letras en Francia* (Madrid: Antonio de Sancha, 1781) included a list of French women writers. A second edition was published in 1792 by the Economic Society of Madrid.

how much her sex is capable of, she did not honour it as it deserves. But there is no need to hold her to this charge, for she rewards merit wherever she finds it. This is proven in the case of the Princess Dashkova,[3] an illustrious heroine who, having displayed her martial spirit to the Russian troops, is like a modern Minerva familiar with all the sciences, and for this and for her poetic genius, her sovereign has appointed her as head and President of the Imperial Academy of Sciences of St Petersburg.

In Spain women have been no less distinguished in the career of letters. If we were to speak of them all with the distinction they deserve, it would take a book of inordinate length. The best-known are Luisa Sigéa, Francisca Nebrija, Beatriz Galindo, Isabel de Joya, Juliana Morell and Oliva de Sabuco.[4] The last of these discovered a new physical system. We could also mention certain famous ladies who today honour the field of literature, but their merits are so well-known that it would be superfluous to refer to them in this paper. The merits of women in general may be read more extensively in the work of Monsieur Thomas entitled *Essay on the Character, Manners and Understanding of Women*[5] and in many others with titles like *Famous Women, Illustrious Women, Treatise on the Education of Women,*[6] *The Friend of Women,*[7] *The Vindication of Women,*[8] etc.

If women have acquired distinction in literature, they have been no less recognised for their wise government of public affairs, a role which is the subject of the greatest argument. But the ancients did not dispute it so much when the Lacedaemonians relied for their actions on the advice of women, and nothing was done without consulting them. The Athenians, in all the matters proposed to the Senate, wished to hear the opinions of the women, as if they were wise and prudent[9] senators. The example of these two peoples, so worthy

---

[3]   Amar calls her 'la princesa de Askoff'. Princess Yekaterina Vorontsova-Dashkova was Director of the Imperial Academy of Sciences from 1783–1796, and also its active head, since unlike some of her predecessors she did not regard her directorship as purely honorary. She also headed a separate organization, the Russian Academy, created in 1783 to compile the *Academic Dictionary of the Russian Language* (1789–1794).

[4]   All these women were included in Juan Bautista Cubíe's *Las Mugeres Vindicadas de las Calumnias de los Hombres* (Madrid: Antonio Pérez de Soto, 1768), which may be Amar's source. They were also included in Feijoo's list of illustrious women, with the exception of Beatriz Galindo (1465–1534), who taught Latin to Queen Isabella of Castile, and Francisca Nebrija (c. 1444–1522), who may have lectured at the University of Alcalá, where her father was an eminent scholar.

[5]   Antoine-Leonard Thomas, *Essai sur la caractère, les moeurs et l'esprit des femmes dans les differens siècles* (Paris: Moutard, 1772). A Spanish translation was published in 1773. Thomas was in fact ambivalent about women's abilities.

[6]   This may refer to Archbishop Fénelon's *Traité de l'Education des Filles* (Paris: Pierre Aubouin, et al., 1687)

[7]   Pierre Boudier de Villemert. *L'Ami des Femmes* (Paris: [n. pub.], 1758).

[8]   Juan Bautista Cubíe, *Las Mugeres Vindicadas* (Madrid: Antonio Perez, 1768).

[9]   Prudence (derived from the Latin *prudentia* meaning foresight or sagacity) was regarded as one of the cardinal virtues, and implied the ability to discipline oneself by the use of

to be followed in all circumstances, should decide the case in favour of women, all the more because they have justified the principle over the ages, since almost all of those who have been in a position to rule entire nations have done so skilfully. Consult the history books, and in particular see whether there were as many kings who governed states who are called heroes, as there were queens who are called heroines.

On the subject of queens, first place should go to Deborah, for she governed the people of Israel in a role chosen for her by God, which should close the argument for good. Gemiamira, mother of Elagabalus, attended the Senate to give her opinion, as a result of her prudence and wisdom.[10] If we wish for more modern examples, everyone knows of the prudence of the Catholic Queen Isabella, who although she did not rule alone, participated in all the important matters that arose during her time; in England the queens Elizabeth and Anne have contributed as much as the wisest kings to extending the power of Great Britain and making her so formidable. In Russia the two Catherines have perfected the splendour begun by Peter the Great. And we could cite many others who, in domains more limited than those just referred to, have shown evidence of their ability to govern.

Prudence is not a talent so alien to the female sex that it cannot be found in many women. Leaving aside what is necessary in public affairs, we shall regularly discover it in many homes. How many examples could we cite in the little republic of the family where a woman covers up and hides the defects of her husband in the management of her household? But the fact that these virtues are so frequent seems to make them less appreciated.

Valour is normally regarded as a specifically male characteristic; but as with everything there are exceptions, as there is with beauty in women. We see handsome men and ugly women, brave women and cowardly men, which helps to prove that there is no virtue that is not common to both sexes. If fewer women than men have distinguished themselves in valour, it is clear that this results from the different ways they are brought up; for women have some sort of secret inclination that has always made them regard cowards and fainthearts with horror. This observation alone can demonstrate that if they do not exercise valour, at least they admire it and always prefer it; but in fact they have exercised

---

reason, and to judge what actions are appropriate in a given time and place. It is broader than the modern English term 'prudence', which has become synonymous with caution.

[10] The name Gemiamira in the text is an error. The mother of Elagabalus was Julia Soaemias Bassiana. The version 'Semiamira' was used by Boccaccio in his *De Claris Mulieribus*, which was published in a Spanish translation in 1528 as *Libro que tracta de las Ilustres Mugeres* — it was in Gothic script and the initials S and G are similar, so this must have been Amar's source. Boccaccio took his information from the *Scriptores Historiae Augustae*, a highly unreliable history of the Roman emperors written centuries after their time, which portrays Semiamira as little better than a prostitute; her son's decision to admit her to the Senate was seen as just another sign of his depravity. Her story is not helpful to Amar's argument.

it when they have found themselves in need of it. We see examples in the Persian women, who were given the main credit for victory over Cyrus; in the Sabine women who were decisive in the triumph of the Romans; in the Roman matrons who saved Rome from the dire peril caused by the army of Coriolanus; in the women of Saguntum[11] who fought valiantly in defence of their country — in a word, in practically all histories, for there is hardly a single one that does not preserve the memory of certain exploits by women when they saw their nation at risk of destruction.

Not only have there been heroic deeds carried out by groups of women, but there have also been individual heroines who have confronted danger. Jael killed Sisera, Judith passed alone through the Assyrian army and killed Holofernes. In Spain we have the example of Juliana de Cibo, who served as a soldier during the war in Granada against the Moors; of Maria de Estrada, who fought with the troops of Hernan Cortes; of Maria Montano, who accompanied the army sent to conquer Algeria in the time of Carlos V; and of Maria Pita, who distinguished herself in the place where the English attacked Coruña.[12] I omit many others, since it is not possible to mention them all in such a short volume.

Such feats are not unknown today, for as I have already mentioned, the Princess Dashkova, who currently presides over the Royal Academy of St Petersburg, previously commanded the Russian troops. And currently there is in France a lady author who having disguised her sex and travelled the world under the name of the Chevalier d'Éon, has obtained the titles of Royal Censor, Doctor of Both Laws, Parliamentary Advocate, Captain of Dragoons and Volunteers, Aide-de-Camp to the Marshal Duke de Broglie, Chevalier of the Royal and Military Order of St Louis, Secretary to the Ambassador in the Courts of Russia and England, and later Minister Plenipotentiary in the latter, in which contrasting and delicate positions she has succeeded in acting with a constancy, prudence and discretion that would do honour to the man most versed in political and military affairs.[13]

From all the above examples it must necessarily be inferred that if women received the same education as men, they would achieve as much or more than they do. But what a contrast between their education! From the time they are girls, women are taught nothing but to read and write and do handiwork. They take a great deal of trouble over adorning themselves, which leads them to acquire a certain habit of always thinking about external appearances. If

---

[11] Saguntum, in Valencia, was besieged by the army of Hannibal in 219 BC in the Second Punic War against the Romans.
[12] Again, all these women appear in Cubíe's *Las Mugeres Vindicadas*. Estrada and Pita are mentioned by Feijoo.
[13] Unfortunately for Amar's argument, it was discovered later that the Chevalier d'Éon was not a woman but a cross-dressing man.

anyone talks to them about talent, it is as a side issue, so it is no great surprise that they gradually lose the idea of being capable of anything else. By contrast, boys apply themselves naturally and are made to learn before they even know what study or knowledge means; they hear tell of universities, colleges and employments for those who study there. In this way application and study grow and become natural for them, and it is not long before they gain the fruit of their efforts through the distribution of prizes.

If a woman dedicates herself to study, she has to do so only for personal development and advantage, for she knows that she cannot aspire to any reward. It takes a truly magnanimous spirit to engage and continue in the difficult career of letters solely for the satisfaction of illuminating your own understanding. We nevertheless see that certain women possess this heroism, but as if all the merit achieved by the few who do this were not already known, the female sex in general are blamed and criticised for their ignorance — as if this were a personal defect, and not more immediately a defect of their education and the circumstances in which they find themselves.

It is essential to acknowledge that we understand nothing in itself, except by comparison with something else. This rule will serve to measure the aptitude of the two sexes, but on a fair basis: that is, between a man and a woman who are both completely ignorant. In this case, which is fairly frequent, it is even demonstrated that the latter prevails over the former with her more lively imagination, quickness to learn and effective way of speaking. At the other extreme, if we compare a capable and educated woman with a scholarly man, her conduct will be no less agreeable than his, and may exceed it in a certain finesse which men hardly ever acquire. Moreover, if we make the comparison between those who have studied extensively and those who know nothing, their inequality will be no surprise, and as long as their situations are consistent, the result will not be against women, and this is conclusive proof that their intellectual disposition is the same.

Finally, time and necessity have accustomed women to the slavery they suffer in one part of the world, and the dependency to which they are subject in the other. The first kind appear to accept being stripped of the use of their reason, while the second take pleasure in it, despite being deprived of any prize or reward. The majesty of the sceptre, solemnity of the toga and glory of military honours have become objects which are shown to women as something to admire but not to aspire to, for the passing of the centuries has taken away the surprise they first felt when they saw all the doors leading to honour and reward closed to them. But they are nevertheless not insensitive to the rebuffs they receive. And none is greater than the new dividing wall between them and the sanctuary that people intend to erect today; and what we are talking about here is more than a sanctuary or a dividing wall. It is the Madrid Economic Society, which is reluctant to admit women into its illustrious assembly. Perhaps it is those who call themselves the Friends of the Nation who will be able to keep them out? Perhaps women are spies, scattered around the kingdom and telling outsiders about the work being done for their benefit? Or are the matters discussed in the Economic Societies so mysterious and intricate that only men can understand them? None of this is true, but the question is equally important, since it means no less than making women equal to men, giving them a seat in their meetings and discussing serious matters with them, something which is apparently out of order and even absurd.

If this is our opponents' motive, it must also be appropriate for women to defend their cause, since on this occasion silence would only confirm the idea they have of them: that they do not care about and are not interested in serious matters. To this reason, which applies to all women in general, must be added one that is particular to the writer of this paper, who received long ago the honour of being admitted into one of the principal Economic Societies of this kingdom; a distinction which she appreciates so much that she would like to see it extended to many others of her sex, so the obligation to toil for the good of the country may be shared equally by men and women.

The question being considered in the Madrid Economic Society, of whether to grant or deny entrance to the fair sex, has exercised the pens of two members of the Society who are admired as much for their eloquence as for their ability, and although they are of opposite opinions, it cannot be denied that both base theirs on ingenious and well-reasoned arguments, but whilst each has the right of defence, these gentlemen do not feel that one or more women should contribute to a cause that is so important for all of them. The advantage men have in this case is no less than that which they have as a judge or advocate. Our sentence is in their hands: if they decide we should be admitted to their discussions, they will always say they are doing it as a favour, and if they refuse us entry, we shall see how much superiority is involved in this decision, but we shall have no reason to lose heart until the final verdict is pronounced.

The respected Member who opposes the admission of women bases his opinion on the claim that if they admit one or two, they will have to extend the favour to all women, which from the beginning will be very damaging to the Society and ultimately will bring about its ruin. He does not deny there may exist somewhere a woman who is capable of profound combination of ideas, constant reflection and the required constancy and discretion, but he believes the characteristics typical of the sex to be petulance, caprice, frivolity and pettiness. There is no age at which women may be suitable, for in their childhood and youth they are useless and distracting, and in old age they are tedious and annoying. He goes on to say they would only add to the tumult and disorder of the sessions rather than enlighten them, for they lack even the elementary principles this body requires. Even their financial contribution is undervalued, if in principle you assume this class may be admitted.

We cannot sufficiently admire the inflexibility of a Member who, amid the corruption against which the current age protests, keeps his heart pure so as to judge the two sexes, openly pronouncing against the one he calls 'alluring'. This is no doubt an example worthy to be imitated! But if men begin to pretend to be saints like this, why should we not follow them to the best of our ability?

It is clear that not all women should be admitted to the Society, any more than should all men. But given that our challenger does not deny that some women are capable of profound combination of ideas, constant reflection and the required constancy and discretion,[14] it would be a manifest injustice to sentence them to the same fate as those who are petulant, capricious or frivolous. The task of choosing and distinguishing between the two groups resides in those who govern the society. May they lay down strict and narrow guidelines, and never deviate from observing them. Confounding the guilty with the innocent and the wise with the ignorant is the height of tyranny; and the Friends of the Nation should never be its tyrants. Let us say, for example, that if a woman has the characteristics indicated above, or is more diligent than others, if she presents to the Society a paper of a sufficient standard on one of the subjects with which it is concerned, or makes some discovery that would benefit the nation; in a word, the type who deserves to be a member, then she should be admitted to the Society, and be entitled to attend whenever she wishes.

In this way, neither will the gentlemen on the Committee have the ability to admit any women who are not qualified, nor will women beg for this distinction because they are beautiful or fashionable, but for being industrious and useful to the country. If what keeps them out today is their constant childishness and lack of attentiveness, the Friends of the Nation should work to correct these defects, and they would repair the damage. Award prizes and incentives to those women who are diligent and industrious, one of them being admission to the Society, and it is natural that they will strive to deserve it. For as long as this is not the case, and they are treated like a rotten limb and separated from the body of society, what progress can they make? We already know the influence exerted on everything by opinion, and thus the contempt which men now have for women is sufficient to keep them in ignorance for ever.

The woman who would deserve the title of Member of the Society, for the reasons we have described above, would also know how to maintain the

---

[14] Amar clearly wishes to emphasise this phrase, since she repeats it from the paragraph above. The 'combination of ideas' was defined by John Locke in his *Essay on Human Understanding* as the way in which the human mind developed from initial sense impressions to complex abstract thought. A number of later writers, including Nicolas Malebranche, denied that women were capable of this. See *La Recherche de la Vérité* (Paris: Christophe David, 1721, 7th edn), Book 2, Part III, ch. 1, p. 121.

appropriate confidentiality, for the belief that women are indiscreet gossips has many and justified exceptions. It is enough to reflect in passing that without women entering into the deliberations of the courts, the councils, the academies or the societies, there is hardly a meeting of any of these bodies, however secret, that does not come to be divulged, often quoted by the very speakers who were on the different sides of the argument. It is certainly not women who reveal the mysteries of state, government or politics, in which they do not participate. Since it is therefore the men who make them public, let them not say that discretion is a distinctive characteristic of their sex. On the contrary, we could cite numerous examples of the wisdom, prudence and valour of women, and of their constancy in keeping a secret, but this is so obvious that everyone knows about it. I would say that since this is a natural result of discretion, the person who has it, whether man or woman, will know how to keep it. Furthermore, if the Society requires the qualities which it has said are necessary to admit women, it cannot be doubted that they could bring a prudent discretion perhaps better than men who, out of competition for talent or position, divulge what happens in their meetings.

To think that the participation of women would be pernicious because of the vices they would introduce into the practices of the Members, is an assumption that is all too fatal to both sexes. The zeal with which they wish to root out these vices and prevent them from spreading is worthy of praise, but let us not believe it to be impossible. Perhaps the modesty and seclusion of the women of old that is so much admired freed them from the assaults of men? We have a number of good examples in sacred and profane history of the customs of our ancestors. When were murders, assassinations, assaults and rapes more frequent, than when women were kept at home and guarded with padlocks? In later times other customs developed that we cannot say were an improvement, but it would not be difficult to demonstrate philosophically that if difficulty augments desire, familiarity attenuates it. It is a constant belief that men and women ought to live entirely separately, but even if this separation ought to be total, for as long as it is not achieved and things stay as they are today, let us not say that adding one respectable motive to a thousand reasons to come together would lead to the destruction of the human race.

The meetings of the Society necessarily include many people, and amongst such a large number there is no danger of dissolute behaviour. Modesty has not been extinguished in the same way as other virtues: everyone wishes to appear good even if they are not, and this maintains the required decency in such gatherings. What is more, if there is no abuse in other groups, why should there be in this one? Is it possible that the men who attend it in order to work for the common good will be instantly transformed into libertines? Is there no restraint or respect in such assemblies? Of course there is, so we should not fear a worse danger than exists on all occasions when men and women have to see each other; a risk which does not cause this to be absolutely prohibited since it is sometimes necessary for them to come together, and since the vices of one individual should not and cannot destroy the common good. Thus, if women can be in any way useful to the Society, there is no reason to keep them out because of a remote risk that does not prevent other similar meetings.

Neither is it a good reason to claim that women lack basic knowledge in the matters dealt with by the Societies. I would love to know how many of the men who join them have this basic knowledge, and attend them all and cast their votes. The matters discussed by the Society are almost all matters of fact, which is why comparing works that come from abroad with ours to see what advances exist and to judge the products that are presented, are things that anyone who has eyes and an average mind would be able to understand. To create new inventions in the arts, improve learning, stimulate manufacturers, workmen and artisans to improve and profit from their work, to calculate what one country lacks and bring it from another in exchange for its surplus through the mechanism of prudent commerce; even though these are things that require reflection and information, they are not such abstract questions that they cannot be understood by a woman of normal talent. The only thing the Society needs so others may understand is someone who can explain these subjects with order, clarity and distinction.

When the Economic Societies were set up, few people knew what subjects would concern them. Many people enrolled blindly, driven more by the curiosity aroused by a new establishment and the glory of seeing their names on a list alongside others they regarded as famous, than by love of their country or the desire for its good fortune. When over time they came to understand the objective of these bodies, some people applied themselves to studying these new subjects, whilst others stopped attending and poured scorn on what they did not understand, finding it easier to do this than to educate themselves. Nevertheless, in all the Societies a significant number of individuals have remained who do not possess the basic knowledge desired by the respected Member who opposes the admission of women on the grounds of such ignorance. Yet it is conceded that when compared with men, women may claim they have an advantage since they pick things up more easily and often propose helpful ideas to resolve certain difficulties satisfactorily.

If it was a mistake for men to enrol in the Societies without having the necessary education to be useful to them, it was equally wrong for those bodies to admit everyone indiscriminately, so as to accumulate a fund of wealth if not of intelligence. The poverty of the patrician groups cries out for a remedy, but as long as they are unable to achieve it through other expedients, they are obliged to increase the number of contributors without examining their other qualifications. But even amongst this class our opponent does not believe women could be useful. I insist that if they are suitable to be admitted for other reasons, they will also contribute through their subscriptions. The money which people complain is wasted today on luxury and vanity will be applied to the public good, providing permanent proof that women are able to take an interest in the nation and the state.

Luxury is excessive and women are the cause of it: of that there is no doubt. But the greater the disorder, the more urgent the remedy. We see how inadequate are the vehement denunciations of the preachers, the wise policies of the government, the poverty of families and the difficulties of married couples. Who knows whether it might not be more effective than all of these to interest women in the national good? This would be achieved if they were encouraged to enter the Society of Friends of the Nation. There they would observe the vigilance of nations that adapt and promote other types of business for the prosperity of their compatriots. They would see that if the merchant, the worker, the manufacturer and the artisan are incentivized, this is designed to provide a stimulus to all, so that in Spain commerce, agriculture, industry and the arts may flourish; with such examples before them, women would never again consider with indifference the common cause.

The objective of the Societies could not be more appropriate, but for them to achieve the ends they desire two things are essential: first, that people apply themselves to hard work and constant improvement, and second, that the fruit of their work and labour can find a market, for without such good fortune no one will go to great efforts to make something which he cannot sell. If we aim to promote our arts and manufactures, it is necessary for us to be content with what is produced at home. At first it will be a wrench to use what is less attractive and in worse taste, and to leave aside foreign materials, which are superior in both qualities, but if we do not start to offer this sacrifice of taste on the altar of patriotic fervour, then our works will never flourish. And these works, which luxury has introduced and to which it gives their value, are they not usually those which deal with the adornment of women? It is necessary to interest them in dressing themselves at a lower cost, so their money does not go to benefit foreign lands, by wearing materials from their own country. Their participation in the Society will inspire them with these principles which are beneficial to the state: there they will hear of the damage caused by extreme luxury, and the means to avoid it. Ask them to contribute to the nation with their minds, their hands and their wealth. Men should have no doubt that women will offer all these things if they allow them to join in their debates and encourage them to think of the general good, which will appeal to them as soon as they observe it.

Another Member, of equal merit and status to the first, has written in favour of the admission of women to the Society. He says that this is not a new idea, that it was intended from the beginning and had eminent supporters, but that despite this it was not put into effect at that time; that is to say, it did not go through the necessary formalities. He praises the qualities of the two ladies who have already been admitted. He points out the rules that need to be followed in order to admit others, and if these are followed, it does not appear that any breach of due process on this point is to be feared. He does not recommend that once they have been admitted, the Section should be closed to new members, and concludes by agreeing that their attendance is good for the Society and for the women themselves: to women because it will encourage them to make good use of their talents, and to the Society because it will provide an increase in understanding and in funds, which it can invest in its praiseworthy activities.

In truth, this respected Member deserves to receive endless gratitude from women for having intervened in their defence. The reasons on which his argument is founded and the grace of his style are worthy of particular praise. The most active form of thanks we can give him is to labour to put ourselves in the state he desires in order to justify our admission, which we ourselves must be anxious to see conceded only on the basis of merit, application and virtue.

Following such an eminent apologist, any other defence in favour of women must seem feeble, but fear of this did not discourage me once I was convinced of the justice of the cause, for this alone could have compelled our defender and those others who are of the same opinion to put forward their arguments. The two ladies admitted to the Madrid Society[15] undoubtedly have great qualities, and for this reason they deserved to be the first, and to have forced the ruling in favour of their sex that has not yet been ratified to be revived, but it should also be extended to others who have the qualities we have described. For the Society would benefit, in addition to all that has been expressed in this paper, from the greater understanding women have than men on various everyday topics which need to be promoted, since they are important to the general good. These are subjects like spinning, weaving, lace-making and other activities proper to the fair sex. It would be a coincidence if a man understood these branches of knowledge, while all women should know about them. Once they are all united in one body, the president may allocate each person to the activities they understand. Little else would be required to rectify many ills, for the arts would flourish if only they were deprived of artifice.

Let us conclude, therefore, from all the above that if women have the same ability as men to educate themselves; if in all ages they have shown themselves capable of learning, prudence and discretion; if they have possessed and continue to possess the social skills; if their efforts may benefit them and the

---

[15] The Duchess of Osuna (wife of the Society's president) and the child prodigy Isidra de Guzmán. See introduction to the text.

state; if applying themselves to the matters undertaken by the Society could be a remedy for the disorders of which we complain so much; if the danger they represent to the Society is remote and could even be reduced by their presence, since no one will be admitted save those who are truly deserving; if it is not a universal novelty that women should participate in discussions; if at this time a woman occupies the Presidency of the Academy of Sciences in one of the Courts of Europe, which is even more important than sitting as an individual member of a group; if the subjects discussed are not excessively abstract; and finally if it is a question of making them friends of the nation, which would be of great utility, then based on this hypothesis admitting women, far from being prejudicial, can and must be the right thing to do.

Josefa Amar, Zaragoza, 5 June 1786

Josefa Amar y Borbón and the Question of Women's Education[1]

Education was a key issue for the reforming ministers of Carlos III's government. They were conscious that the labouring classes received virtually no instruction and were mostly illiterate, while at the other end of the scale Spanish universities were controlled by religious foundations, and continued to teach a scholastic curriculum that had barely changed since medieval times. The only alternative for higher education were the six *colegios mayores*; these were originally founded to educate boys of limited means, but had gradually become the exclusive preserve of the sons of the higher nobility, from which they made a smooth transition into posts in the church or royal administration. What is more, they were controlled by the Jesuits, and regarded with suspicion as a way for them to place their graduates close to the centres of power.

In 1768, the King expelled the Jesuit order from Spain, and two years later an edict placed all universities under royal authority. However, attempts to persuade them to adopt a modernised curriculum met huge resistance, and the reformers resorted to setting up new educational institutions. In 1770 the Royal School of St Isidore was established in Madrid, with a programme of studies that included mathematics, experimental physics, and natural and civil law. Gaspar de Jovellanos, after many years of effort, set up in his home town of Gijón an institute for mining and navigation, to train a generation of technical experts to improve the economy of Galicia by exploiting its reserves of coal and proximity to the Atlantic Ocean. The Basque Economic Society set up a model modern college that taught humanities and modern languages, mathematics and natural science, but also had technical departments specialising in agriculture, mineralogy, metallurgy and architecture.

The many Economic Societies around the country established Patriotic Schools in which girls of the labouring class were taught spinning, weaving and embroidery, while boys learned practical skills, and the prime minister,

---

[1] For a discussion of the context in which Amar's work was written, and the conflicting ideas on women's education, see Bolufer, *Mujeres*, pp. 117–35.

Count Floridablanca, required all the major cities to set up a school of technical drawing.

But this left open the question of what to do with the daughters of the middle and upper classes. They could not go to university like their brothers, and were not going to spend their lives spinning. There was an increasing awareness that the formative years of life were those that young children spent at home, and the greatest influence on their development would come from their mothers. In 1789 the Aragonese Economic Society in Zaragoza asked Juan Meléndez Valdés, a poet and reformer who had been appointed by Jovellanos as a judge in the city, to write a guide for mothers on the early education of children. This may have been the inspiration for Josefa Amar to publish her own handbook on education, which was clearly the fruit of many years of research and consideration. The following year she sent a copy of her *Discurso sobre la educación física y moral de las mujeres* (*Discourse on the Physical and Moral Education of Women*) to the Aragonese Society for its library, for which they recorded their thanks.[2]

The Prologue to the Discourse on the Education of Women

The *Discourse on the Education of Women* is nearly 350 pages long; only the *Prologue* is translated here. In the *Prologue*, Amar sets out her arguments justifying the education of women. She defines the problems that need to be remedied: society regards the education of women as a trivial matter, and women have no external reward to motivate them to learn. The current situation of women is to be pitied: all their self-esteem is based on beauty, which is inevitably fleeting. They have learned to regard their other talents with indifference, and developed no inner resources to comfort them in their old age.

If a solution is found to these difficulties through educating women, this will have great benefits, not only for the women themselves, their husbands and children, but also for the state. This appeal to public utility is key to her argument: Amar claims that the good order of private families contributes to public happiness, and in this the role of women is essential.

The format of the *Prologue* shows the influence of Amar's classical education. She gives examples from antiquity to support her claims, and lists of illustrious women of the past and present (though she keeps these brief), and ends with an invocation to the shades of Thucydides, Demosthenes and Cicero. Her first reference is to Lacedaemonia (or Sparta), famed for the fact that boys and girls practised the same physical exercises, and the women were committed to the success of the state, to the extent of being willing to sacrifice their husbands and sons in war. But these rhetorical flourishes are mere decoration: the core of the work is entirely practical and rooted in her own society.

---

[2] Sarrailh, *L'Espagne Éclairée*, p. 207.

Amar's ambitions are limited to what she thinks is achievable in the short term. She reassures the reader that she does not expect all women to study. She struggles to see a way for them to go to university, since they would have to study in the company of men, which she knows is not acceptable. Alternatively, they would have to have schools of their own; but she does not seem to see this as a practical proposition. The main benefits of educating women are that they will be able to run a household competently, educate their own children and provide intelligent companionship to their husbands.

But behind this conventional attitude lies a subtle interpretation of the different roles of men and women. Amar makes it clear that these are based not on some fundamental fact of nature, but on social practice. She states that it is merely the custom that men are the ones who obtain employment, while women stay at home, though she soothingly says she is not going to try to overturn this. Similarly, it is a practical advantage for women to manage the household, since they spend more time at home and are more familiar with the servants. She insists that both parents have equal responsibility for the care of their children, and it is only because women suckle their babies that 'to a certain extent' they have a greater obligation towards them.

It is interesting that Amar reflected none of the sentimental philosophy of women that had been spreading across Europe ever since the publication in 1762 of Jean-Jacques Rousseau's *Émile or on Education*.[3] Rousseau was convinced that men and women were intrinsic opposites, destined by nature to be entirely different in thought and behaviour. To him, women's restriction to domestic tasks was not just a social expedient, but a reflection of their fundamental physical nature, and their education should be limited to manual labour and the arts of pleasing men. Rousseau regarded a woman who tried to compete with men in the public space as a monster, but he could rise to paroxysms of emotion at the tender sight of a mother surrounded by her children.

Rousseau's works were banned in Spain as being contrary to religion, but Amar was clearly familiar with *Émile*: in the last chapter of her book, she included in her list of recommended works a book called *The Christian Émile*,[4] which she explained was the opposite of Rousseau's original. Despite the attempts by various national authorities to suppress Rousseau's works, his attitude towards women — that they were altogether lovely as long as they remained in their allotted place — had become diffused throughout Europe. Amar is notable for omitting completely from her published works any analysis of the subject of love: her approach was rational rather than romantic, observing that once a man and a woman are permanently in each other's company, the excitement soon wears off, and 'the most secure basis for mutual appreciation

---

[3] Jean-Jacques Rousseau, *Émile, ou de l'éducation* (The Hague: Jean Néaulme, 1762).
[4] C. de Leveson, *Émile chrétien, ou de l'éducation* (Paris: Libraires Associés, 1764).

is confidence and communication of ideas'. It is with this principle in mind that Amar begins her *Discourse on the Education of Women*.

The Text of the Discourse[5]

The style of the *Discourse on Education* is halfway between a handbook and an academic text: Amar attempts to give a comprehensive guide to the upbringing of children, starting from pregnancy and childbirth. She is careful to cite notable authorities and to give precise references to their works. The extent of her own reading is made abundantly clear: her numerous sources include Xenophon and Plutarch (often in the original Greek and Latin, followed by her own translations), François Fénelon's *Treatise on the Education of Girls* and John Locke's *Some Thoughts on Education*. Spanish sources include the *New Philosophy of the Nature of Man* by Oliva de Sabuco (who was included in Feijoo's list of illustrious women), Luisa de Padilla's *Virtuous Nobility* and Luis de León's *The Perfect Wife*.

She imitates Locke by allotting considerable space to the physical care of babies and infants, recommending that mothers should breastfeed their own children wherever possible, that babies should not have their limbs restrained by swaddling clothes, and that both boys and girls should be allowed plenty of physical exercise. She advises on diet (regular meals, and not too much salt or spice) and approves of frequent cold baths. She does not wish to see young girls encouraged to be delicate and timid, which will make them 'useless for everything'.

Much of her advice on the moral education of children is equally applicable to boys and girls. It is parents (and not just mothers) who have the prime responsibility for ensuring that their children are brought up to be obedient, sensible and well-behaved. Mothers will be responsible for educating their sons until they leave home to go to school or start a career, but their care for their daughters must be even greater, since they will never have any other teacher. Children learn from example as well as authority, and a mother should be seen to be thrifty, diligent and modest, on good terms with her husband, and able to keep her children and servants in order. If she wastes every day in visits and entertainments, what kind of example will that be?

Amar recommends that children should be introduced at an early age to the practice of religion, but insists they must learn that true devotion does not merely consist of visiting numerous churches and listening to plenty of

---

[5]   For an analysis of Amar's *Discourse on Education* see Franklin Lewis, *Women Writers in the Spanish Enlightenment*, pp. 38–59, and Isabel Morant Deusa's 'Reasons for Education: New Echoes of the Polemic', in *Eve's Enlightenment: Women's Experience in Spain & Spanish America 1726–1839*, ed. by Catherine Jaffe and Elizabeth Franklin Lewis (Baton Rouge: Louisiana State University Press, 2009), pp. 51–61.

sermons — an error to which women are particularly prone. She quotes Luis de León's admonition that married women should not try to compete with nuns in frequency of prayer, to the neglect of their domestic obligations.

When she turns to the tasks and responsibilities of women, Amar is entirely conventional in stating that these consist principally of manual work and household management. Just as a scholar should be seen in his study, an artisan in his workshop and a labourer in the fields, so a woman of whatever status should be seen with her spinning wheel and sewing needle. This is not just a way of saving money by making clothes that would otherwise have to be bought elsewhere, but is a useful and honest way of spending the time. Girls should be taught as early as possible to knit, sew, spin and embroider.

Amar admits that it will take a considerable change in attitudes for people to prefer such home-made garments to fashionable clothes made by professionals, but she echoes Juan Luis Vives[6] in commending the praiseworthy example of the great Spanish queen Isabella, who despite ruling the kingdom of Castile in her own right, accompanying her husband to the wars and being a patron of literature, was happy to be seen spinning or sewing.

When it comes to household management, Amar quotes the authority of the Greek philosopher Xenophon, who first promulgated the principle that men were made to accumulate wealth and women to preserve it. Thus it is that thrift, prudent purchasing and efficient organisation of the household are necessary to enable a woman to maintain and enhance her family's assets. Amar specifies that her intended audience consists of bourgeois women like herself, and she is careful to explain that she does not mean women actually have to do all the chores themselves, as long as they ensure their servants give a good account of their actions. Women must understand everything that goes on in the house, so they can judge whether things are being done properly.

In order to train girls to take over these responsibilities (remembering that they might expect to be married in their late teens), Amar advises that once they reach the age of ten or twelve, their mothers should occasionally delegate to them the task of making purchases or instructing the servants. Thus they can be prepared for their future destiny.

However, having established these principles, Amar asserts that the domestic role of women does not in any way mean they should not be permitted to cultivate their minds, and recommends a detailed course of study for those women who show the aptitude for it. She insists that all girls should be taught to read and write, and mocks those who wish to keep women illiterate for fear they will spend their time writing love letters.

Amar claims that the course of study she suggests would not be difficult for a girl of normal ability, and could be achieved during the time left over from

---

[6]   *The Education of a Christian Woman* (see volume introduction).

her domestic tasks. In fact, we may think her reading list would be daunting to a modern full-time graduate student. She starts with all the works of the best Spanish authors, including Cervantes' *Don Quixote*, and particularly recommends León's *The Perfect Wife* and Vives' *The Education of a Christian Woman*. She then moves on to the classics, which may be read in Spanish translation, and which include the works of Plutarch, Cicero, Sophocles and Euripides. All of these will be morally improving and help the reader to improve her own style.

Passing on to history, the 'diligent young lady' should first learn the history of her own country from ten textbooks, and then the history of France, England, Italy and Germany, and particularly of ancient Greece and Rome. Arithmetic is important, and she should learn the Italian method of double-entry book-keeping, since this will help her run her household in future. She may learn Latin by reading Cicero, Caesar, Livy and Sallust, and translating passages from them into Spanish. Amar is aware that Latin is the preserve of men, and that some people will be as shocked at this suggestion as if she had suggested women should 'put their hand in the sanctuary'.

As for modern languages, the most interesting are French, English and Italian, the study of which 'does not require much fatigue'. Greek is an option, and some women (such as Anne Dacier in France and the sixteenth-century Englishwoman Lady Jane Grey) have excelled in their knowledge of this language. Geography is useful and entertaining, and poetry is approved as long as it is not about love. Amar does not object to girls being taught the usual feminine accomplishments of drawing, music and dancing, though she clearly regards these as inferior to literary skills, and useful mainly as a way of passing the time in activity rather than idleness.

The rest of the *Discourse* is not about women's practical training or intellectual instruction but their moral development. Amar spends considerable time on the subject of 'adornments', but while recognizing that girls show an interest in dress and finery from an early age, does not attribute this to feminine nature as did many male writers, but blames the people around them who praise them for their looks from the youngest age. She accepts that a degree of elegance is required, but this should be appropriate to the situation and to the woman's social status. She disapproves of the pressures of fashion, which require constant change and excessive expenditure. It is a mother's responsibility to teach her daughters to recognise the limit beyond which a reasonable interest in her appearance tips into the dangers of vanity and luxury. This is also a concern from the point of view of public utility, for men often prefer not to marry, for fear of the excessive financial demands of a fashionable wife.

She then turns to a lengthy discussion of the vices generally attributed to women, and whilst refusing to accept that these are specific to the female sex, recognises that there are certain faults that are more often seen in women than in men. One of these is a taste for flattery, but here she holds men to be at least part of the cause, since they habitually adopt a language of excessive praise whenever they talk to young women, and it is hardly surprising that they find it pleasurable. Women are generally accused of talking too much, but Amar insists this is the fault of female education not natural talent, since girls are never taught to reflect on any serious subject. She observes that men mock ladies' meetings, saying that they all talk at the same time, discuss nothing but trivia and keep going round in circles; perhaps she is recalling the opposition to the Ladies' Section of the Madrid Economic Society four years earlier.

Other supposed feminine failings are a taste for vengeance, curiosity, malicious gossip, envy and a habit of taking everything to extremes. The solution to all of these, she insists, is education: women must be given the opportunity to cultivate their minds and develop their judgement.

Next she turns to the virtues women must display. The first, which moralizing writers had insisted for centuries was essential for women, is modesty. But Amar puts a different spin on this characteristic: modesty, she insists, is not just a case of casting down one's eyes and assuming a hypocritical countenance, but is more a case of well-ordered and well-judged behaviour, of actions and words that show respect for other people. Moderation is also a virtue, and this she interprets widely as the avoidance of all excess. The example she chooses is that of women who, having acquired a modicum of learning, show it off through pedantry; she is particularly concerned about this since it is often used as evidence by those who believe it is improper and ridiculous for women to 'wish to apply themselves to serious matters'. Politeness and courtesy are recommended, and include acquiring a skill in handling other people, and showing respect for those who may be less privileged.

It is noticeable that there is nothing in this advice that would not be equally appropriate for men; these are the characteristics that enable anyone to operate successfully in society. Unlike the earlier writers (such as Juan Luis Vives and Luis de León) whom Amar quotes so copiously throughout the *Discourse*, she does not believe that chastity is a sufficient virtue for a woman, or that women should be restricted exclusively to the domestic environment. A particularly interesting comment is that girls should be taught to 'estimate themselves correctly', in other words should develop an appropriate self-respect. This is very different from those moralizers who had insisted on female humility and self-abnegation, and is reminiscent of Feijoo's desire that 'women should come to understand what they truly are'.

The book now turns to that most important subject for women: the 'choice of estate'. Amar notes that in her society, women have only two options: to be a wife or a nun. To remain single in society is not acceptable for a woman:

she comments with some bitterness that although being unmarried is no barrier to a man in his career, 'a single woman is a zero', whose very existence is condemned by public opinion, 'which is the most powerful of arguments'. There were at the time a thousand convents in Spain,[7] so many women did choose the cloistered life. She is concerned that many women choose to be nuns for the wrong reasons: some may have been brought up in a convent from a young age and are nervous of change, but may come to regret it once they are older, imagining in marriage 'a happiness that hardly ever exists'. Alternatively, they may have been unhappy at home and treated with indifference by their parents, who did not bother to find a good match for them. In neither case does such a decision represent a true vocation, without which they cannot be happy in the religious life.

But the choice of marriage is an equally delicate one. Amar paints a fairly negative view of matrimony: women are frequently, through no fault of their own, treated harshly by husbands who have tired of them, and blamed for everything that goes wrong in the household. She urges that couples should come from 'equal circumstances', without extreme disparities in age or wealth. It is interesting that as far as age is concerned, she approves of the recommendation made by the seventeenth-century Milanese physician Ludovico Settala that the perfect match is between a woman of eighteen and a man of thirty. (We may recall that Amar herself was married at twenty-three to a man of forty-eight, so she clearly did not regard this as ideal.) She insists that parents should take into consideration their daughter's preferences when choosing a husband, thus sharing a common anxiety for contemporary European writers, who observed that parents frequently arranged matches for their children for financial or dynastic reasons, and thus women could find themselves locked into unhappy marriages with total strangers.

Once the marriage has taken place, women need to know what is expected of them. Amar sets out the conventional wisdom that the duty of the husband is to acquire sufficient wealth to keep his family, and the wife's is to manage his assets prudently, take care of the house and children, and be a pleasant companion to her husband when he comes home tired from his day's work. She does not wish to 'pretend that men are saints', and recognises that husbands can be disagreeable and even vicious, but is sure that a sensible woman can correct these faults over time. If her husband takes a mistress, she should overlook the fact and continue to treat him pleasantly, and he will soon come to love her more than ever. If he is irritable and tends to lose his temper, she should not answer back, but wait until he calms down and is able to listen to reason. One may be sceptical about whether these mild expedients were always as effective as she suggests, but they were likely to be the most effective remedy in a society

---

[7]   Herr, *The Eighteenth-Century Revolution in Spain*, p. 29.

where women had no rights, and as Amar states, the knot of marriage 'is formed in an instant, and dissolved only with death'.

One of the biblical texts most frequently quoted by those who wished to prove women's inferiority was St Paul's injunction that they should be taught to be subject to their husbands. Amar confronts this by stating that this type of authority should be seen as a necessary expedient, and not absolute like 'royal and sovereign authority'. It is just as wrong for men to treat their wives with contempt because they believe they are intellectually superior as it is for wives to aspire to 'absolute and despotic control'. She reflects the argument made by Feijoo over seventy years earlier that women were intellectually equal with men, and the only justification for male authority was that someone had to be given the last word.

The *Discourse* closes with a discussion of whether girls should be educated at home or elsewhere. This was an important question: it was traditional in France and Italy for girls to be sent to convent schools for their early education, but although Spain had a thousand convents, few of them offered this service; moreover, those that existed tended to be monopolized by the daughters of the aristocracy, and in any case they offered only a basic level of education. The 1787 census showed there were only twenty-five colleges for girls from noble families, with a mere 642 students, while there were six times as many places for boys. Amar does not in any case favour these establishments: she cannot see how they can effectively teach household management, and fears that the young and impressionable may suffer from mixing with older girls who are already corrupted by exposure to the fashionable world. She therefore recommends that, wherever possible, girls should not be separated from their mothers until they marry or take the veil, unless the mothers themselves are so badly-behaved that their example would be prejudicial. If a mother is incapable of teaching her daughters, she would do better to employ a governess, whom she can supervise in her own house. In order to make such a class of teachers available, Amar finds it 'essential that the government should apply its attention to the education of women in general', an unusually progressive idea at a time when there was no state-sponsored system of education anywhere in Europe.

In a lengthy appendix to the book, Amar lists nearly fifty other works on female education that she has used as sources, in chronological order from Xenophon to the contemporary Englishman Vicesimus Knox. She makes it clear she has read most of them, in a variety of different languages, and in some cases comments on the quality of the available Spanish translations, thus displaying the breadth of her erudition as well as the immense effort she has put into researching her subject.

Even more than the *Discourse on the Talents of Women*, the *Discourse on the Education of Women* demonstrates that Josefa Amar was a well-informed participant in the current of enlightened ideas circulating around Europe in the second half of the eighteenth century. She cites Luis de León six times during the course of the book, sometimes at length, using his words to criticise women who are spendthrift, idle, excessively talkative or obsessed with their looks. She quotes his disapproval of harsh and domineering women, and advises that they will achieve better results by treating their family and servants with consideration. It may seem surprising that she regarded with approval a work containing so much that today appears frankly misogynistic, but we may observe that she does not quote León's statements about the subjection of women to their husbands, but rather those that encourage them to regard domestic economy as a morally honourable and socially important role.

A number of Amar's other opinions would have been regarded with unease by Spanish traditionalists, such as the belief that children are born 'without ideas'. This concept, first found in the works of John Locke,[8] was rejected by those who believed that ideas are put into our minds by God, and who also tended to argue that society's views on the different roles of men and women were based on innate ideas and therefore unchangeable. Like Locke, Amar is sure they are, on the contrary, the result of early conditioning, and thus capable of being amended by education. (This and other views were sufficient for Locke's works to be later banned in Spain.)

Like the men with whom she debated in the Madrid Economic Society, Josefa Amar was a reformer rather than a revolutionary. She did not call for legal rights or civic equality between men and women; as she says in the *Prologue*, she did not intend to invert the natural order of things, but only to 'rectify as far as possible what already exists'. She was, however, convinced that if parents applied themselves to bringing up their daughters and mothers did not throw away their time in mindless entertainments, the happiness of women could be improved. And, most importantly, she joined her voice with many others in the Europe of her day in insisting that women were men's intellectual equals, and demanding that they should be given the opportunity to study and to learn.

---

[8]   John Locke, *Some Thoughts Concerning Education* (London: A. & J. Churchill, 1693).

Josefa Amar y Borbón

Prologue to the *Discourse on the Physical and Moral Education of Women*

It is for good reason that education has always been considered a most serious and important matter. Both public and private happiness depend on it, for if we could contrive that all individuals were prudent, well-informed and of sound and moderate judgment, and each family well-regulated, united and thrifty, then the automatic result would be the general good of the state, which brings together numbers of individuals and families. Thus the better the education, the greater the number of satisfied people and the greater the advantages to the nation. But if, on the other hand, it is poor, then we shall perpetuate those errors and disorders that are passed on through imitation and the power of the first ideas we receive in our childhood. It is not for nothing that the supreme Creator has disposed matters such that the care of the life and health of children, as well as their instruction, is made subject to the vigilance of fathers and mothers, so that in this way they may inspire them with simple and correct principles, and their children may learn at an early age to obey and respect those who have them in their charge.

There is nothing that cannot be taught at this age, and no virtue that cannot be adopted, if those who are responsible for their education take advantage of the opportunity. What prodigies of valour were achieved by the Lacedaemonians! Lycurgus, their wise legislator, saw that he needed to create a warlike people, so he established various laws to this effect, one of which was that boys should constantly exercise the arts of war so that, stimulating each other by example, they should all learn to regard the defence and conservation of the fatherland as their primary obligation. These ideas were so widely communicated that even the women became militant, and desired no quality in their sons other than valour and opposition to the enemies of their republic. They did not mourn their death if it took place on the field of battle. If we were to say that these women did not love their husbands and sons as much as those of more recent times or of other nations, it would be a manifest insult to the rigid virtue they practised.

To what can we attribute this difference? To the power of education to excite valour. The Romans considered education to be the most essential aspect of paternal authority. In Spain there was the same concern, as we see in Lucio Marineo Sículo: 'The Spanish have a reputation for culture and good manners, and also for the great vigilance and attention they pay to the education of their children, which is the greatest virtue: even before they are born they carefully seek out nurses and tutors of good character and habits, a thing that is not seen in other nations'.[1]

The importance of this subject can also be observed from the many authors who have written on the subject. It would be tedious to make a list of them all, but it would be wrong to omit the most important, which will be referenced in the final chapter of this discourse, and given where possible in chronological order. The works cited there will demonstrate that although many authors have written about education, there are few whose ideas are consistent with the present treatise. Most of them talk only of the instruction of boys, and those which also include girls do it with a haste that denotes indifference. We may add to these reasons the fact that we do not have in our language any work that includes the two essential aspects of education, the physical and the moral, and for this reason it does not seem inappropriate to publish this work; although it may be far from perfect, it may serve as a stimulus to worthier authors.

The education of women is generally considered a trivial matter. The state, their parents and, what is more, the women themselves, regard with indifference whether they learn one thing or another, or nothing at all. Who can explain the cause of this universal neglect? To suggest that men contrive this in order to keep women in ignorance and dominate them more easily is a vulgar idea, and one that is easily disproved, if we observe that in all ages there have been various scholars who have written in praise of the intelligence of women, and have made catalogues of the most famous. And to tell the truth, what advantage would they derive from women's ignorance? Since they are destined to marry, there can be little harmony between an educated man and a stupid woman. The institution of matrimony is designed for two persons who have to live permanently in a mutual union and society, and for this there is a need for a community of ideas and interests; without this there can never be united and tranquil marriages. And if we speak of ordinary company and rational society, how much more valuable is an educated mind in making the relationship between people useful and pleasant! For this reason it is essential to seek out the origin of this concern, and there is no doubt that it lies in the method of education given to women.

Women are as subject as men to the common obligations of each individual,

---

[1]   Lucio Marineo Sículo (c. 1444–c. 1533) was an Italian humanist who was born in Sicily and spent twelve years teaching at the famous Spanish University of Salamanca. He published a lengthy history of Spain in 1530.

which are the practice of religion and the observation of the civil laws of their country. Beyond this are the specifics of the province where they live and the circumstances to which they are called: that is to say that in this sense there is no difference between the sexes, and consequently both of them need to be properly instructed in order to carry out their duties. The obligations of a married couple are extensive, and their influence has a major impact on the good or ill of society in general, for the good or bad order of private families transcends their situation and contributes to public happiness and tranquillity.

In these private families the wives have a particular responsibility: the direction and supervision of the house, the care and upbringing of children, and above all an intimate and perfect companionship with her husband. There is no more familiar tale than the one where wives dominate and control the men according to their whim. It is a true one, and for this reason it is appropriate to make this influence and power more useful to one and the other, for these days it is founded only on outward graces which quickly disappear, and even if they were more permanent, there would be no benefit in giving preference to external attractions.

If enlightening women's minds would be useful to the state, for the reasons I have described, it would be no less so for the women themselves, for obliged as they are to base all their esteem on looking good and dressing well, see what effort it costs them to maintain both of these. What anxiety and care to preserve their beauty if they have it, or to feign it if nature has not granted them this advantage, as is the case with the majority. It is certain that beauty is a thing to be admired: there is no greater empire than this, for in an instant it makes itself the ruler of all hearts and the source of extreme emotions; a thing not seen with the other graces, whose influence is more gradual and less obvious. Yet beauty is a merely gratuitous gift which owes little or nothing to our own efforts. Adornment and artifice can compensate to some extent, but will never succeed in completely disguising natural defects; and even if all women were beautiful, unless they obtained the privilege of making this gift more permanent, that is, that it lasted the whole of a woman's life, they would gain nothing.

In the actual state of affairs, there is nothing more fragile and temporary: smallpox, sickness, falls or other accidents can quickly destroy it; and since it has no greater enemy than time, this is sufficient to reduce its value. A woman who has been beautiful but ceases to be so after a given number of years experiences two very different phases in her life. She who has passed through both can energetically describe the misfortune of the second phase: I say misfortune, if she has acquired no other quality to accompany and to survive her looks.

Despite these frequent disappointments, almost all women apply their greatest efforts to their looks, and regard other talents with indifference. This can be attributed mainly to their education, since they are taught nothing from childhood except how to dress up, and they observe that their mothers and friends dedicate most of their attention to the same thing. They hear themselves praised for being pretty and cute, and set themselves to study this art, and despite some difficulties in choosing and arranging their finery, many of them succeed in becoming experts. It is true that women observe each other with great care; they imitate and vie with each other, and it is the most trivial theme of conversation when they visit each other; all of this helps to refine and perfect this interest of theirs. There are nevertheless some who cannot excel in this art, either for lack of opportunity or through a desire to choose the quality that favours them best; and most of all, because it depends on the whim of other people, who if they fail to praise the appearance of a particular lady will leave her feeling hurt at having wasted so many hours.

It is not just personal charms that create true happiness, first because not everyone has them or can acquire them, and more importantly because even if you have them, their brilliance will pass away quickly and their loss will leave behind a bitter void; it is necessary to acquire more solid and permanent talents that will stay with you throughout your life, and to the extent that they are beneficial in daily life, will be useful to their possessor; finally, they should be talents that we can acquire through our own efforts. These are the qualities of the mind, which do not disappear or grow old. Women are desperate for flattery and devotion, and they will surely obtain this when they are young, especially if it is combined with an attractive appearance, but once this disappears, what happens then? The ridiculous farce they played in the world, their role as queens and almost goddesses, is over, and they suddenly find their retinue of courtiers has vanished. One needs a great fund of philosophy to tolerate being dethroned like this, and to see that the same people who just now were so obsequious are now indifferent. It was youth and physical attractiveness that sustained this comedy; once these are gone, the illusion ceases. As for dressing fashionably, we can see that this is ridiculous and even impossible to maintain throughout our lives, for what may look good on a young girl is ugly and laughable on an old woman.

In trying to persuade women to apply themselves to more serious subjects, we come across a greater problem than the one described above, and that is the lack of reward. Reward is the most powerful and universal stimulus that we know of to motivate all our actions, and since women cannot count on it, they have to apply their efforts solely for their own benefit. In this sense they have to be nobler than the men, who study in the security that this will lead to employment, honours and advantages. Once a boy starts on a course of study, he has a well-founded hope that he will achieve in time his preferred destiny in ecclesiastical or secular life. Many of them are aware that they can count on earning great wealth without knowing more than how to read and write.

Despite these hopes, they are set to study from a young age, first because is it necessary to take advantage of these years, and secondly because if it were left to their own choice, many boys would be likely to flee from the hard work it takes at first to absorb the dry elements of the sciences. Education compensates for a lack of knowledge or reflection. The same should be done for girls, in their case pointing out that its own usefulness is its unique recompense. This is no small thing if we consider it properly, for wisdom carries its own sufficient reward. What greater advantage than the power of making good use of your time, developing resources that will last through all the ages and events of life, acquiring new ideas and being content to stay apart from the clamour of other people? Apart from this, fame and immortal glory will always seek out merit wherever it may be found.

In all ages and all nations there have been women who, rising above the obstacles I have referred to above, have made themselves famous for their intellect and learning. Even today we recall the memory of the celebrated Aspasia, wife of Pericles, whose wisdom and counsel were praised by Xenophon; of Sappho, the illustrious poet, and many other Greek women who were distinguished for their erudition. In Spain we shall never forget Luisa Sigéa, Ana Cervatón, Juana Contreras, Luisa de Padilla[2] and Juliana Morell.[3]

In France a large number of women flourished in ancient times and they continue to do so today, and the same is true in other countries. I do not pretend to make a list here of all the illustrious women, for such catalogues exist in all languages, and I do not set out here to prove their aptitude and intelligence. The truth of this is sufficiently demonstrated in a variety of books, and most of all in the evidence the women themselves have left behind. It is enough for a woman to apply herself to study and make progress to prove the fortunate disposition of her sex.

---

[2]   All these women were included in Cubíe's *Las Mugeres Vindicadas*, and Cervatón and Morell were also mentioned by Feijoo. Luisa de Padilla, the Countess of Aranda (1590–1646), published a work called *Virtuous Nobility* on the subject of children's education, and Amar included several quotations from this in the text of her *Discourse on Education*.

[3]   **Amar's footnote:** Her wisdom was universally known, not least for having been in Lyon in France, where there was a literary contest which earned her a doctorate at its university. There is no doubt she was the Spanish lady referred to by Arniseo in a letter written in Lyon on 1 May (year unknown), which said: 'I found here a Spanish girl dedicated to the Franciscan Order, who is said to be only fourteen years old, and who seemed to me to be not much older than that. I have found out that she is already so devoted to the study of philosophy that she composes theses, and debates them in her academy, not indeed with excessive learning, but still more learnedly than one would expect of one of her sex and age. She can genuinely both speak and write, with the greatest accuracy, the Hebrew, Greek, and Latin languages, and in addition to these Spanish, Italian, and French. She is also, next, turning her mind to canon law, in which she hopes to obtain a doctoral degree. Her father, because of some crime, fled Spain, and has established himself in Lyon.' [Quotation from letter appears in Amar's text in Latin.]

Besides, what more can we say, given that there are so many and they are so famous? Any man who doubts this truth is closing his eyes to the light. We are far from needing further evidence of the talents of women when, despite the defective education they are commonly given, which appears designed to stifle the seeds planted by nature; despite this, I repeat, there are many women who, with no help other than their natural reason, understand better than men who have never studied, and can engage quickly with matters discussed in their presence.

As for culture and appropriate use of words, it is rare for a woman not to equal or excel certain men who are speakers by profession. The famous Locke, speaking of a certain lady, said that 'in praise of her natural eloquence, it would be an insult to say that she spoke better than many schoolmasters, for this is very common, but in fact she was better than some of the most cultivated and educated men in England'.[4]

The talent and application of women have not degenerated in recent times. In our own century we have seen the famous Sophia Elizabeth Weber, wife of Elias Brenner, a scholar employed in the Royal Archive in Sweden. She was born in 1659 in Stockholm, and became celebrated for her vast erudition and poetic talent. She had fifteen children to whom she gave an excellent education, and cultivated literature without neglecting the necessary obligations of domestic management. She maintained a correspondence with various literary men, and the fame of her writing was such that medals were struck to perpetuate her memory. One of these showed her bust on one side, and on the reverse a laurel with the inscription: 'Crescit cultura' (culture increases). Another showed the figures of herself and her husband, with the epigraph: 'Conjuge vir felix, felix erat illa marito' (the husband was happy in his wife; the wife was happy in her husband). She died in 1730.[5]

Neither should we overlook the evidence of appreciation given to the female sex by the celebrated Pope Benedict XIV, on the occasion of the election of Señora Gaetana Agnesi to the Chair of Mathematics. This lady thought she should inform his holiness and confirm whether this met with his approval, and he replied in his own hand with these words, which are worthy of being engraved in bronze: 'It is with great pleasure that I give my approval, and I am delighted that women are put in a position to display their learning and intellect. I urge you to train up other women like you, to prove that you are at least as good as we are once you apply yourselves. Understanding is futile if it

---

[4] The quotation is taken from Locke's *Some Thoughts on Education*. The original is somewhat different, and says, 'there are ladies who [...] speak as properly and as correctly (they might take it for an ill compliment if I said as any country schoolmaster) as most gentlemen who have been bred up in the ordinary methods of grammar schools'.
[5] **Amar's footnote:** Her life story may be found in Latin in the 1731 *Literary Memorials of Sweden*, p. 118.

is wasted on trivia, but it is enlarged and elevated as it becomes accustomed to meditation. I confess that when I am searching in a library, I should like to find alongside our doctors some admirable women who know how to set their learning in a frame of modesty. In this way women would come to inhabit the palace of the popes, and I would have more opportunities to bring them to mind.'[6]

This same pope also referred with distinction to Madame du Bocage, well known for her poetry and her letters on Italy, and knowing that when she was in Rome she was always accompanied by Cardinal Passionei, who was over eighty years old, he exclaimed with his usual grace: 'O what a noble union between age and talent!'.

Despite what I have said about the aptitude of women, it is not to be wished, nor would it be the case, that all of them without distinction should dedicate themselves to study as if they were to follow a trade or profession. This would necessarily create confusion, for either they would have to attend a university in the company of men, which would cause more harm than good, or they would need schools of their own. We can see that there are different classes and occupations, as is the case with men, some of whom dedicate themselves to letters, others to arms, these to agriculture and those to the various arts and trades needed by society; for if such variety did not exist, we would not be able to supply our various needs.

For the same reason there are certain tasks that are particular to women, such as sewing and spinning, which men could not carry out without neglecting their respective obligations. It also falls to them to manage the household, for they spend more time at home and are more familiar with the servants and can keep them in order. If we wished to invert this order so they could spend the whole day studying, then the men would have to look after the house, and if we also inverted the custom that they are the ones who obtain employment, they would be useless at both activities. Let us not, therefore, make some fantastic plan: let us work only to rectify as far as possible what already exists. To achieve this, women would cultivate their minds without prejudice to their duties, first so they may behave in such a way as to make the yoke of matrimony more pleasant and agreeable; secondly, so they may fully perform the respectable duty of mothers; and thirdly, for the usefulness and benefit that instruction conveys in all the ages of life. But while education does not aim at these ends, its benefits will never spread.

It seems that in proposing a system of education, we should include all classes

---

[6] Cardinal Prospero Lambertini came from Bologna, and continued to support his native city after becoming pope as Benedict XIV. As well as awarding a professorship to Maria Gaetana Agnesi, he also appointed the mathematician Laura Bassi to Bologna's Academy of Sciences.

of society, but this is impossible in practice, if we recognise that in this world everything is relative. It is certain that the essential obligations apply to all types of people without distinction, but they do not all need the same instruction to fulfil them. For this reason we shall not discuss those women of the lower class for whom it is sufficient to know how to carry out practical domestic tasks themselves. Their fate will normally unite them with husbands of equal simplicity, for whom beauty is not a necessity. In these marriages mutual felicity will be achieved if the husband works hard and the wife assists him in his tasks. Not all people require the same things to be happy, and this helps to reduce disappointment. The wise distributor of gifts and talents has given to some people simpler ideas, so they may more easily satisfy their desires and necessities, whilst others, gifted with greater sensibility and energy, are afflicted by the very delicacy and variety of their desires.

Thus it is that an enlightened and cultivated mind may be very useful to the class of women who, to put it bluntly, will marry men who are educated and cultivated, for this will strengthen and improve the harmony of their perpetual union. It is clear that they do not always seek such characteristics when entering into matrimony, for we see many men marrying because they are in love with a woman's looks or personal charms; but in the same way we see this enchantment quickly disappear, and once they are permanently in each other's company, these charms vanish in an instant and offer little variety; once they are used to it they grow tired of the sight of each other, and run the risk of gazing with indifference on the same thing that used to delight them most. *Sit formosa aliis uxor, tibi sit bona.*[7] This is the most infallible rule. If these examples were not so common of people who have been passionately in love before marriage, and afterwards have come to detest each other as intensely as they once loved, we could go further into this subject; but no one is unaware of it.

The main problem is that their love is not founded on any solid merit. The most secure basis for mutual appreciation is confidence and communication of ideas. A man who spends his whole day occupied in business, much of it disagreeable, regards his home and family as a centre of relaxation and a relief from the pressures of work or the tasks of a strenuous profession. This relaxation and relief will be complete if he has a wife who is placid and discreet, to whom he can confide his secrets and share in a rational conversation. On the other hand, what annoyance and unpleasantness will he experience from a stupid wife, or one who can talk about nothing but her appearance? We can hardly be surprised by the lamentable consequences that arise from the latter case.

---

[7] 'Let other men's wives be beautiful, as long as yours is virtuous.' The quotation comes from the *Distichs* of Michael Verino, published in 1487 in Italy and in Spain in 1489. It became popular with schoolmasters as an aid to teaching Latin. Verino was quoted by Cervantes in *Don Quixote*, in a way that suggests the work was already familiar to Spanish readers.

The care and education of children is the equal responsibility of fathers and mothers; but since nature has deposited them for a period of time in the lap of their mothers and given them what is needed to feed them during their early months, it seems that to a certain extent they have a greater obligation to preserve and look after them. Another reason is that mothers spend more time at home and have their children before their eyes for most of the time, so they may understand them better and know how to correct them. From this it ensues that the faults of children are generally blamed on their mothers; and in truth many of them, through total negligence or misplaced indulgence, not only fail to give them a good education but prevent them benefiting from the efforts of their fathers or teachers. Others show a preference for one child over another, and do not allow him ever to be scolded or chastised, not realizing that true love consists in using all possible methods to improve them, and that parents have the same obligation to take care of their youngest as their oldest child.

But now the time has come to discuss the two essential aspects of a perfect education: the physical and the moral. The first because it determines the strength and functioning of the body, which is so importance throughout life; and the second because it is aimed at developing the understanding and habits, and is the only way to achieve a real and continual happiness. O that I had the eloquence of Thucydides, Demosthenes or Cicero, to persuade women to apply their talents in this way! Whoever could achieve this would do no less a service to the human race than that which these wise men gave to their republics.

Inés Joyes y Blake and the
War between the Sexes

It has been estimated that during the eighteenth century there were fewer than two hundred Spanish women whose works appeared in print, a small number compared with France and England. Many of these women published translations rather than original works, which was considered more acceptable than publicly expressing their own opinions. It was especially frowned upon for women of the highest social class to write for publication, which carried the implication of working for money and resulted in a loss of social status. Despite this, the Countess of Montijo, first Secretary of the Madrid Ladies' Committee, had at the tender age of nineteen published a translation from French of a work on the sacrament of marriage, but this was considered acceptable since it was on a religious subject, and the foreword was written not by her but by the priest who was her spiritual adviser.[1]

Translations made up an important proportion of books published in Spain in the 1780s, rising to over a quarter of the total in the period from 1784 to 1788. Women played a significant part in this; it was particularly common for them to translate works by other women, especially from French, and many of these were on the subject of education and the upbringing of children. Thus the works of Louise d'Épinay, Marie Le Prince de Beaumont, Françoise de Graffigny and Stéphanie de Genlis were made available to a circle wider than the Spanish elite, who were habitually taught French and were able to read them in the original. A selection of the works of Madame de Lambert, whom Josefa Amar particularly admired, were translated in 1781 by Cayetana de la Cerda y Verda, Countess of Lalaing, who boldly added her own foreword.[2]

Inés Joyes y Blake was thus participating in an existing tradition when in 1798 she published her translation of Samuel Johnson's moral fable, *The History of Rasselas, Prince of Abissinia*. She was, however, exceptional in taking the opportunity to insert at the end of this work a thirty-page addition which

---

[1] Maria Francisca de Sales Portocarrero, Countess of Montijo, *Instrucciones cristianas sobre el sacramento del matrimonio* (translation of Nicolas Le Tourneux's *Instructions chrétiennes sur le sacrement de mariage*) (Barcelona, 1774).
[2] See López-Cordón, *Condición Femenina y Razón Ilustrada*, p. 87

had nothing to do with the main text: her own entirely original *Apologia de las Mugeres* (*Apology for Women*). (The term *Apologia* did not imply any admission of guilt or regret, but a desire or justification for a belief or a course of conduct.)

Inés Joyes was born in Madrid in 1731.[3] Her father Patrick was Irish, a native of Galway, and her mother was born in France but was also of Irish extraction; Inés was the third of their six children. Patrick Joyce (who adapted his name to Patricio Joyes) was a member of a community of Irish refugees who had started to arrive in Spain following the English 'Glorious Revolution' of 1688 which had driven the Catholic King James II from the land, with more following after the failed Jacobite uprisings of 1715 and 1745. These exiles were welcomed into Spain and ancient Irish documents were readily accepted as proof of noble status, which entitled their holders to join the royal administration or become officers in the army, where a number of them rose to exalted positions: Richard Wall served as the King's chief minister from 1754 to 1763, General O'Neill was a successful governor of Zaragoza in the 1780s, and General Alexander O'Reilly was a senior military commander in Cuba and Puerto Rico, and later in southern Spain.

Other Irish refugees in Spain made their living, and often their fortune, in the fields of banking and commerce. Patricio Joyes and Sons became one of the most important banking houses, supplying funds to the monarchy, and was one of the shareholders of the Bank of San Carlos (a prototype central bank), founded in 1782 by Francisco Cabarrús, Josefa Amar's opponent in the controversy over the Madrid Economic Society.

The Joyes family sought to improve their social status by sending sons into the army and the administration, and marrying their children into the Spanish nobility. It is, however, notable that none of their members entered the church, and it would appear the family identified itself with the secular, reforming class. Joyes' ability to translate fluently from English (a language that Spanish women were rarely taught) also suggests they maintained a link with their anglophone roots, and their enlightened ideas included giving a good education to their daughters.

Inés' father died in 1745, when she was only thirteen years old, which was often the signal for a family to plunge into penury, but her mother took over the reins of the family business and kept it going until her own death fifteen years later. This example of female enterprise seems to have been a model for Joyes' own life: like her mother, she was an educated woman who brought up her own children and acted as their tutor during her widowhood.

In 1752, at the age of twenty-one, Joyes married Agustín Blake, her second cousin, like her a descendant of Irish immigrants, who used his wife's dowry and

---

[3]   For biographical information on Inés Joyes, see Bolufer, *La vida y la escritura en el siglo XVIII.*

a substantial gift from his aunt to establish his own trading-house in Malaga. This town was a significant port, and Agustín appears to have specialized in trading agricultural produce. Its concentration of inhabitants from different nations also gave it a cosmopolitan culture.

Agustín died after thirty years of marriage, when Joyes was fifty-one, leaving her with nine unmarried children and few assets, since the business had gone bankrupt. As was often the case with widows, she was plunged into lawsuits over her children's inheritance and negotiations over the financial settlements related to their marriages. She maintained close links with her own family in Madrid, as is demonstrated by their involvement as witnesses to documents and executors of wills; a number of her children were to marry cousins, as she had done (the genetic risks of doing so were not then understood, and it was seen as a useful way of keeping wealth within the family).

Joyes' eldest son, Joaquín, joined the army and proved to have great skill in training young officers; one of his protégés was Pedro Girón de Pimentel, son of the Duchess of Osuna, and despite the disparity in their social status, the Duchess corresponded with him on terms of friendship and familiarity. Joyes did not live to see Joaquín rise to the position of Captain General during the war against Napoleon, a post which he filled creditably until he was finally overpowered by the French forces and imprisoned in France. Two other sons, José and Juan, also pursued a military career, while Agustín and Manuel joined the family business.

Joyes also had four daughters: Teresa died at the age of twenty and Maria Josefa at the age of thirty-four. Ana Maria married and spent her life in Malaga, where she lived to the age of seventy, and Inés married a soldier of Irish descent when she was twenty-eight, giving birth to three sons, who all followed a military career, and one daughter.

The 1780s saw Malaga go through a period of dynamic expansion, with increased economic activity and the growth of social and cultural institutions. Malaga set up its own Economic Society of Friends of the Nation, as did the nearby town of Vélez-Malaga, where Joyes and her children lived. However, these Societies did not admit women or even establish a Ladies' Committee. Her name does not appear in any of the official subscription lists of philanthropic societies, but judging from the *Apology*, she was a frequent guest (and acute observer) of more informal social gatherings. She may even have hosted such meetings in her own house: an English traveller, Joseph Townsend, recorded that he was 'happy in being received under the hospitable roof of Mrs Blake, the sister of my banker, Mr Joyes' in 1787, and expressed his satisfaction at the 'agreeable society' he found in her home.[4] We can imagine her pleasure at being able to converse with this English visitor in his own language.

---

4   Townsend, *A Journey through Spain*, III, p. 45. Cited in Bolufer, *La vida y escritura*, p. 106.

Joyes was not the only contemporary Spanish woman of Irish extraction to venture into print. Margarita Hickey (d.1793) was born in Barcelona to a colonel of the Irish Dragoons and his Milanese wife; at a young age she married a soldier who was in his seventies, and after his death in 1778 was able to dedicate the remaining twenty-five years of her life to literature. Much of her poetry includes defences of women, using terms that are often far more vehement than those used by Josefa Amar or Inés Joyes, to typify men as insolent, lustful, domineering monsters, and women as innocent and suffering victims.

María Gertrudis Hore (1742–1801) was born to parents who both came from prosperous Irish commercial families and was born in Cadiz, a port city that, like Malaga, was considered to be cosmopolitan and free-thinking. She married at the age of twenty but separated from her husband after sixteen years of marriage and retired to a convent in Cadiz, where she took the veil. Like Hickey, Hore used the remaining twenty-three years of a life free from the obligations of marriage to write poetry, in her case on religious subjects. Many of these poems use the image of the caged bird, but it was not the convent that she regarded as a prison, but the constraints put on women in wider society.[5]

The History of Rasselas, Prince of Abissinia

We can only speculate what led Inés Joyes, at the age of sixty-seven, to decide to translate an English work into Spanish, but what is certain is that the choice of Rasselas was highly unusual. Samuel Johnson was virtually unknown in Spain: his reputation in England rested on his journalism and his famous Dictionary of the English Language, neither of which was of obvious interest to foreigners. Rasselas was first published in England in 1759, and is a slim volume, a simple fable about a prince and a princess who travel the world with two companions, seeking to discover the best way to live. They experience a number of adventures and eventually return to their country without having answered their question: all ways of life prove to have their drawbacks, and there appears to be no ideal solution.[6]

---

[5] For a discussion of Hickey and Hore, see Elizabeth Franklin Lewis, 'Hispano-Irish Women Writers of Spain's Late Enlightenment Period', in *Routledge Companion to Iberian Studies*, ed. by Javier Muñoz-Basols, Laura Lonsdale and Manuel Delgado (London: Routledge, 2017); and the same author's chapter 'Situating Feminine Happiness: María Gertrudis Hore's Ascent to the Sacred Parnassus', in her *Women Writers in the Spanish Enlightenment*, pp. 61–96. Also Frédérique Morand's 'Enlightenment Experience in the Life and Poetry of Sor María Gertrudis de la Cruz Hore' (pp. 33–50), and María A Salgado's 'Margarita Hickey's Guide to the Traps of Love' (pp. 62–83), both in *Eve's Enlightenment*, ed. by Jaffe and Franklin Lewis.

[6] See Jessica Richard (ed.), *The History of Rasselas, Prince of Abissinia* (Peterborough, Ontario: Broadview Editions, 2008); Marlene R Hansen, 'Sex, Love, Marriage, and Friendship: A Feminist Reading of the Quest for Happiness in *Rasselas*', *English Studies* 66 (1985), 513–25.

The book fell into a genre that was to prove increasingly popular in eighteenth-century Europe: a voyage by outsiders used as a pretext to comment on and criticise the manners of contemporary society. French writers were particularly keen on this approach: Montesquieu's *Persian Letters*[7] had a pair of oriental travellers writing home to express their shocked and bewildered observations of Paris, and Françoise de Graffigny's *Letters from a Peruvian Lady*[8] did the same from a feminine perspective, but also took the opportunity to condemn the Spanish enslavement of native peoples in South America. The most famous example is Voltaire's *Candide*,[9] where the naïve young couple suffers all sorts of trials during the course of their discovery that this is not 'the best of all possible worlds'.

Rasselas is full of themes that were important to writers of the European Enlightenment: the search for happiness, the education of a prince, good government, the distinction between useful and speculative knowledge, and virtue as the exercise of reason. But there are a number of reasons why it may have particularly appealed to Inés Joyes. The prince Rasselas is accompanied on his quest by his sister, the princess Nekayah, who shares his adventures and comments in the philosophical discussions on an equal basis. Her attendant Pekuah is also shown to be an intelligent and thoughtful woman, who extracts herself from a dangerous situation through her prudent behaviour.

In one adventure, Pekuah is captured by an Arab chieftain, who hopes to exchange her for a ransom, and in the meantime imprisons her in his harem among his women. The Muslim enslavement of women was, as we have seen, a theme that had been used by both Feijoo and Amar, and Johnson describes Pekuah's boredom and frustration among a group who, being completely deprived of education, pass their time aimlessly, with nothing to do but needlework, quarrelling frequently over the most trivial matters. It was impossible to converse with them, for they had nothing to talk about: they could not read and had spent their entire lives in the same place. Pekuah observes that though these women might be beautiful, they could not provide satisfactory companionship for the Arab chief, who was an intelligent man, and what passed between them under the name of love was 'only a careless distribution of superfluous time'.[10] This scene must have struck a chord with Joyes, whose

---

[7]   Charles-Louis de Secondat, Baron de Montesquieu, *Lettres Persanes* (Paris: Pierre Marteau, 1754); Montesquieu, *Persian Letters*, trans. by Margaret Mauldon (Oxford: Oxford World's Classics, Oxford University Press, 2008).

[8]   Françoise de Graffigny, *Lettres d'une Péruvienne* (Paris: A. Peine, 1747); Françoise de Graffigny, *Letters of a Peruvian Woman*, trans. by Jonathan Mallinson (Oxford: Oxford World's Classics, Oxford University Press, 2009).

[9]   Voltaire, *Candide, ou l'Optimisme* (Paris: Marc-Michel Rey et al., 1759); *Candide, or Optimism*, trans. by Theo Cuffe, ed. by Michael Wood (London: Penguin Classics, 2005).

[10]   Samuel Johnson, *The History of Rasselas, Prince of Abissinia* (London: Penguin Classics, 2007), p. 89.

Apology begs contemporary Spanish women to give up their obsession with external appearances, and to be aware that the flattery bestowed on them by men is insincere and manipulative.

The discussion of marriage and family life in *Rasselas* is equally disillusioned. Nekayah observes that a family is like a little kingdom 'torn with factions and exposed to revolutions', and that once they are past the age of infancy, children become rivals to their parents. When Rasselas protests that this is too harsh a view, Nekayah insists that 'domestic discord [...] is not inevitably and fatally necessary; but yet is not easily avoided'. She paints a picture of families dominated by servants or tormented by rich relations, with imperious husbands and perverse wives, and goes so far as to say that she is not sure 'whether marriage be more than one of the innumerable modes of human misery'. Rasselas has to admit that nothing but disappointment and repentance can be expected from 'a choice made in the immaturity of youth, in the ardour of desire, without judgment, without foresight, without enquiry after conformity of opinions, similarity of manners, rectitude of judgment, or purity of sentiment'.[11] These are observations that were reflected in the *Apology*.

At one point Nekayah makes a comment that would have been particularly shocking in eighteenth-century Europe, when she observes that it is not her responsibility to populate the world. This highly individualistic statement would have been almost incomprehensible at a time when women's principal function was believed to be giving birth to children. For Nekayah, even as a princess, to consider this as a matter of choice, and moreover one she may decline, was remarkable. Again we shall see Joyes express in the *Apology* her own opinions about the dangers of childbirth and the dignity of the single life.

As a translator, Joyes was faithful to Johnson's text, rendering the English accurately into fluent Spanish. She did not imitate many of her contemporaries by adding comments of her own and passing them off as part of the original work. The only sections she omitted or changed were those that criticised celibacy and the monastic life, a wise precaution in view of the need to obtain the approval of the Spanish censor.

The book that contains the *Historia de Rasselas* and the *Apologia de las Mugeres* was published in 1798 by one of the leading publishing houses in Madrid, Antonio de Sancha. Notice of its publication was given in two of the newspapers, but it was not reviewed or summarized and no information was given about its author. Few references to it can be found in later correspondence or publications. It was, however, mentioned in the *Memoirs* of Manuel de Godoy, who under King Carlos IV was for many years the most powerful man in Spain: in a eulogy of Spanish women writers he includes the *Apology*, describing it as

---

[11] Johnson, *Rasselas*, pp. 59–66.

'written with talent and skill'.[12]

Inés Joyes y Blake died in Malaga in March 1808 at the age of seventy-seven. Her book was not reprinted until 2009, and the *Apology for Women* has not been translated into English until now.

The Apology for Women

The *Apology* begins with a brief dedication to the Duchess of Osuna, a highly appropriate choice given that the Duchess was one of the most distinguished ladies in the kingdom, a member of a leading aristocratic family, the hostess of an important salon and, as we have seen, the first president of the Ladies' Section of the Madrid Economic Society of Friends of the Nation. She was, moreover, on friendly terms with Joyes' son Joaquín Blake.

The foreword consists of standard declarations of modesty commonly used by authors, and particularly women, to excuse any faults or weaknesses in their work, and justifying it on the basis that it was not originally intended for publication, but as advice for her daughters. However, the statement that it arose out of a family discussion may be doubted, unless it was drafted many years earlier, since by 1798 two of Joyes' daughters were dead, a third married and only one still living with her mother.

Joyes goes straight into her theme, which is the way women suffer from the injustice and deceitfulness of men. She echoes Josefa Amar in observing that men express praise and contempt for women in equal measure, but is more outspoken than her predecessor in pointing to the double standard that prevails in relations between the sexes. Women's reputation is at the mercy of men who will despise them if they submit to their seductions and condemn them if they do not. However, this is not just an anti-male polemic, for she believes that women share responsibility for their unfortunate situation, and can improve it by their own efforts.

Like Feijoo and Amar, Joyes has to deal with the biblical story of Eve, so often used as evidence that women were ordained by God to be inferior to men. She chooses to interpret the story as indicating a temporary hierarchical authority, like the ranks in the military, where an officer may be in command over men who are his social superiors. (This was exactly the position of her son Joaquín, who had risen to high rank in the army.)

Joyes' vocabulary is forthright and challenging. Men want women to serve them like slaves, yet they are normally the ones found guilty of vicious and immoral behaviour. If a woman falls into degradation, her troubles can usually be found to originate in 'the deceitful behaviour of some wicked man'. But she does not let women off the hook: they have laid themselves open to attack by

---

[12]   Manuel Godoy, *Memorias Críticas y Apologéticas* (Madrid: Imprenta de I. Sancha, 1836), p. 248.

deserting their true destiny, which is that of a wife and mother and manager of a household. Instead of developing the skills and attitudes necessary to succeed in this occupation, they have become obsessed with external appearance.

Like her predecessors, Joyes is convinced this is the fault of women's inadequate education. Their intellectual training is superficial — 'comedies in their hundreds, a few novels and the odd saint's life' — and they quickly learn to despise practical tasks. The social pressure to compete with other women through luxury of dress and appearance, and to spend their lives in an endless round of balls, plays and visits, is inescapable. But once youth and beauty have gone, women find themselves abandoned by their admirers and lacking the inner resources to cope with their situation. They cannot turn to other women for friendship, since they have become accustomed to seeing each other as competitors for the attentions of men. Even women who try to be virtuous suffer, for men take pleasure in blackening their reputation by spreading malicious gossip.

Many visitors to Spain during the latter part of the eighteenth century had expressed surprise at the prevalence in the upper of echelons of society of the *cortejo* or gallant; a man who accompanied a married woman in public as her escort, and was assumed to be her lover. The *cortejo* was tolerated by the lady's husband, and indeed it seemed that every newly-married woman needed to have one.[13] Joyes spends a considerable part of the *Apology* warning women against gallantry. At the end of his *Defence of Women*, Feijoo had expressed understanding for women with unkind husbands who succumbed to the blandishments of a lover, but Joyes insists that such men will turn out to be dominant and manipulative, and eventually abandon them.

However, she takes an equally jaundiced view of marriage, and speaks up in support of women who, through choice or necessity, remain single. Here again the double standard prevails: men may remain unmarried as long as they like without loss of status, whereas women are condemned for not accepting an offer from even the most unattractive man. It is interesting to note that one of Joyes' sons remained single until he was fifty-three, and her daughter Inés did not marry until she was twenty-eight. Her mother may have had the opportunity to observe directly how differently the two were treated by society.

It would be wrong to fall into the trap of suggesting that everything contained in the *Apology* was based on the author's personal experience, as if women were incapable of learning from reading or observation. We may, however, observe that Joyes speaks at length and with considerable vehemence about the torment of women living with bad husbands, which she describes as an 'earthly hell'. A man may be charming while he is her suitor, but 'once the fatal knot is tied, she

---

[13] See volume introduction for an explanation of this concept. See also Carmen Martín Gaite's *Usos amorosos del dieciocho en España*.

finds she has a tyrant who wishes to control her very thoughts'.

Men and women locked into ill-assorted marriages are unlikely to make good parents, which is a problem since they are destined to be the teachers of their children. However, Joyes declines to go into detail about the bringing up of children, with the exception of the subject of breast-feeding, where she is very forthright. During the eighteenth century, acres of print had been filled on this subject; the practice of high-status women across Europe was to hand their newborn babies over to wet nurses, who brought them up at some distance from the family home. Writers both male and female objected strongly to this: sometimes for practical reasons — Josefa Amar pointed out that half of the children who died before the age of three had been put out to wet-nurses.[14] But there were more insidious arguments, related to the desire among writers such as Jean-Jacques Rousseau to restrict women to a life of domesticity; they painted a horrifying picture of negligent mothers passing a life of pleasure at theatres, balls and gaming-tables, while their children suffered at the hands of lazy nurses.

By the time of the *Apology*, the social pressure on women to suckle their own children was intense. Even Josefa Amar devoted several pages to encouraging the practice, but she took up just as much space recommending that care should be taken in the choice of nurse, if for some reason it was not possible. Joyes, by contrast, is positively angry as she exposes the cruelty of husbands who enforce the practice on their wives regardless of any ill effects it might cause, and wryly observes that the many treatises on the value of breast-feeding have all been written by men. In a dramatic twist, she contrasts the pressure on women to conform in this way with social indifference towards men who infect their wives with a venereal disease.

The *Apology* ends with a plea for an improved education for women. She says that she has personally heard gentlemen pronounce that it is enough for a woman to be able to cook and sew, and women who wish to develop their intellect are mocked as *bachilleras*, a term that expressed the same derision as the French *précieuse* or the English 'bluestocking'. Perhaps it was her fury at this condescending approach that motivated the widowed Inés Joyes, living quietly in a provincial town and nearing the end of her life, to undertake the translation of an English work of Enlightenment philosophy, and to attach to it her own personal defence of women.

---

[14] Josefa Amar, *Discurso sobre la Educación de las Mugeres*, p. 27.

Inés Joyes y Blake

Apology for Women

Foreword

It is well-known that the dispute over the superiority or pre-eminence of the sexes is one of the most common topics of conversation in society today. On one occasion when I had been discussing this in a particularly heated way, I wanted afterwards to set down my principal arguments for my daughters, so I wrote them this letter that today I make public; but from the defence of women I passed on to commenting on some of their defects and giving advice on the upbringing of children. In a word, I wandered almost without realizing it far from the limits of my original theme, as so often happens in family conversations.

I beg my readers to overlook this imperfect and careless style, and to concentrate on my true intention: and I recommend they abstain from cruel or irrelevant criticism. I am confident in any case that there will be no shortage of women to protect me and rush to my defence, and if many of them conspire to shake off the yoke of that belief which unjustly favours men, then we shall soon see how little the pedantry of those who call themselves scholars can do against the sane, natural reason and simple arguments of women.

My Dear Daughters,

I cannot suffer patiently the ridiculous part that women usually play in the world, worshipped as goddesses one minute and despised the next, even by men who have the reputation of being wise. We are loved, loathed, praised, condemned, celebrated, respected, despised and censured. The most grim philosopher takes pleasure in the sight of a beautiful woman, but the most contemptible fop, having put all his efforts into attracting the attention of a group of ladies, makes his exit and proceeds to ridicule them all one by one: he swears that one of them is dying for him and another is furious because he has not courted her with obsequious flattery; he calls the one who is grave a prudish hypocrite and the one who is gay a coquette, the rational one is a bluestocking[1]

---

[1] Joyes uses the word *bachillera*. 'Bachiller' in the masculine was the entry grade for admission to university, from which women were excluded. The feminine form was used mockingly, to indicate a woman who thought she was learned and talked pedantically about subjects she did not truly understand, but merely made herself look foolish.

and she who, like him, talks of nothing but frivolity, is called ignorant, even though his ignorance is the greatest of all.

But what am I saying? I complain of the injustice of men towards our sex, since I have any number of reasons to do so; but it is equally certain that we, through not knowing how to make use of the advantages given us by nature, have found ourselves in a most unhappy state. Let us consider this a little, and we shall see if I am right.

When God created Eve and gave her as a companion to Adam, man was in a state of grace; through doing him this favour, God carried out his will. He allowed Eve to be seduced by the cunning of the serpent, and Adam surrendered to the woman's entreaties: they both sinned, and both received their punishment. I will leave the experts to argue about which of them committed the greater sin; the truth is that both were sentenced to suffer death, both were ejected from Paradise, both remained subject to the miseries of the state of sin; and God gave each of them a particular sentence: the man was to earn his bread with the sweat of his brow, and the woman to bring forth children in pain.

The fact that she had to be subject to the man (a thing thrown in our faces by those who claim to be wise) was a precise consequence of the imperfect state to which human nature was reduced. During the period of grace, reason prevailed without the slightest resistance, but sin was followed by the disorder of the passions which created a variety of opinions, and with this variety and contradiction, since no one was in charge, everything fell into dissension, discord and disorder. Since the man was stronger and had to earn the bread, he was given responsibility for the protection and defence of the other sex, and from this protection resulted a sort of authority.

But this is not an argument for inequality, any more than we recognise a personal or essential inequality in the various authorities in the world which we accept. In the militia an ordinary man has command over many others who by birth and circumstances are by far his superiors. In the church and the law, the same thing happens in all classes, and in these cases the superior should be careful not to say he is better than some other man because his role is more important.

God assigned to each sex its destiny, and gave them accordingly the appropriate properties. To man He gave strength, to woman perspicacity, and since she was by nature milder and more flexible, He granted her the second vote in all discussions. Despite this, we do not find anywhere that women are prohibited from exerting sovereign command, since we see and have seen throughout the ages kingdoms governed by women with great skill and success. The idea that greater talent is linked to greater strength is one which would make all sensible people laugh, though we are not short of fools who defend it so as to maintain their pretended superiority. But if we compare a brawny but ignorant farmhand with an educated and studious man of delicate constitution, we shall see that if they have a fight the labourer will win, but if they have a discussion it will be the scholar.

People constantly point out the ignorance of women, their caprice, love of trifles, curiosity, vanity, falsity, etc.; despite the fact that we all know many books published in our time that have been banned for following the doctrine of the Koran and denying to women the equal possession of a rational soul.[2] There is absolutely no doubt that the way men speak of our sex often includes such statements, for many men treat us either as creatures destined solely for their recreation and to serve them like slaves, or as deceitful monsters that exist in the world for the ruin and punishment of the human race. What profound injustice! What outright delirium!

Men may say what they like, but souls are equal, and if through the greater delicacy of their organs, women are more apt for a particular type of activity, and men through their greater strength for another, nothing makes this a proof against us, for the bee is no less honoured among flying creatures than the vulture, even though the latter is incomparably larger and stronger; nor is the sheep less than the lion, for whilst one does nothing but destroy and devour, the other meekly provides mankind with food and clothing. The bee governs its colony and fills it with delicate honey and useful wax, whilst the vulture wanders over sites of cruelty in search of its food.

Let us be clear: the vices and defects commonly identified in women have already been mentioned, but it is extremely rare to see a woman fall into the enormous faults commonly found among men, and which are too numerous to count. For this reason, when theft, murder, drunkenness, gambling which ruins families, dissolute behaviour, insolence, law-breaking and other such crimes are occasionally found in women, they inspire great horror for being so alien to their nature. They may tell me that illicit love affairs are also common among women, and I would not deny it; but it would be difficult to find a depraved woman sunk into a life of vice who, if she looked back to the beginning of her disgrace, would not find it in the deceitful blandishments of some wicked man. Once she has lost all respect, the misery in which she finds herself drags her, most often with repugnance, into this wretched way of life.

It may be argued against me that women do not of necessity have to succumb to this widespread fashion for the *cortejo*. And I with all honesty would respond with sincere grief that this is true; and for this reason I said at the beginning that we ourselves, not knowing how to make use of the advantages bestowed on us by nature, have created for ourselves this unhappy state. Yes, it is our own fault. We were created for the noble destiny of being respectable mothers

---

[2] Joyes shared with Feijoo and Amar the erroneous belief that Muhammad denied that women had souls and excluded them from paradise.

of families and wives who with an attitude of cheerfulness help their husbands
to bear the heavy burden of their life's cares; and those whose character and
circumstances distance them from the yoke of matrimony are destined to
maintain the good order of the homes of their fathers, brothers and relatives —
for it would be difficult to find a well-governed and organised house that is not
controlled by a woman.

Why then do we found our glory on being praised by men for our external
attractions, and allow this ill-founded ambition to cause such constant rivalry
between us, so that anyone who wants to be polite, when praising a woman
in the presence of others, is careful to say 'saving all those present'? For this
reason, men often begin to flatter one group of women by mocking and
ridiculing another, taking advantage of this shameful weakness in order to
deceive them. And our frailty extends so far that, however much men may say
that women adorn themselves only to look good in their eyes, it is absolutely
sure that a woman takes more care over her appearance when she has to appear
in a group of ladies than when she is going to be with any number of men; for
the propensity of most women to satirise each other makes them fear its sting,
and make efforts to avoid it. What a truly arduous undertaking this is, and the
cause of an infinite number of ills!

To this desire to stand out from the crowd we owe the excessive luxury
which consumes even the largest fortunes. An infinite, yes, infinite number of
women know and inwardly lament the consequences, and wish to reduce their
expenditure, but — what a shameful reflection on our nature! (here I speak of
men as much as of women) — we fear to be thought ridiculous more than to
be thought vicious, and thus we are carried away by the social whirl and spend
the best part of our lives doing what our reason condemns and we do not wish
to do, and failing to do what we approve and desire; and in order not to appear
inconsistent, we defend to the world what we condemn in ourselves. Let anyone
put their hand on their heart, and unless they are the kind of person who never
thinks at all, they will admit that I am speaking the honest truth.

Let us consider the way in which women are generally brought up. They
have hardly begun to walk and talk before people are already speaking to them
about beauty and grace, and even to many of them, as a joke, of a *cortejo*; so
some become familiar with this doctrine even before they hear of Christianity.
They learn to read and write, but not all of them, for there are in Spain fathers
who are so stupid, despite being respected as gentlemen, that they resist their
daughters being taught to write on the pretext that this will enable them to send
love letters. What folly! As if, in the case that they were inclined to such caprice,
they could not find secretaries! We concede that most of them learn to read
in a mumble and scrawl pothooks, but as for good writing, spelling, style and
choice of books ... of these there is no question. Comedies in their hundreds,

a few novels and the odd saint's life — that is the height of their erudition. They learn in their childhood the kind of women's work which appears acceptable in every class and time, but usually reluctantly and regarding it as an imposition, and they are accustomed from an early age to conversations in which women's domestic tasks are treated as things worthy only for those of humble spirit or limited horizons. At the same time they hear of one woman admired for her good taste in dress, of another who was the belle of the ball, and of the hearts that were lost to another whenever she passed.

If a stranger arrives in a town, the first question people ask is if she is pretty or fashionable, but never if she is intelligent or sensible. Most people will admire her keen wit, her charm, her mocking humour which, if examined more carefully, may turn out to be pedantry, trivial gossip, haughtiness and brazen effrontery. If on the other hand she is a little shy or timid, they brand her a fool. It is good to display a degree of confidence in the way you speak and present yourself, but this is acquired over time through mixing with people, and I will never regard a young girl as stupid if she is embarrassed on meeting people she is not used to dealing with.

I was pleased to read in Feijoo that he never held a good opinion of a boy who showed too much boldness.[3] And if this is said of boys, what shall we say of our own sex, whose most attractive characteristic is modesty? Who is not enchanted by a face that is easily covered with the blush of shame? Let us clearly recognise that self-love is innate in us as it is in men, and however much we are told that we should follow virtue because it is a worthy thing, and should always do good without consideration for praise or blame, nevertheless the desire for the former and distaste for the latter are embedded in the human heart. What is more, if the day were to come that these two motives were uprooted and replaced by a complete indifference to the opinion of the world, we would be overwhelmed by a torrent of evils, to the extent that those few people — if there are any — who love virtue only for itself, would have to flee to the mountains. I say 'if there are any' because in reality I am far from regarding as a vice a noble imitation and a just and moderate desire to conserve our honour.

Once we accept this principle, I say that people are naturally inclined to do what they hear praised from their tender years, and to avoid what they hear blamed and mocked. And thus, as I have said, the impressions women usually receive from the beginning are contrary to their own happiness and that of their families, and to the well-being of society as a whole. This is obvious, for during their whole existence they are, as girls, the playthings of their parents and families, and once they are of age, idols vainly worshipped and blinded by the flattering tributes they receive. What determination to stand out from the others! What envy, what fury when they see another woman better dressed or

---

[3]   *Defence of Women*, ch. V, para. 33.

coiffed than they are, or could ever be! What outrage when an admirer leaves them for another! What lamentations when the hairdresser does not arrive on time, or has not done their hair to the height of perfection they require! And what misery if in the middle of all this comes one of those malevolent attacks of the pox to disfigure the face they adore with a greater degree of truth than they so often hear from those fops!

Finally, the reign of beauty is in any case of short duration; its bloom fades imperceptibly, and then what desperation there is to preserve it, what attempts to cover up the ravages of time! But despite all these efforts, the day comes when, whatever they do, the world disappoints them. No longer do they see in people's faces that pleasure evoked by the sight of their beauty; no more do they hear admired as charming that trifling talk which, set off by their beauty, once appeared to be sharpness and wit: in short, the enamel has worn off and nothing is left but the value of the metal. How wretched if it is of base quality! Now nobody comes to court them, their husbands are bored with them, their children do not respect them, they are the object of mockery, and divide the rest of their days between gossip and fits of the vapours.

It is fortunate if this disappointment is followed by a desire to be virtuous; but the pity is that if a woman has not accustomed herself in time to turn her thoughts in a useful direction, it is difficult in such circumstances for them to be capable of giving her serenity and inner peace. Friendship is denied to them, since they have never appreciated this gift from heaven. No help can be expected from men, who abandon them, nor from their own sex, since the young ones take revenge for their envious criticism and laugh at their grey hair; their contemporaries regard them as competitors, and friendship is not a fruit that buds, blossoms and ripens in a few short days.

How different is the lot of a woman accustomed to know her own mind and use her reason, who does not give superficial appearances greater value than they deserve. Even in the prime of life, when everything conspires to make her conceited, she bears in mind that her beauty will be of short duration, and is aware that if those men who pay her court most assiduously observe that she takes pleasure in their flattery, they will boast of a relationship that does not exist or, if rejected, will avenge themselves with the most bitter satires. She knows how to do justice to the merits of other women, and is a true friend to her friends, overlooking their faults — for who is without fault?

It is a hard thing for our sex to live without the only satisfaction that exists in the world — that of sincere friendship. This is undoubtedly rare, but it does exist, and I insist that women are naturally more prone to it than men. People may say that history contains stories of heroic friendship between men and none of true friendship between women, but this is meaningless. Strong friendships between men are rare, and this is why the few examples are so famous. On the other hand, since men are more exposed to the theatre of the world, many of their actions become public knowledge, whereas equally heroic actions by women do not interest the public, so they remain buried in oblivion.

No one will deny that true friendship cannot exist unless it is founded on virtue; and it is certain that in general greater care is taken to inspire in women a love of virtue and a horror of vice. Moreover, women's more placid, flexible and benevolent temperament naturally inclines them to friendship. Unfortunately these fine dispositions can be corrupted early on by the bad example or deliberate efforts of men to win them over; thus what was once the seed of happiness turns into bitter suffering. There are many girls who experience in their early years a tenderness that gives them great satisfaction. But this lasts only until they mount the world's stage, where there is no shortage of frivolous men who take pleasure in disturbing those innocent hearts, running back and forth with gossip and praising the woman before them at the expense of the one who is absent. And since nothing wounds a sincere heart more deeply than falsehood, they persuade them that a woman they regarded as their true friend has betrayed them, and this is enough to make them suspicious of all others; or if there are still some they call their friends, this is only out of social convention, so there will be no shortage of competitive situations where they may amuse themselves by outshining them.

But those women who were brought up to be truly thoughtful are ashamed of such envy, and pride themselves on recognizing other women's true deserts. If in this they mean that vanity plays a role, it is because they display their discernment. But since they truly love their own sex, they praise all those who possess admirable qualities; they know what they can contribute to the reform of manners; they wish all women to know their true worth and not to limit their ambition to something as base as being flattered by men. For men generally believe this is what we want and progressively lose the respect they had for us when we treated them more dismissively.

I am not one of those who likes to keep going on about the good old days, since I know the world has always contained both good and evil, but it is generally believed that less than fifty years ago there was not so much uncouth language, and bands of young men did not toss about the names of even the most distinguished ladies, inventing stories that never happened and boasting of conquests they never achieved. Seeing this, more than a few people wonder whether women will have to go back to living their lives under lock and key.

I am far from sharing this opinion, since we can never regard it as a good thing if evil is avoided purely through fear or lack of opportunity. No, my daughters, my ideas are nobler than this: our good judgement and self-respect must be the only chains that bind us; but let us be clear and guard ourselves from that devil who, under names such as gallant and *cortejo*, has been introduced into society and become a plague that ruins the peace of many families.

I believe the majority of those who follow this pernicious way of life do so only because they are carried along by that vain desire to stand out from the crowd that is encouraged by their frivolous education; but there is nevertheless no doubt that once they have engaged in this kind of distraction they are embarrassed to retrace their steps, and lose all taste for the simpler, more innocent and longer-lasting pleasures that may be found in the heart of a well-ordered family, and the rational and friendly behaviour of a society of sensible and agreeable people. And in return for this, what do they get except to be the object of a feigned or inconstant adoration, and the butt of public gossip?

Men who take on the role of *cortejo* hide behind their apparent submission more malice than those who listen to their words ever suspect. They come in full of humility and then start to act like masters, even daring to show off their wicked ways to the household servants! It is quite a thing for fashion to tyrannise women so strongly that, while rejecting any suggestion that a husband may wish to control them or find fault with their behaviour, they permit a *cortejo* to dare to lord it over them, often even in their private family affairs, and if he shows displeasure, they cannot do enough to please him.

It is an intolerable thing to suffer from a husband who is jealous, insolent, vicious, etc., but at least there is the hope that with patience and persistence he may mend his ways; and above all it is a virtue to put up with him, and this acts as a good example. But to tolerate a tyrant who, solely because he knows the weakness of your heart (and despises you for it) dares to speak with a tone of authority and wishes to make himself feared, is base and vile and ... what more can I say? Believe me, if a woman who follows the fashion for a *cortejo* is married, she is undoubtedly seeking satisfaction, but she will achieve this only for that short time that she is dazzled by vanity, for soon either she will tire of him or he of her, and they will end up falling out. It is bound to turn out exactly like this if both of them have frivolous minds; if Madame has a quick understanding she will soon be irritated by an Adonis who values her only for her pretty face; and similarly if he has any sense at all he is bound to tire quickly of repeating sweet nothings. And what do they do then? If they give up their *cortejos*, people will say they have lost their power to attract, and if they go from one to another, they will forever be branded as fickle.

If an unmarried woman gives herself up to this madness she deceives herself completely, for if her idea is to find a husband, she should know that the most obsequious man will be the last who really thinks of marrying her, and however much he convinces her, he doesn't really mean it, for although he converses with her everywhere and follows her like a shadow, as soon as he hears people start to hint at marriage, he slyly slips away; and will even assure at great length anyone who inquires that marriage had never occurred to him, and it is not his fault if people gossip without reason, or that the young lady is of the same mind. Believe me, this is the kind of man who is bored by a woman who gives in easily.

A young lady should be pleasant to everyone in general but when one-to-one must be always elusive, always suspicious, always sceptical. You should be aware that among men it is generally believed that you cannot converse with young ladies without making love to them, talking about fashion and gossiping about other women; and that if their declarations of love are welcomed and the conversation is not cut short, they are entitled to believe they have captured your heart; and it is a rare man who does not go off to tell his friends about the conquest he has made. Finally, you may be sure that those women who have the largest number of *cortejos* marry either late or never, or make bad marriages.

But why should it be necessary for them to get married? Why do we have to regard as losers in life those women who arrive at the age when they are vulgarly called 'Auntie'? An infinite number of men (including many who are wealthy enough to support a family) spend many years as bachelors, saying they do not wish to lose their liberty and are afraid to end up with a wife who is impertinent, jealous, foolish, etc. There are indeed women like this, but there are also large numbers who would be capable of making a sensible man happy. But among these one looks ugly to them, another does not have sufficient fortune, this one knows too much, that one is ignorant, one is too young and the other is not young enough. God help the poor women and the perfections required of them! At the same time a man who is old, ugly and stupid, as long as he has a fortune, is still regarded as having the right to claim even the most perfect of women. And the worst is that there are women who would condemn a poor girl who hesitates and displays reluctance to accept the party offered to her, without realizing that it is a great effort for a woman of discernment to take as her companion and the head of her household a man whom she cannot admire — I do not say love, which is a passion of short duration, but even the sort of respect that can be turned into a firm friendship.

Men have the advantage that custom gives them the right to propose, and he who proposes can choose where to direct his suit. It falls to us only to accept or reject. And even if we receive numerous proposals, but not from one who pleases and suits us, would it not be much better to remain single than to expose ourselves to losing our liberty to someone who repels us? Would this not mean tricking the suitor, and risking your happiness in this life and the next? Is there any greater torment than living permanently with someone who disgusts you? And if in addition this natural aversion to submit to the marital yoke we find that he is an imperious, insolent, jealous, spendthrift, vicious gambler, is this not this earthly hell as bad as the eternal one?

It will be said that men are also prone to encounter misfortune, and this is very true, but if they proceed with prudence and caution they will not run much risk. What is more, no one can deny that a woman with a bad husband suffers much more than a man with the worst of wives, since he is not obliged to stay at home except when he chooses, except on particular occasions. He comes and goes, goes off on his travels, turns a deaf ear to her voice (if she is the kind who raises it) and has a thousand ways to bend her to his will if he chooses. But the unfortunate wife, what recourse does she have? However prudent she is, she suffers and endures much more. She sees herself flattered, caressed and pursued by a man who is her slave while he is her suitor, but once the fatal knot is tied, she finds she has a tyrant who wishes to control her very thoughts.

Even sensible people often say that men have a choice of destinies but women have only two, for they must become either wives or nuns. What a pernicious maxim, an erroneous concept which is the cause of an infinite number of unhappy and ill-assorted marriages, so often regretted! Throughout our lives we need prudence, the queen of all the virtues, but nowhere is this more important than in our choice of estate. Prudence tells us that before making our decision we must pray to God, consult our parents or those who stand in their place, our priest, and our own mind and temperament. It is an established rule that it is not up to us to seek out marriage, but if we are called by a true vocation to the state of a nun, this must be examined long before it is entered into. But let us be sure that God does not call us to the state of matrimony without making available a marriage that is suited to our circumstances. I am firmly persuaded that one of the main causes of the corruption of manners, a miserable consequence of the poor education girls generally receive, is the casual way in which many of them enter into this important relationship. Greed, ambition and vanity are the only motivations in marriages arranged by parents for their children, or in those which the latter, who may have reached the age of reflection but are imbued with the reigning principles of the age, seek for themselves; whilst others are driven by no more than a blind impulse of love.

What kind of upbringing can a couple give their children if they themselves are constantly besieged by hunger and lack of basic necessities, if they once lived in homes that may not have been grand but at least had sufficient to live according to their estate, but now spend their time worrying about how they will earn their daily bread, and see the arrival of each baby as another source of anxiety? It would be a surprise if they did not tire of each other, but even if this does not happen, they cannot retain that serenity of mind which is needed to form the hearts of their children, a care which falls mainly to the parents, and must begin from the cradle.

I am not suggesting that the parents should be the only teachers, for although many people say and write that they should, in practice it is virtually impossible. There are teachers for the alphabet and others for the things they need to learn in their early years, depending on their circumstances or their destiny. (Although in fact this is not available in many towns in Spain, owing mainly to the limited respect shown to schoolteachers, which is the reason that people who are well-suited do not commit themselves to this useful and respectable occupation). But to study the temperament of the children, to accustom them to restraint at an early age, to give them the idea of virtue, truth, compassion, charity, generosity — in a word, of love of good and horror of evil — this, I repeat, can be done by the parents without great effort if they do it together.

It is a shame that the idea of good education is generally mistaken, and people often confuse what is essential with what is incidental. Many people think a man is poorly educated if he has not learned to bow like a Frenchman, dance gracefully, be at ease in company, speak several languages and converse elegantly, even if he has many excellent qualities, a variety of useful knowledge, an honest and generous heart and a devotion to religion. Perhaps his parents may not have disapproved of such accomplishments but did not have sufficient fortune to allow him to learn them; but in return they gave him a wealth of solid virtues which made him a useful citizen, able to take his place in the company of all kinds of sensible people, however elegant, and making up for his lack of other studies by a solid judgement that allows the mildness of his conduct to make up for his mode of address.

But what can we say of those marriages conducted with great ceremony that unite an Adonis obsessed about his appearance with a wife who is equally satisfied with her own? Or two children; or a jealous old man and a coquette; or ... but let us leave it at that. It is more than certain that when children observe discord between their parents (and they notice it much earlier than we imagine), they quickly lose respect and once they have lost it they take less notice of what they are taught or of the statements they hear. On the other hand, couples who resent their way of life to the extent of being uninterested in their own children, will hand them over to the care of others without examining whether the masters and governesses are suitable. As long as they are fashionable and highly-recommended, that is enough. The child will emerge well or badly educated according to whether it is lucky with its teachers.

It is undeniable that men receive their first impressions of women from those to whose care they are entrusted until the age of at least five years old. Anyone who has looked after children has observed that at the age of one, or even before that, they begin to discern things, and if they are scolded for something they are conscious of it, or if they are praised they cheerfully repeat their childish babble. It is easy to conclude from this principle that it is necessary to take advantage of the age of infancy to implant the virtues in these delicate hearts, and that through these efforts, which should be our responsibility, we could achieve an important reform of manners.

Let us teach them to imagine that enclosed in their fragile bodies there is a soul, the image of their Creator, that they are destined to possess for eternity; and just as we try to bring them up healthy and good-looking, let us make even greater efforts to uproot whenever possible the seeds of vice from their minds. Let us do all we can in this direction, let us serve as example and entertainment, and instead of those foolish tales people tell them, let us always tell them true stories, so they will become used to hearing in a pleasant way about the creation of the world and those other interesting passages from sacred history that any properly-brought up person ought to know — instead of the fables of giants, dwarves, witches, spells, etc., with which we stuff their heads. In this way they will have the advantage of learning truths which will make them love virtue and fear God.

This has started to turn into a treatise on education, but enough of them have been written. The trick is to choose the good ones, and not to prefer what is brilliant to what is solid, a stumbling block that has never been so common as at the present time. Let us begin with the spirit of religion: that is, the fundamental maxims of truth, fidelity, docility and application. We should regard it as certain (and I speak from experience) that any maxim impresses itself more on children when it is expressed as a warning about something that is before their eyes, than through two hours of sermonizing. We must be careful not to put dangerous ideas before them even as a joke, for at that tender age they are unable to distinguish and everything they hear makes an impression on them, may it be criticism of priests or nuns, or the rites of devotion, even the unnecessary ones. All these things should be spoken of in their presence with extreme veneration and respect, for they will be all too exposed during the course of their lives to the risk of losing their love of religion. And at a time when it has become fashionable to laugh at the most sacred things, it is essential to work constantly so the spirit of piety may put down deep roots in those tender hearts.

Some of those who write about the raising of children begin by making strenuous efforts to persuade mothers to breast-feed their own babies. They are right, but it is unfair to treat as bad mothers those who do not do so. There are many women whose delicate constitution means they could not withstand such a task, and I have known some who undertook it at the cost of their lives. The worst thing is that some husbands who have read such treatises take this to be the first and only important point, and take pride in seeing their poor wives suffer from an abscess on the breast, loss of appetite and other such evils, without wishing to find an alternative solution. These unfortunate women suffer more from the harshness and lack of compassion of their husbands than from the original problem; and the more intelligent and sensitive they are, the more they are afflicted.

On the other hand, how can you prove that the mother's milk is always better for the child if she suffers from poor health (and many women's health suffers as soon as they marry, through the fault of their husbands)? Here we could cite the fable of the man and the lion walking through the picture gallery.[4] Women are rarely authors, and yet it is fashionable for modern experts to write about the physical education of children, who always condemn the serious shortcomings of women who do not suckle their children; but I have never read one that touches on the inhumanity of men who, having lived a life of unparalleled vice, proceed without scruple to enter into matrimony with a woman as pure as a dove, who within a few weeks starts to display the contamination he has passed on to her and hence to all his descendants. I don't want to go too far with this: I have said enough, and hope you will understand and believe what I am saying. This is certainly more prejudicial to society than a few women (who are always a small number) who for reasons of excessive delicacy decline to suckle their children, for usually they will seek out a wet-nurse who is healthy and of good physique; and I assure you there are many women who cannot suckle but are nevertheless excellent mothers. If I were to respond to all the claims made by modern writers about physical education, it would lengthen this discourse beyond the limits of time and subject that I have set myself. It is better for me to plead for some impartial physician to write about the various illnesses that afflict those women who suckle, and methods to prevent and cure them.

Let us return to my main theme, that children's hearts should be formed early, so as to uproot the seeds of vice and incline them towards virtue. For mothers to know how to do this, it is essential for women to be educated more than, to our shame, is permitted today. I have heard various academic gentlemen in their caps and gowns say to learned audiences of would-be philosophers that it is enough for a woman to know how to sew and run her kitchen, and complain that anything more than this would be inappropriate pedantry.[5] I haven't the patience to listen to such arrant nonsense. Have all the men you hear holding forth on a daily basis about politics, history, etc., studied these subjects at university? By no means: few of them know a word of Latin, and many of them have picked up such knowledge as they have after reaching adulthood, since their parents failed or were unable to give them an education when they were young. But once they have the opportunity to mix with cultured people, they are anxious to be able to join in their conversations, so they acquire good books and apply themselves to reading them, and this and the talk of good companions dissipates the fog of ignorance that obfuscated their minds. They participate in discussions without fearing their statements will be treated as

---

[4]   See Feijoo's different version of the story in chapter IX of his *Defence of Women*. It appears that Joyes was familiar with Feijoo's work, but was quoting from memory.

[5]   Joyes uses the term *bachillería*. See note 1 to the *Apology*.

nonsense, whilst always taking care not to express an opinion about something they do not understand.

So if with only that natural talent God has given them, men can be admitted to any conversation, I would like to know what law exists, and when it was passed or by whom, to say that women should always be reduced to talking about gowns, ribbons, flowers, etc. Why must they converse only about gallantry, gossip and domestic quarrels, show off their skills at cookery, boast about their housekeeping, celebrate their children's talents and the fine arts of dancing, card-playing, the theatre and the *paseo*?[6] If we find in a drawing room six or eight men and a similar number of women and a conversation begins about some rational subject, there may be one woman who is interested in it, but the others either start to yawn or engage each other in talking about the domestic or trivial subjects I have mentioned; and they will not fail to scowl at a woman who joins in with the men, for since they are ignorant, they will be cast in the shade by one who is not.

Men generally prefer women to be ignorant, since this is the only way they can maintain that superiority that they believe is theirs. And it is not surprising they think like this, when an eminent man like the Marques de San Felipe can say in his book on the Hebrew kings, when talking of Deborah, the Judge of Israel: 'Everything is dangerous in women, including knowing what danger is. The philosopher was not mistaken when he said that knowledge in a woman is an imperfection: the way to dominate them is to bring them up in ignorance.'[7]

I wish I could cry to women from the top of the highest mountain, so they may hear these words of advice: 'Listen, O women', I would say, 'do not belittle yourselves: your souls are equal to those of the sex that wishes to tyrannise over you. Use the intelligence the Creator gave you: it is for you, if you so wish, to bring about the reform of manners, which no one will achieve without you. Respect yourselves and others will respect you; love one another; be aware that your true worth does not consist in a pretty face or in external graces that will last only a short time, and that once men see you faint before their praise, they take your surrender for granted. Show them that you support your own sex, that you can spend hours with each other in various occupations and conversations without missing them; send away the fops and fribbles: none of these will seek you out once they lose hope of tricking you with their false blandishments; but the men of sense, those of true good breeding, will seek your company, respect you and admire you. You will achieve the glory of reforming manners by making virtue truly amiable; love of luxury will decline, since your example

---

[6] The *paseo* was the custom of the upper classes to take an evening walk or carriage drive in order to greet their friends and be seen by the public. It was an opportunity for women to show themselves off in the latest fashions.
[7] Vicente Bacallar y Sanna, Marques de San Felipe, *Monarchia Hebrea* (Genoa: Matteo Garbizza, 1719).

will moderate that of men; your husbands will love and appreciate you; your children will honour you; your family will count themselves blessed to be associated with you; you will live as happily as the world allows and die with the glory of leaving behind you a virtuous posterity.

BIBLIOGRAPHY

Primary Sources

Works by Benito Jerónimo Feijoo

1726–1740 *Theatro critico universal, o Discursos varios en todo género de materias, para desengaño de errores comunes*, 8 vols (various publishers)

1731 *Defensa de las mujeres*, in *Theatro critico universal*, 4th edn (Madrid: Viuda de Francisco del Hierro), I, 16, pp. 331–400

1749 *Justa repulsa de iniquas acusaciones: Carta en que manifestando las imposturas que contra el Theatro critico y su autor dio al publicó el R.P. Fr. Francisco Soto Marne* (Madrid: Antonio Perez de Soto)

1753 *Suplemento de el Theatro critico, o Adiciones y correcciones*, 3rd edn (Madrid: Herederos de Francisco del Hierro)

1742–1760 *Cartas eruditas y curiosas en que por la mayor parte se continua el designo de el Teatro critico universal*, 5 vols (various publishers)

1754 *Ilustración apologética al I y II tomo del Theatro critico universal*, 7th edn (Madrid: Eugenio Bieco)

1852–1853 *Teatro Crítico Universal* (Madrid: Ayguals de Izco)

1863 *Obras Escogidas de Padre Fray Benito Jerónimo Feijoo y Montenegro* (Madrid: M. Rivadaneyra)

1997 *Defensa de la mujer: Discurso XVI del Teatro crítico*, ed. by Victoria Sau (Barcelona: ICARIA)

1998 *Biblioteca Feijoniana: Edición digital de las Obras de Benito Jerónimo Feijoo* (Biblioteca Filosofia en Español, Fundación Gustavo Bueno, Oviedo) <www.filosofia.org/bjf>. Electronic reproductions of eighteenth-century editions of the *Teatro Crítico*, *Cartas eruditas* and miscellaneous works, including the *Adiciones*, the *Justa repulsa* and the *Ilustración apologética*.

2011 *Teatro crítico universal*, ed. by Ángel-Raimundo Fernández González, 9th edn (Madrid: Cátedra). Selected *discursos*.

2014 *Cartas Eruditas y Curiosas*, I, ed. by Inmaculada Urzainqui and Eduardo San José Vázquez (Oviedo: KRK Ediciones)

Translations of works by Benito Jerónimo Feijoo

Translations anonymous unless attributed.

1743 *Defense, ou Eloge des femmes*, trans. by Nicolas-Gabriel Vaquette d'Hermilly (Paris: Pierre Clément). Reprinted in *Sommets de la littérature espagnole*, X (Lausanne: Editions Recontre, 1962)

1743 'Defense, ou Eloge des femmes', in *Mémoires pour l'histoire des sciences et des beaux arts*, II, Article 86, pp. 770–91 (Paris: Chaubert)

1743 'Difesa, od Elogio delle donne', in *Memorie per la storia delle scienze, e buone arti*, I, Article 86, pp. 301–14 (Pesaro: Niccolò Gavelli)

1755 'Apologie des femmes, par Dom Feijoo, benedictin espagnol', trans. by Antoine François Prévost, in *Journal Étranger*, May 1755, pp. 189–226; July 1755, pp. 208–37

1768 *An Essay on Woman, or Physiological and Historical Defence of the Fair Sex; Translated from the Spanish of El Theatro Critico* (London: W. Bingley)

1774 *An Essay on the Learning, Genius, and Abilities, of the Fair-Sex: Proving Them Not Inferior to Man; From a Variety of Examples, Extracted from Ancient and Modern History; Translated from the Spanish of El Theatro Critico* (London: D. Steel, 1774). Reissue of 1768 *Essay on Woman*.

1778 *Three Essays or Discourses on the Following Subjects: A Defence or Vindication of the Women; Church Music; A Comparison between Antient and Modern Music; Translated from the Spanish of Feyjoo; by a Gentleman*, trans. by John Brett (London: T. Becket, 1778). This later appeared in John Brett's *Essays, or Discourses* (1780), with the same pagination and typesetting.

1778 'On the Political Abilities of the Female Sex', in *The Gentleman's and London Magazine, or Monthly Chronologer*, 48, June 1778, pp. 329–30. (Dublin: J. Exshaw). Unattributed extract from pages 24–30 of *Three Essays* (London 1778), trans. by John Brett.

1780 *Essays, or Discourses, Selected from the Works of Feijoo, and Translated from the Spanish, by John Brett, Esq.*, 4 vols (London: H. Payne, C. Dilly, and T. Evans, 1780)

1810–1811 'A Defence of Women', in *The Lady's Magazine, or Entertaining Companion for the Fair Sex*, November 1810 to August 1811, trans. by Elener Irwin (London: G. Robinson)

The Controversy over the Teatro Crítico

ARDANAZ Y CENTELLAS, JAIME, *Tertulia histórica y apologética, o Examen crítico* (Madrid: [n.pub.], 1728)

ARMESTO Y OSSORIO, IGNACIO, *Theatro anti-critico universal sobre las obras del muy R.P. Maestro Feyjoo, de el Padre maestro Sarmiento, y de Don Salvador Mañer* (Madrid: Francisco Martínez Abad, 1737)

BASCO FLANCAS, RICARDO, *Apoyo a la defensa de las mugeres que escrivió el Rmo. P. Fr. Benito Feyjò, y crisis de la contradefensa critica que a favor de los hombres y contra las mugeres diò a luz temerariamente Don Laurencio Manco de Olivares* (Madrid: por la Viuda de Blàs de Villanueva, 1727)

CASCAJALES, TIBURCIO, *Carta que escribe Tiburcio de Cascajales, al señor D. Pedro Mendez Diaz de Arellanano, sobre lo mal, que le ha parecido el papel de la contradefensa crítica a favor de los hombres, que escribio Don Laurencio Manco de Olivares* ([Madrid? n.pub.], 1727)

CASTEJON, AGUSTIN DE. *Dudas y reparas sobre que consulta a Feijoo un escrupuloso* ([Madrid? n.pub.], 1727)

MANCO DE OLIVARES, LAURENCIO, *Contradefensa critica a favor de los hombres, que en justas quexas manifiesta contra la nueva defensa de mujeres que escrivió [...] Fray Benito Gerónimo Feyjoo, en su Teatro crítico* (Madrid: Francisco Sánchez Assensio, 1726)

——*Defensiva respuesta a favor de los hombres, contra los antagonistas, que han escrito favor de las mugeres* (Madrid: Francisco Sànchez Assensio, 1727)

MAÑER, SALVADOR JOSÉ, *Anti-theatro critico sobre el primero y segundo tomo del Teatro Crítico universal* (Madrid: Juan de Moya, 1729)

——*Crisol critico, theologico, politico, physico, y mathematico, en que se quilatan las materias del Theatro critico, que ha pretendido defender la* Demonstracion critica *del M. R. P. Fr. Martin Sarmiento* (Madrid: Bernardo Peralta, 1734)

——*Replica satisfatoria a la Ilustración apologética del Padre Feijoo, Benedictina* (Madrid: Juan de Zúñiga, 1731)

MARICÁ LA TONTA [PSEUD.], *Papel* [...] *en defensa de su sexo y respuesta al escrito por D. Laurencio Manco de Olivares en defensa de los hombres* ([Madrid]: Calle del Olivo Baxa, 1727)

MARTÍNEZ Y SALAFRANCA, MIGUEL, *Desagravios de la muger ofendida contra las injustas quexas de la Contradefensa critica de D. Laurencio Manco de Olivares* (Madrid: Puesto de Pedro Diaz, 1727)

La razón con desinterés fundáda, y la verdad, cortesanamente vestida: Union, y concordia de opiniones, en contra, y favor de las mujeres: Documentos a estas, y advertencias a los hombres para el mondo de tratarlas (Madrid: Francisco de Fábriga, 1727)

SANTARELLI, JUAN ANTONIO, *Estrado critico en defensa de las mujeres contra el Teatro Critico universal de errores comunes* ([Madrid? n.pub.], 1727)

SARMIENTO, MARTÍN, *Demostración critico-apologetica de el Theatro critico universal*, 4th edn (Madrid: Fernandez de Arrojo, 1757)

SOTO Y MARNE, FRANCISCO DE, *Reflexiones critico-apologeticas sobre las obras del RR. P. maestro Fr. Benito Geronymo Feyjoo*, 2 vols (Salamanca: Eugenio Garcia de Honorato i S. Miguel, 1749)

Works by or Concerning Josefa Amar y Borbón and Inés Joyes y Blake

AMAR Y BORBÓN, JOSEFA, *Discurso en defensa del talento de las mujeres, y de su aptitud para el gobierno, y otros cargos en que se emplean los hombres*, in *Memorial literario*, Madrid, 8, 32 (1786), 399–430

——*Discurso en defensa del talento de las mujeres, y de su aptitud para el gobierno, y otros cargos en que se emplean los hombres*, in Negrín Fajardo, *Ilustración y educación*, pp. 162–76

——*Discurso en defensa del talento de las mujeres, y de su aptitud para el gobierno, y otros cargos en que se emplean los hombres*, in Maria Victoria López-Cordón Cortezo, *Condición femenina y razón ilustrada: Josefa Amar y Borbón* (Zaragoza: Prensas Universitarias de Zaragoza, 2005), pp. 265–96

——*Discurso sobre la educación física y moral de las mujeres* (Madrid: Benito Cano, 1790)

——*Discurso sobre la educación física y moral de las mujeres*, ed. by María Victoria López-Cordón Cortezo (Madrid: Ediciones Cátedra, Universitat de València, Instituto de la Mujer, 1994)

AYALA, IGNACIO LÓPEZ DE, *Papel sobre si las señoras deben admitirse como individuos de las Sociedades* (2 September 1786), in Negrín Fajardo, *Ilustración y educación*, pp. 176–83

CABARRÚS, FRANCISCO, *Memoria de D. Francisco Cabarrús sobre la admisión y asistencia de las mujeres en la Sociedad Patriótica*, 18 February 1786, in Negrín Fajardo, *Ilustración y educación*, pp. 150–56

CAMPOMANES, PEDRO RODRIGUEZ, *Memoria presentada a la Sociedad de Madrid por D. Pedro Rodriguez Campomanes sobre la admisión de las señores en ella*, 18 November 1755, in Negrín Fajardo, *Ilustración y educación*, pp. 143–47

IMBILLE, LUIS DE, *Memoria de D. Luis de Imbille sobre la admisión de asociadas*, April 1776, in Negrín Fajardo, *Ilustración y educación*, pp. 147–50

JOHNSON, SAMUEL, *The History of Rasselas, Prince of Abissinia*, ed. by Thomas Keymer (New York: Oxford University Press, 2009)

JOVELLANOS, GASPAR MELCHIOR DE, *Memoria de M. G. de Jovellanos sobre la admisión de señoras en la Sociedad Económica* (27 March 1786), in Negrín Fajardo, *Ilustración y educación*, pp. 156–61

JOYES Y BLAKE, INÉS, *Apología de las mugeres*. Epilogue to *El príncipe de Abisinia: Novela*, translation by Joyes of Samuel Johnson's *Rasselas* (Madrid: Sancha, 1798), pp. 177–204

—— *Apología de las mujeres*, in Mónica Bolufer Peruga, *La vida y la escritura en el siglo XVIII: Inés Joyes: Apología de las mujeres* (València: Universitat de València, 2008), pp. 275–98

—— *Apología de las mujeres*, in *Historia de Rasselas, príncipe de Abisinia*, ed. by Helena Establier Pérez (Salamanca: Ediciones Universidad de Salamanca, 2009). Translation by Joyes of novel by Samuel Johnson, with the *Apologia* as epilogue.

LAMPILLAS, FRANCISCO JAVIER, *Ensayo histórico-apologético de la literatura española contra las opiniones preocupadas de algunos escritores modernos italianos*, 6 vols plus supplement (Zaragoza: Blas Miedes, 1782–1786). Supplement (VII) includes *Respuesta del señor abate Don Xavier Lampillas a los cargos recopilados por el señor abate [Girolamo] Tiraboschi en su carta al señor abate N.N. sobre el Ensayo historico-apologetico de la literatura española, traducida del italiano por Da. Josefa Amar y Borbón.*

MARIN, MANUEL, *Memoria del señor D. Manuel José Marin sobre la utilidad que puede resultar al establecimiento de la Sociedad, la admisión de mujeres*, 28 October 1775, in Negrín Fajardo, *Ilustración y educación*, pp. 133–43

NEGRÍN FAJARDO, OLEGARIO, *Ilustración y educación: La sociedad económica matritense* (Madrid: Editora Nacional, 1984)

Other Primary Sources

CLARKE, EDWARD, *Letters Concerning the Spanish Nation: Written at Madrid during the years 1760 and 1761* (London: T. Becket and P. A. De Hondt, 1763)

CUBÍE, JUAN BAUTISTA, *Las mugeres vindicadas de las calumnias de los hombres: Con un catalogo de las españolas, que mas se han distinguido en ciencias y armas* (Madrid: Antonio Perez de Soto, 1768). Facsimile edition (Valladolid: Maxtor, 2001)

ESPINOSA Y BRUN, JOSÉ DE, *Discurso sobre el luxo de las señoras y proyecto de un traje nacional* (Madrid: Imprenta Real, 1788). Facsimile edition (Madrid: Mondadori, 1987)

FISCHER, FREDERICK AUGUSTUS [PSEUD. CHRISTIAN AUGUST FISCHER], *Travels in*

Spain in 1797 and 1798: With an Appendix on the Method of Travelling in that Country (London: A. Strahan for T.N. Longman and O. Rees, 1802). Translated from German original published 1799.

JARDINE, ALEXANDER, *Letters from Barbary, France, Spain, Portugal, Etc., by an English Officer*, 2 vols (Dublin: H. Chamberlaine, P. Byrne, J. Moore, and Grueber and McAllister, 1789). 1st London edn by T. Cadell, 1788.

LEÓN, LUIS DE, *La perfecta casada* (Madrid: Juan González, 1632). Bilingual edition by John A. Jones and Javier San José Lera (Lewiston, NY: Mellen, 1999).

POULAIN DE LA BARRE, FRANÇOIS, *De l'égalité des deux sexes: Discours physique et moral, où l'on voit l'importance de se défaire des préjugez* (Paris: Jean Dupuis, 1673). Reprint, Paris: Fayard, 1984. Trans. by Marcelle Maistre Welch and Vivien Elizabeth Bosley in *Three Cartesian Treatises* (Chicago: University of Chicago Press, 2002)

ROUSSEAU, JEAN-JACQUES, *Émile, ou de l'Éducation* (The Hague: Jean Néaulme, 1762); *Emile, or Education*, trans. by Barbara Foxley (London: Dent Everyman's Library, 1963)

SOUTHEY, ROBERT, *Letters Written During a Short Residence in Spain and Portugal*, 2nd edn (Bristol: T. N. Longman and O. Reeves, 1799)

SWINBURNE, HENRY, *Travels through Spain in the Years 1775 and 1776*, 2 vols, 2nd edn (London: P. Elmsley, 1787)

TOWNSEND, JOSEPH, *A Journey through Spain in the Years 1786 and 1787*, 3 vols, 2nd edn (London: C. Dilly, 1792)

VILLARS, MARIE GIGAULT, MARQUISE DE BELLEFONDS, MARIE-MADELEINE PIOCHE DE LA VERGNE, COMTESSE DE LA FAYETTE, and CLAUDINE-ALEXANDRINE DE TENCIN, *Lettres de Mmes de Villars, de La Fayette, et de Tencin: Accompagnées de notices biographiques et de notes explicatives*, ed. by Louis-Simon Auger (Paris: Chaumerot Jeune, 1823)

VIVES, JUAN LUIS, *The Education of a Christian Woman: A Sixteenth-Century Manual*, ed. and trans. by Charles Fantazzi (Chicago: University of Chicago Press, 2000)

—— *De institutione feminae Christianae*, ed. and trans. by Charles Fantazzi and Constant Matheeusen, 2 vols (Leiden: Brill, 1996–1998)

—— *Libro llamado Instruccion de la muger christiana: el qual contiene como se ha de criar vna virgen hasta casarla, y despues de casada como ha de regir su casa, y viuir prosperamente con su marido, y si fuere biuda lo que es tenida a hacer.* Translated from Latin to Spanish by Juan Justiniano (Zaragoza: Bartholome de Nagera, 1555). Reprinted as *Instrucción de la mujer cristiana*, ed. by Elizabeth Teresa Howe (Madrid: Fundación Universitaria Española, 1995).

ZAYAS Y SOTOMAYOR, MARÍA DE, *Exemplary Tales of Love and Tales of Disillusion*, ed. and trans. by Margaret R. Greer and Elizabeth Rhodes (Chicago: University of Chicago Press, 2009)

Secondary Sources

ARENAL, CONCEPCIÓN, 'Juicio Crítico de las Obras del P. Feijoo', in *Revista de España*, LV, 218 (1877), 187–224. Digital version available at: <http://www.filosofia.org/hem/dep/res/n218p187.htm>

ASTIGARRAGA, JESÚS, ed., *The Spanish Enlightenment Revisited* (Oxford: Voltaire Foundation, 2015)

BARREIRO FERNÁNDEZ, XOSÉ RAMÓN, 'O estudio crítico das obras do P. Feijóo de Pardo Bazán, Concepción Arenal e Miguel Morayta: O certame de Ourense de 1876', in *La Tribuna: Cadenos de Estudos da casa-Museo Emilia Pardo Bazán*, 1, 1 (2003), 47–97. Digital version available at: <http://www.cervantesvirtual. com/obra/o-estudio-critico-das-obras-do-p-feijoo-de-pardo-bazan-concepcion-arenal-e-miguel-morayta-o-certame-de-ourense-de-1876>

BAUM, ROBERT, II, 'The Counter-Discourse of Josepha Amar y Borbón's *Discurso*', in *Dieciocho: Hispanic Enlightenment*, 17, 1 (1994), 7–15

BLANCO CORUJO, OLIVA, *La polémica feminista en la España ilustrada: La 'Defensa de las Mujeres' de Feijoo y sus detractores* (Ciudad Real: Almud, Ediciones De Castilla-La Mancha, 2010)

BOLUFER PERUGA, MÓNICA, 'Conversations from a Distance: Spanish and French Eighteenth-Century Women Writers', in *A Companion to Spanish Women's Studies*, ed. by Xon de Ros and Geraldine Hazbun (Rochester, NY: Tamesis, 2011), pp. 175–88

——'Inés Joyes y Blake: Una ilustrada, entre privado y publico', in *Mujeres para la historia: Figuras destacadas del primer feminismo*, ed. by Rosa María Capel Martínez (Madrid: Abada Editores, 2004), pp. 27–55

——'Josefa Amar e Inés Joyes: Dos perspectivas femeninas sobre el matrimonio en el siglo XVIII', in *Historia de la mujer e historia del matrimonio*, ed. by María Victoria López-Cordón Cortezo and Montserrat Carbonell i Esteller (Murcia: Universidad de Murcia, Servicio de Publicaciones, 1997), pp. 203–17

——*Mujeres e ilustración: La construcción de la feminidad en la ilustración española* (València: Diputació de València, Institució Alfons el Magnànim, 1998)

——'Neither Male nor Female: Rational Equality in the Early Spanish Enlightenment', in *Women, Gender and Enlightenment*, ed. by Sarah Knott and Barbara Taylor (New York: Palgrave Macmillan, 2005), pp. 389–409

——'Traducción y creación en la actividad intelectual de las ilustradas españolas: El ejemplo de Inés Joyes y Blake', in *Frasquita Larrea y Aherán: Europeas y españolas entre la Ilustración y el Romanticismo*, ed. by Gloria Espigado Tocino and Maria José de la Pascua Sánchez (Cádiz: Universidad de Cádiz, Servicio de Publicaciones, 2003), pp. 137–55

——*La vida y la escritura en el siglo XVIII: Inés Joyes: Apología de las mujeres* (València: Universitat de València, 2008)

——'Women of Letters in Eighteenth-Century Spain: Between Tradition and Modernity', in *Eve's Enlightenment: Women's Experience in Spain and Spanish America, 1726–1839*, ed. by Catherine M. Jaffe and Elizabeth Franklin Lewis (Baton Rouge: Louisiana State University Press, 2009), pp. 17–32

CARIDI, GIUSEPPE, *Carlos III: Un gran rey reformador en Nápoles y España* (Madrid: La Esfera de los Libros, 2015)

CHAVES MCCLENDON, CARMEN, 'Josefa Amar y Borbón y la educación femenina', *Letras femeninas*, 4, 2 (1978), 3–11.

——'Josefa Amar y Borbón: Essayist', *Dieciocho: Hispanic Enlightenment*, 3, 2 (1980), 138–61

——'Josefa Amar y Borbón, Forgotten Figure of the Spanish Enlightenment', in

Seven Studies in Medieval English History and Other Historical Essays: Presented to Harold S. Snellgrove, ed. by Richard H. Bowers (Jackson: University Press of Mississippi, 1983), pp. 133–39

COUGHLIN, EDWARD V., 'The Polemic of Feijoo's *Defensa de las mujeres*', *Dieciocho: Hispanic Enlightenment*, 9, 1–2 (1986), 74–85

DELPY, GASPARD, *L'Espagne et l'esprit européen: L'œuvre de Feijoo* (Paris: Librairie Hachette, 1936)

DEMERSON, GEORGES, and PAULA DE DEMERSON, *La decadencia de las reales sociedades de amigos del país* (Oviedo: Universidad de Oviedo, Cátedra Feijóo, 1977)

DEMERSON, PAULA DE, *La condesa de Montijo, una mujer al servicio de las luces: Conferencia pronunciada en la Fundación Universitaria Española el día 13 de junio de 1975, con motivo del Año Internacional de la Mujer* (Madrid: Fundación Universitaria Española, 1976)

—— *Maria Francisca de Sales Portocarrero, Condesa de Montijo: Una figura de la Ilustración* (Madrid: Editora Nacional, 1975)

DEMERSON, PAULA DE, GEORGES DEMERSON and FRANCISCO AGUILAR PIÑAL, *Las sociedades económicas de amigos del país en el siglo XVII: Guía del investigador* (San Sebastian: Gráficas Izarra, 1974)

DONATO, CLORINDA, and RICARDO LÓPEZ, eds, *Enlightenment Spain and the 'Encyclopédie méthodique'* (Oxford: Voltaire Foundation, 2015)

FERNÁNDEZ DÍAZ, ROBERTO, *Carlos III: Un monarca reformista* (Barcelona: Espasa, 2016)

FERNÁNDEZ-QUINTANILLA, PALOMA, 'La junta de damas de honor y mérito', *Historia*, 16, 54 (1980), 65–73

—— *La mujer ilustrada en la España del siglo XVIII* (Madrid: Ministerio de Cultura, 1981)

FRANKLIN LEWIS, ELIZABETH, 'Feijoo, Josefa Amar y Borbón and the "Feminist" Debate in Eighteenth-Century Spain', *Dieciocho: Hispanic Enlightenment*, 12, 2 (1989), 188–203

—— 'Feminine Discourse and Subjectivity in the Works of Josefa Amar y Borbón, María Gertrudis Hore and María Rosa Gálvez' (unpublished PhD dissertation, University of Virginia, 1993)

—— 'Hispano-Irish Women Writers of Spain's Late Enlightenment Period', in *Routledge Companion to Iberian Studies*, ed. by Javier Muñoz-Basols, Laura Lonsdale and Manuel Delgado (London: Routledge, 2017)

—— 'The Sensibility of Motherhood in Josefa Amar y Borbón's *Discurso sobre la educación física y moral de las mujeres* (1790)', *Eighteenth-Century Women*, 2 (2002), 209–42

—— *Women Writers in the Spanish Enlightenment: The Pursuit of Happiness* (Burlington, VT: Ashgate, 2004)

FREIRE LÓPEZ, ANA MARÍA, 'Feijoo en el siglo XIX (Concepción Arenal, Emilia Pardo Bazán y Marcelino Menéndez Pelayo)', in *El siglo que llaman Ilustrado: Homenaje a Francisco Aguilar Piñal* (Madrid: Consejo Superior de Investigaciones Científicas, 1996), pp. 369–76

GARRIGA ESPINO, ANA, 'Defensa de las mujeres: El conformismo obligado de Feijoo en la España del siglo XVIII', in *Tonos digital: Revista electrónica de estudios filológicos*, Universidad de Murcia, numero 22 (January 2012)

GLENDINNING, NIGEL, *Influencia de la literatura inglesa en el siglo XVIII* (Oviedo: Facultad de Filosofía y Letras, Universidad de Oviedo, 1968)

HANSEN, MARLENE R., 'Sex, Love, Marriage, and Friendship: A Feminist Reading of the Quest for Happiness in *Rasselas*', *English Studies*, 66 (1985), 513–25

HERR, RICHARD, *The Eighteenth-Century Revolution in Spain* (Princeton, NJ: Princeton University Press, 1958)

HESSE, CARLA, *The Other Enlightenment: How French Women Became Modern* (Princeton, NJ: Princeton University Press, 2001)

JAFFE, CATHERINE M., and ELIZABETH FRANKLIN LEWIS, eds, *Eve's Enlightenment: Women's Experience in Spain and Spanish America 1726-1839* (Baton Rouge: Louisiana State University Press, 2009)

KAMEN, HENRY, *Philip V of Spain: The King who Reigned Twice* (New Haven, CT: Yale University Press, 2001)

KITTS, SALLY-ANN, *The Debate on the Nature, Role, and Influence of Woman in Eighteenth-Century Spain* (Lewiston, NY: Mellen, 1985)

—— 'La prensa y la polémica feminista en la España del siglo XVIII', in *Periodismo e Ilustración en España*, special issue of *Estudios de Historia Social*, 52–53 (1991), 275–73

LARSON, DONALD R., *The Honor Plays of Lope de Vega* (Cambridge, MA: Harvard University Press, 1977)

LÓPEZ-CORDÓN CORTEZO, MARÍA VICTORIA, *Condición femenina y razón ilustrada: Josefa Amar y Borbón* (Zaragoza: Prensas Universitarias de Zaragoza, 2005)

—— 'Josefa Amar y Borbón y sus escritos sobre educación', in *Famille et éducation en Espagne et en Amerique latine: Actes du [5e] Colloque de Tours, [du] CIREMIA, Centre interuniversitaire de recherche sur l'éducation dans le monde ibérique et ibéro-américain*, ed. by Jean-Louis Guereña (Tours: Publications de l'Université François Rabelais, 2002), pp. 509–20

—— 'Texto y contexto de una dama española: Josefa Amar y Borbón', in *El modelo femenino: Una alternativa al modelo patriarcal?*, ed. by Inés Calero Secall and Maria Dolores Fernández de la Torre Madueño (Málaga: Universidad de Málaga, 1996), pp. 105–37

—— 'Women in Society in Eighteenth-Century Spain: Models of Sociability', in Jaffe and Lewis, eds, *Eve's Enlightenment*, pp. 103–14

LÓPEZ TORRIJO, MANUEL. 'El pensamiento pedagógico ilustrado sobre la mujer en Josef Amar y Borbón', in *Educación e ilustración en España*, ed. by Buenaventura Delgado (Barcelona: Barcelona Universidad, Departamento de Educación Comparada e Historia de la Educación, 1984), pp. 114–29

MACKENZIE, ANN L., and JEREMY ROBBINS, eds, *Hesitancy and Experimentation in Enlightenment Spain and Spanish America: Studies on Culture & Theatre* (Abingdon: Routledge, 2011)

McCLELLAND, I. L., *Benito Jerónimo Feijoo* (New York: Twayne, 1969)

—— *Ideological Hesitancy in Spain, 1700-1750* (Liverpool: Liverpool University Press, 1991)

MARAÑÓN Y POSADILLO, GREGORIO, *Las ideas Biológicas del Padre Feijoo*, 4th edn (Madrid: Espasa Calpe, 1962) (1st edition 1934)

MARTÍN GAITE, CARMEN, *Usos amorosos del dieciocho en España* (Madrid: Siglo Veintiuno de España Editores, 1972). Translated as *Love Customs in Eighteenth-*

Century Spain by Maria G. Tomsich (Berkeley: University of California Press, 1991)

MARTÍN-VALDEPEÑAS YAGÜE, ELISA, 'Afrancesadas y patriotas: La Junta de Honor y Mérito de la Real Sociedad Económica Matritense de Amigos del Pais', in *Heroínas y patriotas: Mujeres de 1808*, ed. by Irene Castells Olivan, Gloria Espigado Tocino and María Cruz Romeo Mateo (Madrid: Cátedra, 2009), pp. 343–70

—— 'Del amigo del país al ciudadano útil: Una aproximación al discurso patriótico en la Real Sociedad Económica Matritense de Amigos del País en el Antiguo Régimen', *Cuadernos de historia moderna*, 11 (2012), 23–47

—— 'El eco del saber: La Junta de Honor y Mérito de la Real Sociedad Económica Matritense de Amigos del País y la ciencia en la Ilustración', *Historia social*, 82 (2015), 97–114

MORANT DEUSA, ISABEL, 'Mujeres ilustradas en el debate de la educación: Francia y España', *Cuadernos de historia moderna*, 3 (2004), pp. 59–84

—— 'Reasons for Education: New Echoes of the Polemic', in Jaffe and Lewis, eds, *Eve's Enlightenment*, pp. 51–61

MORANT DEUSA, ISABEL, and MÓNICA BOLUFER PERUGA, 'Josefa Amar y Borbón: Une intellectuelle espagnole dans les débats des Lumières', *Clio*, 13 (2001), pp. 69–97

NEGRÍN FAJARDO, OLEGARIO, *La educación popular en la España de la segunda mitad del siglo XVIII: Las actividades educativas de la Sociedad Económica Matritense de Amigos del País* (Madrid: Universidad Nacional de Educación a Distancia, 1987)

—— *Ilustración y educación: La sociedad económica matritense* (Madrid: Editora Nacional, 1984)

OÑATE, MARÍA DEL PILAR, *El Femenismo en la Literatura Español* (Madrid: Espasa-Calpe, 1938)

PAQUETTE, GABRIEL B., *Enlightenment, Governance, and Reform in Spain and its Empire, 1759–1808* (Basingstoke: Palgrave Macmillan, 2008)

PARDO BAZÁN, EMILIA, 'Estudio crítico de las obras del Padro Feijoo', in *Certamen Literario en conmemoración del Segundo Centenario del Nacimiento de Fray Benito Jerónimo Feijoo* (Madrid: Perojo, 1877)

PÉREZ-RIOJA, J. A., *Proyeccion y Actualidad de Feijoo* (Madrid: Instituto de Estudios Politicos, 1965)

SARRAILH, JEAN, *L'Espagne éclairée de la seconde moitié du XVIIIe siècle* (Paris: Imprimerie Nationale; C. Klincksieck, 1954)

SMITH, THERESA ANN, *The Emerging Female Citizen: Gender and Enlightenment in Spain* (Berkeley: University of California Press, 2006)

SULLIVAN, CONSTANCE A., 'Constructing Her Own Tradition: Ideological Selectivity in Josefa Amar y Borbón's Representation of Female Models', in Vollendorf, *Recovering Spain's Feminist Tradition* (New York: Modern Language Association of America, 2001)

—— 'Josefa Amar y Borbón', in *Spanish Women Writers: A Bio-Bibliographical Source Book*, ed. by Linda Gould Levine, Ellen Engelson Marson and Gloria Waldman (Westport, CT: Greenwood, 1993), pp. 32–43

—— 'Josefa Amar y Borbón and the Royal Aragonese Economic Society', *Dieciocho: Hispanic Enlightenment*, 15, 1–2 (1992), 95–148

——'The Quiet Feminism of Josefa Amar y Borbón's 1790 Book on Education', *Indiana Journal of Hispanic Literatures*, 2, 1 (1993), 49–73

TROUILLE, MARY SEIDMAN, *Sexual Politics in the Enlightenment: Women Writers Read Rousseau* (Albany: State University of New York Press, 1997)

URZAINQUI MIQUELEIZ, INMACULADA, 'Campomanes y su noticia de Feijoo', in *Homenaje a la profesora María Dolores Tortosa Linde*, ed. by Remedios Morales Raya (Granada: Universidad de Granada, 2003), pp. 481–92

——'Los espacios de la mujer en la prensa del siglo XVIII', in *Del periódico a la sociedad de la información*, ed. by Celso Almuiña and Eduardo Sotillos (Madrid: Sociedad Estatal España Nuevo Milenio, 2002), pp. 53–80

——'Feijoo y la Ilustración: Desde Marañon', in *Ilustración, Ilustraciones*, ed. by J. Astigarraga, M. V. López-Cordón and J. M. Urkía (Donostia-San Sebastián, Real Sociedad Bascongada de los Amigos del País-Sociedad Estatal de Conmemoraciones Culturales, 2009), II, pp. 921–50. Digital copy available at <http://www.cervantesvirtual.com/obra-visor/feijoo-y-la-ilustracion-desde-maranon/html/af83ca2d-cc23–437b-bod5–3a8a6373247e_9.html>

——'La ilustración sonriente: Feijoo y la Risa', *Bulletin hispanique*, 104, 1 (2002), 443–87

——'Nuevas propuestas a un público femenino', in *Historia de la edición y de la lectura en España (1472–1914)*, ed. by Victor Infantes, François López and Jean-François Botreó (Madrid: Fundación Germán Sánchez Ruipérez, 2003)

——'Visiones de las Españas: Feijoo, Cadalso, Ramón de la Cruz y Salas', *Dieciocho: Hispanic Enlightenment*, 22, no. 2 (1999), pp. 397–422

VIÑAO, ANTONIO, 'La educación en las obras de Josefa Amar y Borbón', *Sarmiento: Anuario galego de historia da educación*, 7 (2003), 35–60

VOLLENDORF, LISA, *The Lives of Women: A New History of Inquisitional Spain* (Nashville, TN: Vanderbilt University Press, 2005)

——'No Doubt it Will Amaze You: María de Zayas's Early Modern Feminism', in Vollendorf, ed., *Recovering Spain's Feminist Tradition*, pp. 103–120

—— ED., *Recovering Spain's Feminist Tradition* (New York: Modern Language Association of America, 2002)

YARBRO-BEJARANO, YVONNE, *Feminism and the Honor Plays of Lope de Vega* (West Lafayette: Purdue University Press, 1994)

ZUCKERMAN-INGBER, ALIX, *El Bien Más Alto: A Reconsideration of Lope de Vega's Honor Plays* (Gainesville: University Presses of Florida, 1984)

INDEX

Lightning Source UK Ltd.
Milton Keynes UK
UKHW03f2339280818
327970UK00004B/356/P